The Chinese Writing System in Asia

The Chinese Writing System in Asia: An Interdisciplinary Perspective integrates a diverse range of disciplinary approaches in examining how the Chinese script represents and actively shapes personal and social identities in and beyond Asia. It is an ideal read for students and scholars interested in a broad and culturally rich introduction to research on the Chinese writing system. It can also serve as the main text of an undergraduate course on the subject.

Key features of this volume include:

- Insights from studies of the Chinese writing system in linguistics, script reform and technology, gender, identity, literature, and the visual arts;
- Examples embedded in inquiries of the cultural history and contemporary society of Asia;
- Rigorous yet accessible discussions of complex concepts and phenomena that assume no prior knowledge of Asian languages or linguistics;
- Supplementary multimedia materials and resources, including instructional support, available online.

Yu Li is Assistant Professor of Chinese in the Department of Modern Languages and Literatures at Loyola Marymount University, USA. Her research interests include Chinese linguistics, Chinese language pedagogy, East Asian calligraphy, and the Chinese linguistic landscape in the diaspora.

"This is a comprehensive introduction to the Chinese writing system from a wide range of disciplinary perspectives. The author writes beautifully on the linguistic, socio-cultural, anthropological, literary and artistic aspects of Chinese characters."

— **Hongyuan Dong**, *Assistant Professor of Chinese Language and Linguistics, The George Washington University in Washington DC, USA*

"This book is a welcome new introduction to the Chinese writing system. I see the strengths of the book in three areas: its wide scope in the topics it covers, its thoroughness in the treatment of the topics, and its balance between scholarly discussions of the topics and its attention to popular interest in the topics."

— **Guohe Zheng**, *Professor of Japanese, Ball State University, USA*

The Chinese Writing System in Asia

An Interdisciplinary Perspective

Yu Li

Routledge
Taylor & Francis Group

LONDON AND NEW YORK

First published 2020
by Routledge
2 Park Square, Milton Park, Abingdon, Oxon OX14 4RN

and by Routledge
52 Vanderbilt Avenue, New York, NY 10017

Routledge is an imprint of the Taylor & Francis Group, an informa business

© 2020 Yu Li

British Library Cataloguing-in-Publication Data
A catalogue record for this book is available from the British Library

Library of Congress Cataloging-in-Publication Data
Names: Li, Yu, 1978– author.
Title: The Chinese writing system in Asia : an interdisciplinary
    perspective / Yu Li.
Description: Abingdon, Oxon : New York, NY : Routledge, 2020. |
    Includes bibliographical references and index.
Identifiers: LCCN 2019025053 (print) | LCCN 2019025054 (ebook) |
    ISBN 9781138907317 (hardback) | ISBN 9781138907324 (paperback) |
    ISBN 9780429345333 (ebook) | ISBN 9781000698343 (adobe pdf) |
    ISBN 9781000698701 (mobi) | ISBN 9781000699067 (epub)
Subjects: LCSH: Chinese characters—Asia.
Classification: LCC PL1171 .L387 2020 (print) | LCC PL1171 (ebook) |
    DDC 495.11/1—dc23
LC record available at https://lccn.loc.gov/2019025053
LC ebook record available at https://lccn.loc.gov/2019025054

ISBN: 978-1-138-90731-7 (hbk)
ISBN: 978-1-138-90732-4 (pbk)
ISBN: 978-0-429-34533-3 (ebk)

Typeset in Minion Pro
by Apex CoVantage, LLC
Visit the eResources: www.routledge.com/9781138907324

Contents

Preface

The idea of this book came about in the second year of my teaching career. After having taught a few Chinese language courses, I was eager to create something new to offer my students, something that would spark their curiosity, challenge their thinking, and inspire their creativity. I wanted them to see, as I did at the time and still do now, that learning Chinese was not just about being able to communicate in the language; it could be and should be, in no small measure, a journey of intellectual discovery and growth. And so was my experience researching for and teaching the course *Chinese Writing Systems in Asia* at Emory for nearly ten years since then.

Now this book almost feels like a gift to myself: the next time when I teach this course, I will be able to use it as a main text. I have had to rely on a collection of scholarly writings that was challenging to present as a coherent body of text in an introductory course. Having a systematic and accessible set of readings on hand will be a welcome change. I hope it will make it easier for interested colleagues in the field to offer similar courses as well. Besides what is in the print edition and the electronic version of the book, I have also made available additional materials and tips for teaching on the companion website, including exercises and activities that can be integrated into classwork or assigned as homework.

Although intended as a textbook for a college course, this volume is by no means restricted to a classroom audience. General-interest readers curious or enthusiastic about the Chinese script will also find the broad-ranging topics interesting and accessible. This book is designed to be an interdisciplinary introduction to the Chinese writing system. The chapters integrate studies of the Chinese language, writing, and linguistics into inquiries regarding script borrowing, writing reform, technology, gender, identity, visual art, and literature, and they assume no prior knowledge about any of these topics or about Chinese language or linguistics in general. Parts I and II are foundational and will be best read first, but the remaining ones can be more flexibly sequenced.

It is also with the development of my pedagogical field in mind that I have written this book. As strongly as ever, I believe that there is much more to be said and done about teaching Chinese than the worthy endeavor of raising students' communicative proficiency. Language and writing are at the core of humanistic flourishing – as we see in this volume, the Chinese writing system has been and will continue to be part and parcel of the forging and reshaping of social, cultural, and certainly personal identities – of those who've embraced it and those who've abandoned it. Language and culture instructors of Chinese are obligated to bring our students closer to such understandings, and I hope this book is a step in that direction.

A small step, that is. The subject of Chinese characters is endlessly fascinating, and I have had to limit the topics to the selected few that there is room to accommodate and worry about their uneven treatment. Indeed, among the numerous decisions made during the writing process, I suspect not all were wise, and any true wisdom that does come through is probably rubbing off the many works I have consulted and to which I am greatly indebted.

I also owe a great deal to the many individuals who have helped with this project and wish to thank them here: my Emory colleagues and friends Juliette Apkarian, Julia Bullock, Bumyong Choi, Cheryl Crowley, Seth Goss, Sun-chul Kim, Aya McDaniel, Maria Sibau, and Amanda Wright, who gave me invaluable feedback on various parts of this project; my editor Kelly Besecke, who patiently read through every word and offered key insights on making them fit better together; my research assistant Tianqi Wang, who created most of the illustrations, helped obtain permissions to use copyrighted images, and organized materials for the companion website; and my dear friends Ron Janssen, Jin Liu, and Qi Wang as well as my family in China, for inspiring me and keeping me going. It is to them that I dedicate this book.

PART I

Linguistic preliminaries

1 Foundational concepts

THE KEY TO UNDERSTANDING how a writing system works is to understand how its symbols systematically represent the units of the language it writes. This is often an intricate matter that involves linguistic concepts of which we may not be intuitively aware. It is therefore necessary to familiarize ourselves with these concepts first, so that we will be able to discuss the working mechanisms of writing systems with more clarity and efficiency. In what follows, we will start with defining and distinguishing between a pair of terms that provide the disciplinary setting in which we will discuss the other terms: phonetics and phonology. From there we will look at three analogous pairs of concepts: phoneme and allophone, morpheme and allomorph, and grapheme and allograph.

Phonetics and phonology

Phonetics and phonology are both branches of linguistics that study the sounds of human languages. They are different yet closely related. **Phonetics** deals with speech sounds as concrete physical entities, and it is primarily interested in their articulatory and acoustic aspects, for example: How are speech sounds made? What are the gestures and movements involved? What are the articulatory features that distinguish one speech sound from another? What are the physical properties that differentiate them from each other? How are speech sounds represented, analyzed, and read on a computer? As you see, phonetics treats speech sounds as concrete and physical elements that have stable inherent qualities. However, it is important to understand that speech sounds do not function as isolated entities in fulfilling their linguistic roles. They interact with each other, often causing phonetic – that is, articulatory and acoustic – changes, and they tend to behave in ways that form predictable patterns. This is where phonology comes in.

Phonology is primarily concerned with the patterns in which speech sounds behave as members of a linguistic system. In investigating the regularities and patterns in sound distribution, phonology views speech sounds as abstract linguistic units. Such abstraction is necessary, because – for example – a given speech sound may pattern differently with other sounds in different languages, so that the same phonetic entity may have a different phonological status in a different language. One example is the consonants /θ/ and /s/ in English vs. French. θ is an International Phonetic Alphabet (IPA) symbol we use to represent the final sound in the English word *myth*, and *s* is the IPA symbol for the final sound in *miss*.[1] In English phonology, /θ/ and /s/ are regarded as two distinctive sound categories, because changing from one to the other would change the meaning of the word (i.e., from "myth" to "miss," or vice versa). In other words, /θ/ and /s/ **contrast** with each other (i.e., they are used to differentiate word meaning) in the English phonology. In French, however, the [θ] sound is normally not used, so no two words are different from each other solely on the basis of [θ] vs. [s]. If a speaker for some reason substitutes [θ] for a [s] in a French word, the result may sound odd to a native French person, but it would not be interpreted as a different word. Thus, in the subconscious mind of the French speaker, [θ] and [s] are two possible physical realizations of the same sound category: they are phonetically different, but phonologically the same. By contrast, /θ/ and /s/ are phonologically distinctive in English. This example tells us that in order to be able to describe the distribution of speech sounds in different languages, we would not only want to talk about them as concrete entities in the physical world (i.e., phonetics), but would also need to understand at an abstract level how they relate to one another in a particular language (i.e., phonology).

THE STORY BEYOND

Speaking with a French accent

English distinguishes [θ] (*myth*) vs. [s] (*miss*), or their voiced counterparts [ð] (*breathe*) vs. [z] (*breeze*) phonologically, while French does not normally use [θ] or [ð]. In fact, the sounds [θ] and [ð] are rare in human languages, while [s] and [z] are very common. Someone speaking English with a French accent would tend to substitute [s] for [θ] and [z] for [ð]. For example, *thank you very much for these* would become something like *sank you very much for zese. I think of you all the time* would sound like *I sink of you all ze time*.

Emes and Allos

Speech sounds may have different relationships in the same language as well. Take English as an example: some sounds contrast with each other while others complement each other. What do we mean by "contrast" or "complement" in this context? When speech sounds can occur in exactly the same phonological environment, and switching from one to another creates differences in meaning, we say that they **contrast** with each other, or that they are **in contrastive distribution**. For instance, the initial consonants of the English words *mac* /mæk/, *tack* /tæk/, and *lack* /læk/ are /m/, /t/, and /l/, respectively. They can all occur at the beginning of a word and in front of the vowel /æ/. In fact, they constitute the only differences in the words given, and changing from one to another alters the meaning of the word. In this case, these three sounds are contrasting with one another, and we say that they belong to distinctive phonological categories, or phonemes, in English. **Phonemes** are abstract sound categories in the speaker's mind that contrast with each other in a given language. *Phone* here means "speech sound." It comes from the Greek word *phōnē* 'sound, voice.' The English suffix *-eme* indicates a significant contrastive unit in linguistics at the level the stem of the word suggests. In this case, a *phon*-eme is a smallest contrastive *sound* unit. We will soon learn about *morph*-eme and *graph*-eme.

A phoneme may sound different depending on the context, and the concrete phonetic realizations of a phoneme are called **allophones** of this phoneme. *Allo*- means "other." Its origin is the Greek form *állos* 'other.' In linguistics, *allo*- is used to indicate non-contrastive, alternative forms of *-emes*. Besides *allo*-phones, we will also learn about *allo*-morphs and *allo*-graphs in this chapter. As an example for understanding the concept of allophones, think about how the phoneme /t/ in English may be pronounced differently based on the context. When it occurs at the beginning of a word, most speakers pronounce it as an aspirated consonant [tʰ], as in *tack* [tʰæk]. **Aspiration** refers to the strong puff of air that accompanies the production of the consonant, and it is marked as a raised *h* ([ʰ]) in IPA. When /t/ occurs after the sound [s] in the same word, by contrast, most English speakers use the unaspirated version of the sound, [t], as in *stack* [stæk]. If you place your hand close in front of your mouth when saying *tack* and *stack*, you should be able to feel a stronger puff of air in *tack*. Thus, [tʰ] and [t] are phonetically different sounds. In fact, native speakers of English are fully able to hear the difference between them.

Allophones are context-dependent, so that the phonological environments in which they occur do not overlap with each other. In other words, they are **in complementary distribution**. In the example of *tack* and *stack*, [tʰ] is always at the beginning of a word and never occurs right after [s] in the same word, while [t] always occurs immediately after [s] and never at the beginning of a word. Thus, as allophones of the same phoneme /t/ in English, [tʰ] and [t] complement each other in distribution. For this reason, an allophone is also a **predictable** phonetic realization of a phoneme as determined by the phonological context: at the beginning of a word, the English /t/ is always [tʰ], while immediately after [s] within a word, it is always [t].

Companion website

Exercise 1.1 Phonemes or allophones

Now that we understand the terms phoneme and allophone as defined in phonology, we will learn two additional pairs of concepts analogous to them, both of which will be very useful to us in the discussion of writing systems: morpheme and allomorph, grapheme and allograph. A **morpheme** is the smallest combined unit of sound and linguistic meaning or function in a given language. It is a word-like unit but more rigorously defined than word. In fact, "word" is notoriously difficult to define in linguistic terms: Is *hot dog* one word or two words? What about *bookcases*? And *fun-filled*? This is one reason why we need the concept of a morpheme. It allows us to say for sure how many basic units there are: *hot dog* contains two morphemes, *hot* and *dog*; *bookcases* consists of three morphemes, *book, case*, and the plural marker *-s*; and *fun-filled* also has three morphemes, *fun, fill*, and the past participle suffix *-ed*. Each of these morphemes is a smallest meaningful or functional unit and cannot be further divided without losing its meaning or function. Indeed, different from phonemes, morphemes not only involve sounds but also come with meanings or grammatical functions. In this sense, morphemes are at a linguistic level higher or more complex than phonemes.

Like phonemes, however, a morpheme is also an abstract representation in the speaker's mind, and its actual phonetic realizations, or **allomorphs**, depend on phonological contexts. For example, the plural morpheme in English is /-z/. It is realized as the voiceless [s] when following a voiceless consonant. Thus, we have /-s/ in *cats* [kæts], where [t] is a voiceless consonant. The plural morpheme /-z/ becomes [-əz] with a short vowel inserted in front when it comes right after the sounds [s] (as is the final sound in *kiss*), [z] (*buzz*), [ʃ] (*wish*), [ʒ] (*mirage*), [tʃ] (*church*), and [dʒ] (*judge*). Therefore, we have *kisses* [-səz], *buzzes* [-zəz], *wishes* [-Þəz], *mirages* [-ʒəz], *churches* [-tÞəz], and *judges* [-dʒəz]. All elsewhere, the plural morpheme /-z/ is realized simply as [-z]. The allomorphs [-s], [-əz], and [-z] are context-dependent, they are in complementary distribution, and we can also say that they do not contrast with each other.

The concepts phoneme, allophone, morpheme, and allomorph apply to speech; in writing, we may use the terms "grapheme" and "allograph" to think about the roles graphic symbols play. **Graphemes** are abstract representations of contrastive graphic categories in the writer's mind. In writing English, for example, <m> and <t> are two graphemes that can distinguish word meaning: <smart> is a different word than <start>. **Allographs** are actual realizations of a given grapheme that are determined by context. They are written differently in different contexts, but we still recognize them as the same letter or character. In the printed text below, the grapheme <m> has two allographs, each in a different typeface:

> smart [Times New Roman]
> **smart** [Helvetica]

The Times New Roman {m} and the Helvetica {m} are each consistent with their neighboring letters in terms of typeface, as is usually the case in printing practice. Here is another example: the uppercase {M} and the lowercase {m} are also allographs of the same grapheme <m>. Based on the convention for writing English, for example, {m} is used at the beginning of a sentence, while {m} is used elsewhere, unless it is the first letter of a proper name or part of an acronym, where it should be capitalized:

> May you have a good vacation.

> You may have a good vacation.

> May is my favorite vacation month.

> My favorite vacation month is May.

Notational conventions

Following the notational conventions in linguistics, in this book, phonemes and morphemes are placed between slashes (e.g., /p/). Allophones and allomorphs use square brackets ([p]). We use angle brackets (<p>) for graphemes and braces ({p}) for allographs.

Note

1 Transcriptions of speech sounds in the rest of the book are also in IPA. In IPA, each symbol represents a unique speech sound. The use of IPA allows us to specify and communicate with clarity what sounds we are referring to. IPA is also designed to be able to transcribe all speech sounds in human languages, which makes it an indispensable tool for documenting languages not yet written down. We will not discuss IPA in detail in this book. If you are interested in learning how to transcribe English in IPA, many resources are available on the Internet. The companion website has links to such resources.

2 What is writing?

The definition of writing

In our day-to-day use of the English language, the word "writing" may mean a number of different things. It can be the act of composing an essay or a poem. It can be a noun, such as "the writings of Edgar Allen Poe." It can refer to the rhetorical style in which the essays are written, as in "Hemingway's writing is terse and succinct." When handwriting is employed, "writing" can also refer to the penmanship of the writer.

Which of the above is the writing with which we are concerned? Well, none of them. For our purpose, **writing** is defined as graphic representation of language in a specific and systematic manner. For the purpose of this course, we will not be concerned with the connotative, or figurative, uses of the word "writing" – that is, the action or outcome of writing, the style of putting words together to express ideas, or the aesthetic appearance of marks made on paper. We will solely use the term in its denotative, or literal, meaning of the visual representation of linguistic utterances with graphic symbols.

Companion website

Exercise 2.1 The definition of writing

To fully understand what constitutes writing, let us think further about what is *not* writing.

Language is not writing

The distinction between "writing" and "language" is a necessary and important one in our discussion of writing systems. By defining writing as graphic representation of language, we mandate that writing be seen as separate from language: **language** refers to the speech one produces or hears, while writing refers to the visual representation of speech using graphic marks. Writing is not one kind of language, and the concept of language does not incorporate writing.

Yet, perhaps because many of us today live in a highly literate society, confusion between the two, especially in using "language" to refer to "writing," is pervasive. You may have heard statements like these:

Chinese has tens of thousands of characters.
Hebrew has no vowels.[1]
Nǚshū is a secret language invented by women.

Such statements are linguistically problematic. "Chinese" or "Hebrew" each refers to a language.[2] The Chinese language is not composed of characters but speech sounds – one does not need to write or read any characters in order to speak or understand it. Hebrew is clearly not lacking in vowels, though it is true that vowels are generally not represented in writing the language. Thus, the first two statements are in fact comments on how the languages are written rather than on the languages themselves. The third statement may require a little more explanation. *Nǚshū* (女书/女書 'Women's Script') is the name of a script created by and once used among women in rural Jiangyong county, Hunan province in China. It is not a language but a writing system designed for writing the local Chinese dialect. We will learn about *nǚshū* in detail in Chapter 19 of this book.

Statements like these may reveal a lack of understanding about what constitutes language. In cognitive terms, **language** is a complex system residing in our brain that allows us to produce and interpret utterances. For our purpose, since we are primarily concerned with graphic rendering of linguistic utterances, language can be understood specifically as the **speech** produced or potentially produced by this system.

Visual representations of non-languages are not writing

Writing is visual representation of language, and language *only*. Although language conveys information or ideas, not all graphic renditions of ideas or information are writing. A good example to illustrate this point would be **pictography**,[3] or so-called picture writing, that is, the use of usually highly stylized or stereotyped pictures to communicate information or serve as memory aids. International airports are where modern pictography abounds: a figure in a skirt or dress indicates the ladies' room, a person seated in a wheelchair signifies accessibility, and a set of a fork and knife suggests places to eat. Because these symbols are not tied to any particular language, they, to some extent, transcend linguistic barriers and function effectively in assisting travelers navigating the airports. However, precisely because they are not tied to any particular language and do not correspond to any specific linguistic utterances, they cannot be considered writing. They are merely visual cues employed to suggest information with which the viewers are already familiar.

The rule of thumb is that writing represents *specific* utterances of a language in a *systematic* way, so that proficient readers are able to reliably reproduce what is written and consistently render it back into speech intelligible to the community of speakers of that particular language.

Companion website

Exercise 2.2 Examples of writing

Indeed, systematicity is one of the fundamental features of writing, and this is why linguists use the term **writing system** to refer to what we commonly call **writing** or **script**. In the remainder of this book, we will use these three terms interchangeably.

Now let us further examine the ways in which writing is systematic.

Writing is systematic

Writing, first of all, has a systematic relationship to language. A script generally consists of a set of visual symbols (graphemes) linearly or otherwise arranged to represent the speech units of a language. For this to work efficiently, a high degree of consistency is required. Each grapheme in the script usually represents a constant unit of the language, such as a single phoneme or a single morpheme. For example, the letters <a k i l m> in writing English each represent a phoneme in the most ordinary cases. In writing Chinese, a character, such as <人 走 文>, corresponds to a morpheme: *rén* 'person,' *zǒu* 'to walk,' or *wén* 'writing.' Of course, the relationships between a grapheme and a speech unit as exemplified by the writing of English and Chinese are not the only possible relationships between script and language. In writing Cherokee or *Yí*[4] (彝), for example, an individual symbol represents a meaningless syllable. As another example, the graphemes of the Japanese *hiragana* (平仮名) and *katakana* (片仮名) scripts represent speech units that may be slightly smaller than syllables. The nature of the relationship between language and script serves as the basis on which linguists categorize writing systems. For example, Cherokee and *Yí* scripts are both syllabic writing systems. We will look at the classification of writing systems in more detail in Chapter 3 of this book. For now, it is sufficient to understand that the corresponding relationship between a grapheme and a speech unit is generally constant in that it applies to the entirety of a writing system.

Writing systems in general also have internal organizations of their own. For instance, English is usually written horizontally from left to right, while Arabic writing is normally right to left. English letters are arranged sequentially. In writing Korean, however, letters are combined into blocks of syllables, often with some letters stacked on top of others. In both English and Korean, words are separated by spaces, but in Chinese they are strung together with no spaces in between. In English, the first letter of each sentence is usually capitalized, while in writing German, the first letter of each noun is capitalized regardless of its position in the sentence.

The internal structure of a writing system has little to do with the language being written and is primarily a matter of convention. For this reason, it may change over history. For example, some ancient Greek texts of the 6th century BCE were written in alternate lines of opposing directions. That is, the text flowed from left to right in one line, and then right to left in the line below it, and then left to right again below that, and so on. This pattern was likened to how an ox turned in ploughing a field and was given the name *boustrophedon*, a word Greek in origin meaning "to turn like oxen (in plowing)." Chinese text is another example. Today Chinese is usually written in horizontal lines from left to right and the lines are arranged from top to bottom on a page, just like in writing English. Before the 20th century, however, most Chinese texts used a very different arrangement: writing proceeded from the upper right corner of the page in columns arranged from right to left with each column starting at the top. This change was the result of Western influence on China.

Writing is secondary to speech

To say that writing is secondary is to make the point that speech is primary. The primacy of speech has been one of the cardinal principles of modern linguistics – it is one of the features that distinguishes this modern scientific discipline from its earlier state in the European tradition prior to the 20th century.[5] Evidence for this principle comes from historical, cultural, and developmental sources. The history of writing is much briefer than that of human language or speech. Speech is a naturally evolved, defining characteristic of the human species. Writing, on the other hand, is a cultural invention that emerged much later in history. We know from archaeological findings that the history of writing goes back only about 5,000 years, while scholars have estimated that human speech emerged between 200,000 and 60,000 years ago.[6]

That writing is secondary to speech is also evident when we consider that, although all languages are spoken, not all languages have been written down. In literate societies today, it is not uncommon for bilingual or multilingual communities to use one language purely in spoken form, usually for ordinary conversations such as in the home setting, and another language in writing (and/or speech) for more formal purposes. For example, a student native to the city of *Shànghǎi* may speak the *Shànghǎi* dialect, which is not mutually intelligible with Mandarin, with her friends and family, but converse and write in Mandarin for schoolwork. In linguistics, such a phenomenon is referred to as **diglossia**. The local speech variety in a diglossic situation, in this case the *Shànghǎi* dialect, is often not officially written.

Another set of evidence comes from language acquisition. All people, who are physically able, acquire the ability to speak as children. Only some learn to write, while others may never do so. The acquisition of speech happens naturally for children, regardless of the particular language involved. The learning of writing, on the other hand, requires a conscious effort.

Further insight for the primacy of speech comes from the relationship between language and writing. The same language may be written using a variety of writing systems. In theory, in fact, a given language can be written in any kind of writing system. Which system is in use is, to a great extent, a matter of cultural convention rather than determined by the nature of the language involved. Furthermore, writing systems can be and also have been artificially designed or reformed. In this sense, writing is very much a cultural phenomenon.

Last but not least, the primacy of speech is reflected in our definition of language and writing. Given that language refers to speech, and writing is visual representation of language, it logically follows that speech comes before writing and serves as the basis for writing. A pair of terms that we often hear is "spoken language" and "written language," as if speech and writing were equal alternative forms in which language could be rendered. However, these terms may cause confusion about the relationship between language, speech, and writing. The term "spoken language" in itself is redundant – it is equivalent to saying "spoken speech," since by our definition language refers to speech[7] and all languages are spoken.

The term "written language" may cause considerable confusion as well, for it has been found to mean a range of different concepts. Some use it to refer to a language that has been out of use (or has never been in use) for oral communication and is now primarily used in the written form, such as Latin or Classical Chinese. Others use it to mean the writing system with which a language is recorded or represented. Still others find the term applicable to anything that is written down. To avoid confusion, we will restrict the meaning of the term to the first sense. That is, a **written language** is a language whose current use is limited to writing, and it may or may not have been used in speech in the past. Latin and Classical Chinese were both spoken at an earlier point in history. Today, they may be used to compose text, and such text may be read aloud by someone on appropriate occasions, but the languages are no longer employed in daily oral communication as they once were. In essence, a written language is a language that is usually represented in the written form.

Defined as such, a written language is very different from a writing system or script. The term "writing system" may appear rather technical to those not trained in linguistics. In its place, "written language" has been used in non-specialized (and sometimes specialized) publications to refer to script. A written language, however, is not the same as a writing system; in fact, it can be represented using multiple systems of writing. For example, Classical Chinese is usually written in Chinese characters, but we can conceivably write it in *pīnyīn* (拼音 *lit.* 'spell sound'), a writing system based on the Roman (Latin) alphabet.

With the above clarification in mind, it is helpful to be aware that we may still encounter loose usage of these terms in writings by linguists or non-linguists alike. In such cases, we will need to pay close attention to the context and determine the exact connotation of the terms to avoid further confusion. In our own writing, of course, it will be beneficial to adhere to the exact definitions.

Notes

1   This example is from Rogers (2005, p. 2).

2   The term "Chinese language" in fact encompasses a wide variety of speech, some of which are not mutually intelligible. Linguists in China and the West debate over whether these speech varieties should be considered dialects of the same language or separate languages. We will talk more about this in Chapter 5.

3   The term "pictography" is not to be confused with "pictographs" (象形字 *xiàngxíng zì*), which is usually the term used to refer to Chinese characters created based on visual resemblance to the objects or phenomena they represent. Pictographs are part of the Chinese writing system, while pictographic symbols, such as the female figure for "ladies' room" in public places, are not part of any writing system.

4   *Yí* is the standard language spoken by the *Yí* people, one of the 55 officially recognized ethnic minority groups in China.

5   The focus of linguistic study before the 20th century was predominantly on what was written down. Even among modern linguists, the primacy of speech has not been without controversy. George Sampson (1985), for example, argued for a status of writing on par with that of speech. He considered writing and speech both aspects of language (pp. 11–13). In the context of our discussion, assuming the primacy of speech makes more sense and will help avoid much confusion.

6   Berwick and Chomsky (2016).
7   It should be acknowledged that a speech-based definition for "language" has its limitations. Sign languages are full languages (more broadly defined) as well, yet they are excluded from this definition. Defining language as speech, however, makes sense in the context of this book, because we are primarily concerned with writing systems used to represent speech, not sign languages.

3 What kinds of writing systems are there?

Classification of writing systems

What makes one writing system similar to or different from another? Is it the appearance of the symbols, the number of the letters or characters, or something else? Recall how we have defined writing: writing is a systematic representation of language using graphic marks. This tells us that what fundamentally distinguishes writing systems from each other is in how the written symbols (graphemes) represent the units of speech – or at what linguistic level such representation takes place. In other words, the nature of the script changes depending on whether a writing system's graphemes correspond to phonemes, syllables, morphemes, or some other units of speech. This correspondence is the basis on which we classify writing systems.

Broadly speaking, we can divide writing systems into two categories: those whose graphemes represent speech sounds only and do not involve meaning are called **phonographic** scripts. Many familiar languages, such as English, Spanish, modern Korean, Arabic, Hebrew, and Cherokee, are typically written using phonographic scripts.

Phonographic scripts can be further differentiated from each other based on the specific unit of speech a grapheme represents. In a **phonemic** writing system, a grapheme corresponds to a phoneme. The Roman alphabet is perhaps the most widely used phonemic writing system – and the most widely used writing system in the world – in terms of the variety of languages it conventionally encodes. Aside from languages with European origins such as Irish, Hungarian, Romanian, and Czech, it is also used for non-European languages including modern Vietnamese, Indonesian, Turkish, Afrikaans, and Hawaiian. The current total number of languages primarily written in the Latin script is more than 130. Languages typically written in other scripts also often have official alternatives in Roman letters. For example, the main East Asian languages we discuss in this book, Chinese, Japanese, and Korean, have all been **Romanized**, or represented in the Latin alphabet, to take advantage of its more universal currency.

A second kind of phonographic writing system is the so-called **consonantal** script. Arabic and Hebrew, for example, are usually written without representing vowels. Rather, each grapheme corresponds to a consonant. This works because the use of vowels in these languages is generally predictable based on the consonants, and a proficient reader will be able to fill out the vowels as she reads.

In a phonographic writing system, a grapheme may also correspond to a single syllable in the language. For example, the *Yí* language in China is usually written this way (Table 3.1). Scripts like this are referred to as **syllabic** writing systems, or **syllabaries**.

Table 3.1 *Yí* symbols representing syllables

Yí syllabogram	Romanization
ꀉ	ap
ꀘ	bi
ꀁ	gguot

It is also possible for a grapheme of a phonographic script to represent a speech unit whose size is between a single speech sound and a syllable. Japanese *hiragana* (平仮名) and *katakana* (片仮名), collectively known as *kana*, are such writing systems. In *kana*, each symbol represents a **mora**, a phonological unit intermediate between a phoneme and a syllable. More specifically in Japanese, a mora can be a single vowel (V), e.g., *a*; a consonant-vowel sequence (CV) within a syllable, e.g., *ka-*; a nasal (N) at the end of a syllable, e.g., -(ka)*n*; or the first segment of a double consonant (C(C)), e.g., *t(t)*. As you see, a mora can be either a single sound (V, N, C(C)) or a syllable (CV, V). Table 3.2 shows a few examples.

Table 3.2 Japanese *kana* symbols representing morae

Hiragana	Katakana	Romanization	Moraic structure
あ	ア	a	V
か	カ	ka	CV
ん	ン	-n	N
まった	マッタ	(ma)t(ta)	C(C)

Why do we need the concept "mora" after all, if it is so cumbersome to define? It has to do with the timing and rhythm of the language, in this case Japanese. Apparently, mora is the timing unit on which the Japanese speech is based. That is to say, each mora is given about the same amount of time in speaking Japanese. The concept of mora, therefore, is indispensable for describing and understanding the Japanese sound system. We will talk more about Japanese morae in Chapter 11 of the book. For now, it is sufficient to know that **moraic** writing systems are also a type of phonographic script.

Unlike phonographic scripts, which represent speech sounds only, the character-based writing system for Mandarin Chinese consists of symbols that do involve meaning. A Chinese character, in most cases, represents the smallest combination of sound and meaning – that is, a morpheme – in speech. We refer to such a writing system as a **morphographic** or a morphemic script. More specifically, since a character usually corresponds to a syllable in terms of speech sounds, we can also say that Chinese uses a **morphosyllabic** writing system.

THE STORY BEYOND

Morphographic? Logographic?

You may have heard of another term that is often used to characterize the Chinese script: logographic. Some also refer to Chinese characters as "logographs" or "logograms." How is "logographic" different from "morphographic"? Which adjective offers a more accurate description of the Chinese writing system?

The "logo-" part of the word "logographic" derives from the Greek *lógos*, meaning "word." A logographic script is thus a writing system in which a grapheme typically represents a word or a phrase. This is not exactly the case for Chinese characters, however. A great portion of the words in Modern Chinese contains more than one morpheme (and more than one syllable in pronunciation) and so must be written using more than one character. In other words, a large number of Chinese characters represents morphemes that cannot stand alone as words and must be combined with other morphemes to form words in Modern Chinese. This is why Chinese writing is not entirely logographic, and "morphographic" is a more accurate characterization.

We can summarize the different types of writing systems in Table 3.3.

Table 3.3   Classification of writing systems

Category	Type	Examples
Phonographic	Phonemic	English, (modern) Korean, (modern) Vietnamese
	Consonantal	Arabic, Hebrew
	Moraic	Japanese (*hiragana* and *katakana*), Cherokee, Cree-Inuktitut
	Syllabic	*Yí* (in China)
Morphographic	Morphosyllabic	Mandarin (Chinese)

So far, we have been assuming that the grapheme-speech relationship for a given pair of writing system and language is uniform. In the case of English written in the Roman alphabet, for example, such an assumption would mean that each Roman letter consistently represents a phoneme in English: <p> would usually be a consonant and <a> would normally represent a vowel – even though the specific consonant and vowel might not always be the same ones.[1]

In reality, however, this grapheme-speech relationship is almost never completely consistent. English, in particular, is notorious for its pervasive spelling irregularities. One letter may represent multiple speech sounds, and a single speech sound may be written as two or more letters. One often cited example, to push this point to a certain extreme, is the artificial word *ghoti* as an alternative spelling for the English word "fish." If we extend the grapheme-phoneme correspondences in the words listed below to *ghoti*, we will indeed be pronouncing it as "fish." Note that in this form, the letter <i>, which normally represents a vowel, is part of a spelling combination for a consonant.

> *gh*, pronounced *f* /f/ as in *tough* /tʌf/
> *o*, pronounced *i* /ɪ/ as in *women* /ˈwɪmən/
> *ti*, pronounced *sh* /ʃ/ as in *nation* /ˈneɪʃən/

Despite such discrepancies, the Roman alphabet in writing English is still, in essence, a phonemic writing system. The fundamental relationship of "one letter, one sound" still holds

THE STORY BEYOND

The life of *ghoti*

The spelling *ghoti* for "fish" traces its origin to English text written in no later than the mid-19th century. It has been attributed to a number of sources, the earliest of which appears to be William Ollier Jr. (born 1824) in a letter drafted by his father. The word was later on often cited to support English-language spelling reform.

Ghoti has taken on a life of its own in modern popular culture. In Klingon, the constructed language of the Klingons in *Star Trek*, the word for "fish" is spelled as *ghotI'*. In the 1966 *Batman* TV episode "An Egg Grows in Gotham," Ghoti Oeufs Caviar Company is the name of the fictional character Egghead's caviar business. Ghoti Hook was the name of a Christian punk band active during 1991–2002 based in Fairfax, Virginia, though the band pronounced its own name as "goatee" instead of "fish."

The speech synthesizer in Mac OS X pronounces *ghoti* as "fish."[2]

true. This is especially understandable if we view the subject from a historical perspective. Many of the spelling irregularities arose from phonological changes in the English language over time. For instance, why is it that we do not pronounce the <k> in words like *knight, knot,* and *knowledge* yet we spell them with a <k> in writing? In fact, <k> used to be pronounced in Old English before <n>, and it sounded just like the <k> in *kid* today. In modern German, a language genetically related to English, <k> is also still pronounced before <n> in words like *Knecht* (/knɛçt/ 'servant') and *Knoten* (/ˈknoːtn̩/ 'knot').

The linguistic universal of writing systems

Given the variety of existent writing systems, you may wonder: Can any language be written in any writing system? Or, is a language inherently tied to a particular (kind of) script? For example, must the English language be written in the Latin alphabet? Must it be written in a phonemic writing system, more broadly speaking? Can it be represented using a system like the one for Mandarin Chinese – that is, a morphographic script?

We in fact already touched on this earlier, and, simply put, the answer is "yes" – any language can be written using any writing system, at least theoretically. To understand how this is, we need to take a deeper look into the nature of writing and language. Although writing systems employ a wide range of symbol-speech relationships, fundamentally, they are all visual means to represent speech, and in this sense, speech serves as the foundation for all systems of writing, and visually representing speech is the defining feature or purpose of writing. As John DeFrancis pointed out in *Visible Speech* (1989), "all full systems of writing are based on representation of sounds. . . . Just how a particular writing system goes about making sound visible is a secondary matter."[3] We have seen that speech can be made visible by having a grapheme represent a single speech sound (phonemic, consonantal), a combination of speech sounds without meaning (moraic, syllabic), or a combination of speech sounds with meaning (morphemic). These linguistic units are universal to languages – both English and Chinese have phonemes, syllables, and morphemes, for example. So there is no theoretical reason why a language cannot be written using multiple types of scripts. And indeed they already are. You may remember that Mandarin Chinese is written in both the morphosyllabic character-based system and in *pīnyīn*, which uses the phonemic Roman alphabet. Likewise, English may also be written using non-phonemic systems. On the companion website is a simple exercise that shows how this may work.

Companion website

Exercise 3.1 Alternative ways to write an English word

Notes

1   The same letter may be pronounced differently in different contexts. For example, <a> in *far, bad*, and *atop* have different pronunciations.
2   Information about the use of *ghoti* in popular culture comes from the Wikipedia entry *Ghoti*: https://en.wikipedia.org/wiki/Ghoti.
3   DeFrancis (1989, pp. 248–249).

4 *Pīnyīn* tutorial

BEFORE DELVING INTO THE character-based writing system for Chinese, it would be beneficial, if you have not done so, to learn to read and pronounce *pīnyīn* (full name *Hànyǔ Pīnyīn* 汉语拼音/漢語拼音 'sound-spelling system for Chinese language'), the international standard for Romanizing modern Chinese[1] in writing. There are a number of good reasons why. First of all, as a system of writing for Modern Standard Chinese in its own right, *pīnyīn* is naturally a subject of study for this book. In Chapter 14, we will be looking at the history and current uses of this script in more depth and detail. For now, it would be good to be aware that a substantial number of words in this book are represented in *pīnyīn*. In fact, *pīnyīn* has been used to represent Chinese lexical items in Western academic literature and official publications since the 1980s, so chances are that you will encounter *pīnyīn* words in other books about China published in a Western language. Being able to pronounce such words, albeit silently in your mind, would allow for a smoother, more confident, and more enjoyable reading experience.

More broadly, *pīnyīn* is commonly used as a pedagogical aid to learning Chinese by both native and non-native speakers. It is indispensable for dictionaries, language textbooks, and children's books. For many, *pīnyīn* is also the preferred method to input Chinese text on computers and other electronic devices (a topic we will discuss in Chapter 16). Public signage in China, especially those signs containing geographical names for streets, around highway exits, at airports or train stations, or proper names on plaques for shops and restaurants, often has *pīnyīn* accompanying characters to assist foreign visitors. Figure 4.1 shows the name of a convenience store, *Nóngjiā bǎihuò diàn* (农家百货店/農家百貨店 'farm family convenience shop'), run by a local household in a scenic area in rural *Héběi* (河北 '(name of a province in Northern China)').

Another reason for learning to read *pīnyīn* is that it can be accomplished even if you do not yet speak the Chinese language. Chinese syllable shapes are a closed set – that is, there are a limited variety of permissible syllables – so it is conceivable to learn to pronounce every possible syllable. If you master *pīnyīn*, you will be able to pronounce passages of Chinese Romanized in this script even if you do not yet understand the textual meaning, and the ability to do so brings you one step closer to learning the language.

Reading *pīnyīn* involves spelling out syllables by putting together their components. In fact, *pīn* (拼) means "to spell," and *yīn* (音) means "sound," so the name *pīnyīn* reveals the script's working mechanism of "spelling the sounds." A Chinese syllable usually consists of two parts, an initial consonant (which may be absent) referred to as an "initial" (*shēngmǔ* 声母/聲母 in Chinese) and the remainder known as a "final" (*yùnmǔ* 韵母/韻母). A final can be a single vowel, which makes for a "simple final." It may also contain a main vowel and a secondary vowel with or without a nasal consonant (i.e., *-n*, *-ng*) at the end of the syllable, in

FIGURE 4.1   Store signage with Chinese characters annotated with *pīnyīn*

which case the final is referred to as a "compound final." A syllable typically carries a tone that spans across its entirety.[2]

Now, let us get started. We will begin by reading the simple finals first and then move on to the initials. This is because the initials are usually pronounced with simple finals added for greater audibility. After that, we will practice reading the compound finals and learn a few rules about spelling *pīnyīn* in full syllables. Finally, we will learn about tones and practice pronouncing syllables with tones.

Simple finals

There are six simple finals, as shown in Table 4.1.

Table 4.1 Simple finals

a	o	e	i	u	ü

Companion website

Table 4.1 Simple finals

Listen to the recordings on the companion website, and you will see that four of the simple finals are pronounced very much the same way the letters are typically pronounced in Western orthography: *a* sounds like the *a* in *Dada*, *o* is similar to the *o* in *form* when *r* is not pronounced (as in British English), *i* is more or less the same as the *i* in *kiwi*, and *u* the *u* in *truth*.

The *e* in *pīnyīn* may need some special attention. It is not pronounced as in the English word *met*, but is rather like the first vowel in *ago* or *above*. Thus, *he* in *pīnyīn* sounds more like the word *her* (without the *r* sound) than *he* in English.

The vowel *ü* tends to be more difficult for English speakers, because it represents a sound not used in English, and its lip-rounding gesture may be particularly unfamiliar to monolingual English speakers. However, it can be easily pronounced by following a few simple steps. First, say the vowel in *kiwi*. As you sustain this vowel sound, tighten your lips into a circular shape while keeping your tongue in the same position. There, you should now end up with a *ü* sound. The key here is to round your lips as if you were trying to whistle. You can check the shape of your lips in a mirror and make sure they are rounded. As you practice, try to distinguish this sound from *u* and *i*, and also distinguish it from the English word *you*. With sufficient practice, you will be able to pronounce it accurately.

Companion website

Exercise 4.1 Simple finals

Initials

"Initials" refer to consonants that occur at the beginning of syllables. Much like the Roman alphabet, *pīnyīn* initials (and finals) are usually arranged in a chart following a conventional order, as shown in Table 4.2. Syllables in the parentheses annotate how the initials are usually read. Notice here that simple finals are added to the initials to form full syllables in order to make the initials easier to pronounce and more audible.

Table 4.2   Initials

b (bō)	p (pō)	m (mō)	f (fō)
d (dē)	t (tē)	n (nē)	l (lē)
g (gē)	k (kē)	h (hē)	
j (jī)	q (qī)	x (xī)	
zh (zhī)	ch (chī)	sh (shī)	r (rī)
z (zī)	c (cī)	s (sī)	
[y (yī)]	[w (wū)]		

Listen to the recordings on the companion website. You will find most of the syllables straightforward to pronounce. However, in a few places the vowel *i* is not pronounced as an English reader may typically imagine: In the fifth and sixth rows it is not pronounced as *ee*, but rather as a voiced[3] elongation of the consonants *zh, ch, sh, r, z, c*, and *s*. For this reason, the *pīnyīn* syllable *shi* sounds quite different from the English word *she*, and *si* is different from *see*. Listen and see if this makes sense to you.

Companion website

Table 4.2 Initials

Which of the initials are similar to sounds used in English? Which ones may be new to you? The first three rows should be relatively easy for native English speakers, as the consonants in these rows are almost identical to those in English. It may become more challenging as we reach rows four to six, because some of the sounds are not part of the English phonological inventory. We will look at these sounds more closely.

The series *j*, *q*, and *x* may pose the greatest challenge for English speakers. These sounds form a series because they use very similar configuration of the vocal tract. The key gesture here is to press the middle part of the tongue up against the roof of the mouth,[4] and then make the sound by letting air squeeze out between them, resulting in a great amount of friction. For *j* and *q*, start out with the tongue completely touching the roof of the mouth. For *x*, the tongue approximates the roof of the mouth with a slight space in between. The distinction between *j* and *q* is that *q* is accompanied by a much stronger puff of air or aspiration. *J*, *q*, and *x* are somewhat similar to the English *j(eep)*, *ch(eese)*, and *sh(eep)*, respectively, but they really have a different quality. Some say they seem softer, but others feel they are sharper compared to the English consonants. You can decide for yourself which makes more sense; what is important is to be able to tell the difference by listening and imitate as closely as you can. The three sounds also pattern the same way in the Chinese phonology: *j*, *q*, and *x* can only be followed by one of two vowels, *i* or *ü* (written as *u* after *j*, *q*, or *x*). When they are followed by *i*, spread your lips in pronouncing the consonant; when they are followed by *ü*, round your lips.

THE STORY BEYOND

Say "eggplant"!

When taking photos, you get a smiling look when your subjects say "cheese." In Chinese, a popular word for the same purpose is *qiézi* (茄子 'eggplant'). Can you explain why saying these words generates a smiley expression?

You may find close equivalents in English for the next series *zh*, *ch*, *sh*, and *r*. *Zh* is very much like the initial and final consonant in *judge*, *ch* is similar to the first consonant in *chair*, and *sh* is very close to the English *sh* in *shape*. The Chinese *r* is pronounced like the English *r* but without the lip rounding and often with the tip of the tongue curled up.[5] Some Chinese speakers may also pronounce it as something close to the *s* in *treasure*.

Now we move on to the next row: *z*, *c*, and *s*. Be careful about *z* and *c* – they are pronounced differently from what you may assume from an English perspective. *Z* is similar to the final consonants in *heads* represented by *ds*. *C* is very much like the *ts* sound in *cats*, so it is not pronounced like a *k*. *S* is the same as the English *s*.

The bottom row contains two symbols, *y* and *w*. They are not in the official chart of *pīnyīn* initials. However, they occupy the position of initials in writing when the syllables do not have initials in pronunciation: If the syllable starts with the vowel *i*, a letter *y* is added to the initial position, and when it begins with the vowel *u*, the letter *w* is added. In this chart, we pronounce *y* as *yee* and *w* as *woo*.

Companion website

Exercise 4.2 Initials and simple finals

Compound finals

The final of a Chinese syllable may contain two or three vowels. There may also be a nasal *-n* or *-ng* following the vowels, or a retroflex[6] *-r* in the case of *er*. Finals like these are referred to as "compound finals." Listen to the recording for Table 4.3 and practice saying the compound finals. Notice how the vowels *a* and *e* may have different qualities in different syllables. This is because they are affected by the sounds around them. For our purpose, instead of trying to remember the different pronunciations of these vowels in different contexts, it may be helpful to simply memorize the pronunciation of the compound finals as a whole.

Table 4.3 Compound finals

ai	ei	ao	ou					
an	en	ang	eng	ong				
ia	ie	iao	iou	ian	in	iang	ing	iong
ua	uo	uai	uei	uan	uen	uang	ueng	
üe	üan	ün						
er								

Companion website

Table 4.3 Compound finals

Exercise 4.3 Initials and compound finals

Spelling rules

When writing *pīnyīn*, the letters we put down on paper sometimes do not correspond exactly to the sounds we pronounce or hear. The discrepancies are mostly by design and are compromises made to render the orthography more systematic and easier to use. The patterns are quite regular and can be summarized as a few spelling rules.

When a syllable does not have an initial and starts with the vowel *a, o,* or *e*, no initial needs to be added in writing. For example, *ā, áng, ǒu, èn* are legitimate syllables in full form.

By contrast, if a syllable starts with the vowel *i, u,* or *ü*, an initial must be supplied in writing.[7]

Syllables beginning with the *i* sound must be written with the letter *y* at the beginning. If the syllable contains only one vowel *i*, then it is written with a letter *y* added to the front: *yi (i), yin (in), ying (ing)*. If the syllable contains the vowel *i* followed by another one or two vowels, then the letter *y* replaces the letter *i*: *ya (ia), yao (iao), ye (ie), you (iou,* spelled as *iu* elsewhere), *yan (ian), yang (iang), yong (iong)*.

Likewise, if a syllable begins with the sound *u*, then in writing it starts with the letter *w*. If the syllable contains only one vowel *u*, then it is written with a letter *w* added to the front: *wu (u)*. If the syllable contains the vowel *u* followed by another one or two vowels, then the letter *w* replaces the letter *u*: *wa (ua), wo (uo), wai (uai), wei (uei,* spelled as *ui* elsewhere), *wan (uan), wen (uen,* spelled as *un* elsewhere), *wang (uang), weng (ueng)*.

If a syllable begins with the vowel *ü, ü* is replaced with *yu* in writing. When *ü* is the only vowel in the syllable, it is written as *yu (ü)* or *yun (ün)*. Notice that the two dots of the umlaut *ü* are taken off following the letter *y*, but the vowel represented by the *yu* sequence is still just *ü*. If *ü* is followed by another one or two vowels, it is also replaced by *yu*: *yue (üe), yuan (üan)*.

Table 4.4 is a summary of all zero-initial syllables written in *pīnyīn*.

Table 4.4 Spelling rules for zero-initial syllables (syllables in parentheses are written as the forms above them)

yi	ya	ye	yao	you	yan	yin	yang	ying	yong
(i)	(ia)	(ie)	(iao)	(iou)	(ian)	(in)	(iang)	(ing)	(iong)

wu	wa	wo	wai	wei	wan	wen	wang	weng	
(u)	(ua)	(uo)	(uai)	(uei)	(uan)	(uen)	(uang)	(ueng)	

yu	yue	yuan	yun
(ü)	(üe)	(üan)	(ün)

Companion website

Table 4.4 Spelling rules for zero-initial syllables

The compound finals *iou, uei,* and *uen*, when preceded by initials, are abbreviated as *iu, ui,* and *un*, respectively. Thus, *liu* should be pronounced as /liou/, *sui* as /suei/, and *tun* as /tuen/, for example. As stated earlier, as stand-alone zero-initial syllables, *iou, uei,* and *uen* are written as *you, wei,* and *wen*, respectively.

ü is written without the two dots when following the initials *j, q,* and *x* (in addition to when following *y* as previously discussed). This is because the sound *u* never occurs after *j*, *q*, and *x* in Chinese, and leaving out the two dots on ü should not cause any confusion. Just make sure to round your lips when pronouncing the syllables *ju, qu, xu, jue, que, xue, juan, quan, xuan,* and *jun, qun, xun.* Also be aware that both *ü* and *u* can occur after the initials *n* and *l*, so it is necessary to keep the two dots for *ü* here in order to distinguish *nü* from *nu*, and *lü* from *lu*.

The compound final *er* cannot take any initials. When it is a stand-alone syllable, it is written simply as *er*. This syllable may also serve as a suffix used after certain nouns and verbs. In pronunciation, the suffix usually merges with the syllable in front of it, forming one single syllable. For this reason, it is written as a single letter *r*. A few examples are in Table 4.5. You can listen to a recording of these words on the companion website. Note that this is a case in which two Chinese characters are used to represent a single syllable.

Table 4.5   Representation of *er* as suffix in *pīnyīn*

Pīnyīn for individual characters	*Pīnyīn* for word	Meaning of word
花 *huā*; 兒 *ér*	花兒 *huār*	'flowers'
事 *shì*; 兒 *ér*	事兒 *shìr*	'things (to do); business'
玩 *wán*; 兒 *ér*	玩兒 *wánr*	'to play (with)'

Although character writing does not indicate word boundaries, *pīnyīn* writing does.[8] Thus, a space is placed in between two words, while a multisyllabic word is written with its syllables strung together. Sometimes it can become ambiguous as to where one syllable starts and another ends. In such cases, an apostrophe is used to separate the syllables. It is also used to separate two syllables with conjoining vowels. A few examples are in Table 4.6.

Table 4.6   Marking syllable boundaries in *pīnyīn*

Pīnyīn	Chinese characters	Meaning
fāng'àn	方案	'scheme, plan'
fǎn'gǎn	反感	'dislike; be averse to'
dī'àn	堤岸	'embankment'
diàn	電	'electricity'

Companion website

Exercise 4.4 Spelling rules

Tones

When pitch variations are used to distinguish word (morpheme) meaning in a language, we refer to them as **tones**. Chinese makes use of four basic tones. They are simply called "the first tone," "the second tone," "the third tone," and "the fourth tone." It is important to be able to articulate Chinese syllables in correct tones, because changing a syllable from one tone to another may alter the meaning of a word or morpheme. A classic example used to illustrate such tonal contrasts is the syllable *ma*. When pronounced in its high-level first tone, *mā* may mean "mother." In the mid-rising second tone, *má* may mean "hemp." The third tone *mǎ* consists of a dip followed by a rise in the tonal contour and can mean "horse." In its high-falling fourth tone, *mà* may mean "to scold." You can hear these examples on the companion website.

Companion website

Example 4.1 Tones: *mā, má, mǎ, mà*

Does English have tones? English makes use of intonation, but not tones. Both intonation and tones are essentially variations in pitch, like changing from one note to another on the musical scale. However, only when such variations are used to distinguish lexical meaning do they become tones. Intonation in English may indicate whether the speaker is making a statement or asking a question – for example, "yes!" with a falling pitch vs. "yes?" with a rising pitch – but it does not change the fundamental meaning of the word. "Yes" still means "yes."

Chinese tones are conventionally described on a five-level scale. If we divide a speaker's natural comfortable pitch range into five levels – 1 through 5, from low to high – we can represent the contours of the four tones on a diagram as shown in Figure 4.2. The first tone (5–5) is high and level. It starts at level 5 and remains all the way through at level 5. The second tone (3–5) is a mid-rising tone, starting at 3 and ending at 5. The third tone (2–1–4) starts fairly low at 2, dips to 1, and then goes up to 4. The fourth tone (5–1) is a high falling tone, starting at 5 and finishing at 1. Such tonal forms shown in the diagram are referred to as **citation forms**. When a Chinese syllable is pronounced in isolation, its tonal contour is usually close to the citation form. In continuous speech, however, the actual tonal contours may be different. This is especially true for the third tone (2–1–4), which is usually realized only as its first half (2–1) in connected speech, so that it starts low and dips to 1 but does not then rise to 4, unless the syllable bearing this tone ends the utterance. That is, the third tone is usually realized as a low-falling tone. The low-falling tone sounds almost like a low-level tone. Thus, overall it may be useful to think of the Chinese tonal system as an almost symmetrical one that consists of a high-level tone (the first tone 1–1), a low-level tone (the third tone 2–1), a rising tone (the second tone 3–5), and a falling tone (the fourth tone 5–1).

In writing, tones are marked using diacritics on vowels, for example: *mā* (first tone), *má* (second tone), *mǎ* (third tone), and *mà* (fourth tone). What happens when there is more than one vowel in the syllable? This is where the vowel sequence *a-o-e-i-u-ü* comes in handy as a reference tool: the tone mark goes on the vowel that is closer to the beginning of this sequence. For example, *hǎo, tài, mōu, léi, xiè, duì, lüè*. There is one exception to the rule, however. For the compound vowel *iu*, the tone mark goes on *u* instead of on *i*. One way to remember this exception is that when the compound final consists of the two vowels *i* and *u*, regardless which comes first, the tone mark always falls on the second vowel (e.g., *diū* and *duī*).

FIGURE 4.2 Contours of basic tones on a five-level scale

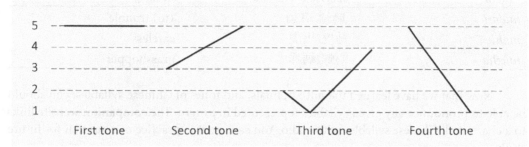

First tone   Second tone   Third tone   Fourth tone

Companion website

Example 4.2 Tones: *hǎo, tài, mōu, léi, xiè, duì, lüè; diū, duī*

Exercise 4.5 Four tones in citation form

When two syllables with third tones are right next to each other, the first syllable changes into the second tone. Thus, *nǐhǎo* (你好 "hello") is actually pronounced as *níhǎo* even though it is written as *nǐhǎo*. Such tonal changes of syllables based on the tones of adjacent syllables are referred to in linguistics as **tone sandhi**. The word sandhi means "fusional change" and is derived from the Sanskrit word *saṃdhi*, meaning "joining" or "juncture."

Companion website

Exercise 4.6 Four tones in bi-syllabic words

In addition to syllables with the four tones as described earlier, sometimes Chinese syllables may be pronounced briefly and lightly with no fundamental tonal contour. Such syllables are said to have a **neutral tone** and do not bear any tone marks in writing. All neutral tones may not be quite the same in pitch value, however, as the pitch value may change based on what tone the preceding syllable has. After a first-tone syllable, a neutral-tone syllable usually has a pitch value of 2. After a second-, third-, and fourth-tone syllable, its pitch value is most often at 3, 4, and 1 respectively. Listen to the examples in Table 4.6 and see if you can tell the difference.

Table 4.7 Pitch variation of neutral-tone syllables

Pīnyīn	Chinese characters	Meaning
māma	妈妈/媽媽	'mother'

(Continued)

Table 4.7   Continued

Pīnyīn	Chinese characters	Meaning
máfan	麻烦/麻煩	'(to) trouble'
mǎhu	马虎/馬虎	'careless'
màzha	蚂蚱/螞蚱	'grasshopper'

Now that we have learned the initials, finals, and tones of Chinese syllables, you should be able to pronounce any given syllables represented in *pīnyīn*. The companion website links to a chart of all Chinese syllables with audio. You can use it to practice or refer to it for future study.

Companion website

Table 4.7 Pitch variation of neutral-tone syllables

Exercise 4.7 Neutral tone

Example 4.3 All Mandarin Chinese syllables with audio

Exercise 4.8 Comprehensive practice

Notes

1 The International Organization for Standardization (ISO) adopted *pīnyīn* as an international standard in 1982. In 2009, after a long debate, *pīnyīn* also became the official standard in Táiwān, although its use has been limited to representing Chinese in public signage in some cities and provinces. For educational or computer-input purposes, the phonemic script *zhùyīn fúhào* (注音符号/注音符號 *lit.* 'sound-annotation symbols'), also known as *bopomofo*, is more commonly used in Táiwān.

2 For a more detailed description of the Chinese syllable structure, refer to Chapter 5.

3 "Voiced" or "voiceless" are terms used in phonetics to describe the state of the vocal cords when pronouncing a given speech sound. If the vocal cords are held tightly together and vibrating, then the sound is said to be voiced; if they are apart and do not vibrate, then the sound is considered voiceless. Vowels are usually voiced, while consonants can be either voiced or voiceless.

4 Some speakers, especially women and children, use a dental place of articulation for *j*, *q*, and *x*. In this case, the tip of the tongue is placed against the back of the lower teeth, and the front-to-middle section of the tongue approximates the roof of the mouth.

5 Speech sounds pronounced with the tip of the tongue curled up are referred to as "retroflex" sounds.

6 See note 5 on what retroflex means.

7 There is a linguistic reason for this convention. When *i*, *u*, or *ü* is not the only vowel in the syllable, and there is another one or two vowels immediately following it in the same syllable, *i*, *u*, or *ü* are in fact realized as their semi-vowel (also known as "glide") counterparts instead of full vowels. In writing, this is represented by changing *i*, *u*, or *ü* into *y*, *w*, or *yu*, respectively. When *i*, *u*, or *ü* is the

only vowel in the syllable, to maintain regularity in orthography, the initial consonant is still added, thus resulting in *yi* for *i, wu* for *u*, and *yu* for *ü*, for example, even though the pronunciation of the full vowels remains unchanged.

8   Word segmentation is a complex issue in *pīnyīn* orthography because it is relatively difficult to define word boundaries in Chinese. Although a set of standards was established in as early as the 1980s, they are usually not taught at school, and native writers are often oblivious to these standards. As a result, it is not rare to see variations in word segmentation in *pīnyīn* writing.

PART II

Writing Chinese

5 The Chinese speech

WHEN WE TALK ABOUT the native speech of the Chinese people, we often simply call it "the Chinese language." But in reality, there is not a singular or unified Chinese language. In its broad sense, "the Chinese language" encompasses hundreds of varieties,[1] much like "the English language" includes Australian, British, and American English as well as many different regional variations – only much more varied. To understand "the Chinese language," therefore, we will need to learn about the different kinds of speech that fall under the umbrella term "Chinese." This is what we will do first in this chapter. We will then take a focused look at the standard variety of the Chinese speech in contemporary China, which we refer to as Modern Standard Chinese (MSC) or Mandarin.

Chinese languages and dialects

"Chinese," as a linguistic construct, is a collective term that refers to the speech varieties of the *Hàn* people (*Hànzú* 汉族/漢族). The vast majority (92%–95%) of the people in Mainland China, Hong Kong, Macau, and *Táiwān* are ethnically *Hàn*, and *Hàn* is also the largest ethnic group in the world, constituting 18%–19% of the global population. The name *Hàn* is derived from the *Hàn* (汉/漢) dynasty (206 BCE–220 CE), the second imperial dynasty of the unified China and the first golden age of China's power and influence over Asia. In fact, the Chinese language is referred to as *Hànyǔ* (汉语/漢語) in Chinese, literally "the language of the *Hàn*," and the square symbols used to write Chinese are called *Hànzì* (汉字/漢字), "characters of the *Hàn*."

Today, the *Hàn* people in China use a diverse variety of speech. Many of them are **mutually intelligible** – that is, speakers of one variety can by and large understand the speech of another without much deliberate learning – while many others are not. Linguists generally use mutual intelligibility as the key measure to determine whether two genetically related speech varieties are dialects of the same language or two separate languages. If they are mutually intelligible, then they are usually considered **dialects**. In the case of Chinese, for example, many of the Mandarin varieties spoken in *Héběi* (河北) or *Shāndōng* (山东/山東) Provinces in Northern China and those in *Sìchuān* (四川) or *Yúnnán* (云南/雲南) Provinces in Southwestern China are regarded dialects of the same language, because the Mandarin speakers in these areas, though thousands of miles apart, are generally able to comprehend each other. The linguistic relationship among them is to a large extent like that among American English, British English, and Australian English, for example. By contrast, any varieties of speech that are not mutually intelligible are considered different **languages,** whether or not they have historically derived from the same ancestral language. By this definition, Mandarin and Cantonese (aka *Yuè* 粤) should be considered distinct languages, even though they are both descendants of (an earlier version of) Chinese: monolingual Mandarin speakers and monolingual Cantonese speakers usually find it quite impossible to understand each other, albeit both speaking a variety of Chinese. Clearly, "Chinese" should be more accurately understood as a group of related languages rather than as a single language. This group also includes *Wú* (吴), spoken in *Shànghǎi*, *Zhèjiāng*, and the southern part of *Jiāngsū*, *Mǐn* (闽), spoken in *Fújiàn*, *Hǎinán*, and *Táiwān*, and a few other languages. We use the term Sinitic to refer to this group, and we say that Mandarin and Cantonese are both **Sinitic languages**. Other examples of language groups with which you may be familiar include Romance languages and Germanic languages. The relationship between Mandarin, Cantonese, *Wú*, *Mǐn*, and so on is quite like, for instance, that between Spanish, French, Italian, and Romanian, members of the Romance group.

Although Chinese consists of multiple languages (and dialects), scholarly literature on Chinese linguistics still commonly uses the term "dialects" rather than "languages" to refer to the Sinitic speech varieties. This has to do with the convention of the discipline. Linguists in China, in particular, have long used the term *fāngyán* (方言 'speech of a geographical region') to refer to the various speech varieties of Chinese. This term encompasses both the languages and the dialects of Chinese and places them on equal footing regardless of their mutual intelligibility. For example, Northeast Mandarin, Southwest Mandarin, and Cantonese can all be referred to as *Hànyǔ fāngyán* (汉语方言/漢語方言 'Chinese regional speech varieties'). This practice is congruent with the shared history and cultural heritage of the speakers of various Chinese speech varieties. For this reason, while keeping in mind that translating *fāngyán* as "dialect" is not accurate, we will use the term "dialect" in this book to refer to the Chinese speech varieties.[2]

How many varieties of Chinese speech are there? Many linguists recognize seven to ten major dialect groups that are not mutually intelligible. (Within a dialect group, there may also be mutually unintelligible varieties of speech.) Aside from Mandarin and *Yuè* (粤 Cantonese), with which we are by now familiar, there are also *Wú* (吴), *Mǐn* (闽), *Kèjiā* (客家), *Xiāng* (湘), and *Gàn* (赣). Some linguists also recognize *Jìn* (晋/晉) as a dialect group separate from Mandarin, *Huī* (徽) separate from *Wú*, and *Píng* (平) separate from *Yuè*. Table 5.1 provides an overview of the dialect groups ranked by the size of their native-speaker population.

Table 5.1 Chinese dialect groups

Dialect group		Example
Chinese name	English name	
Guānhuà (官话/官話)	Mandarin	*Běijīng* (北京) dialect
Wúyǔ (吴语/吴語)		*Shànghǎi* (上海) dialect
Yuèyǔ (粤语/粤語)	Cantonese	Hong Kong (香港) Cantonese
Mǐnyǔ (闽语/閩語)		Taiwanese Hokkien (台湾福建/台灣福建)
Jìnyǔ (晋语/晉語)		*Tàiyuán* (太原) dialect
Xiāngyǔ (湘语/湘語)		*Chángshā* (长沙/長沙) dialect
Kèjiāhuà (客家话/客家話)	Hakka	*Méizhōu* (梅州) dialect
Gànyǔ (赣语/贛語)		*Nánchāng* (南昌) dialect
Huīyǔ (徽语/徽語)		*Jīxī* (绩溪/績溪) dialect
Pínghuà (平话/平話)		*Guìběi Pínghuà* (桂北平话/桂北平話)

Note: *Yǔ* (语/語) and *huà* (话/話) both mean "speech."

FIGURE 5.1   Map of Chinese dialect groups

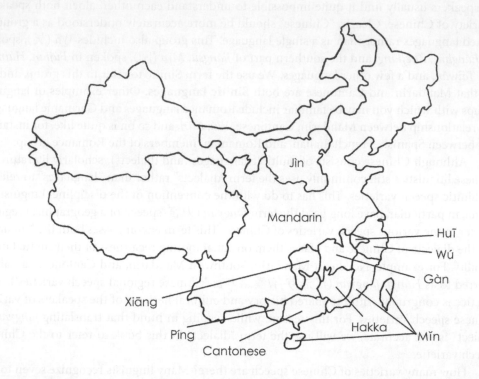

The map in Figure 5.1 shows the primary regions of their native speakers. As you can see, the southeastern area of China is more linguistically diverse than the other parts. In fact, eight of the ten aforementioned dialect groups, that is, all but Mandarin and *Jìn*, find home in this area, while different varieties of Mandarin disperse across Northeastern, Northwestern, and Southwestern China, and *Jìn* speakers concentrate in the central area of Northern China.

Geographical factors contributed to the formation of this pattern. With its dense mountains and rivers, Southeastern China affords much less mobility to its residents compared to the other regions (especially to the Northern plains). When speakers settled in various pockets of this area, it was more difficult for them to maintain contact, and as a result, their speech changed in divergent ways. In time, the diverging speech forms became so distinctive that their speakers could no longer understand each other.

To understand the linguistic diversity in China, it is also important to know that, while the majority ethnic group (i.e., the *Hàn*) speaks Sinitic languages, the ethnic minority groups (*shǎoshù mínzú* 少数民族/少數民族) in China mostly speak other languages in addition to Sinitic. Some examples of these languages are Mongol in Inner Mongolia; Kazakh, Kirghiz, and Uighur in Northwestern China; Tibetan in Western and Southwestern China; Burmese, Thai, and Vietnamese in Southwestern China; and Malayo-Polynesian languages in *Táiwān*.

Modern Standard Chinese

Now that we have gained some basic understanding of the linguistic diversity in China, it is apparent to us that the term "the Chinese language" must be clearly defined if it is to be used for any meaningful or effective discussion. It obviously may refer to only one variety of Chinese, so which one should it be? In today's China, what we call **Modern Standard Chinese** (MSC) is the variety most widely promoted and used for public and official purposes, including in governmental administration, education, commerce, and the media, so it may make sense that this is the variety we refer to when we speak of "the Chinese language." In this book, we will also use "Mandarin" as an alternative term, in keeping with the convention in the field, but "Mandarin" in this case is much more narrowly defined and needs to be differentiated from the "Mandarin" used as the name of a language group in our earlier discussion. MSC or Mandarin is the speech variety on which the writing of Chinese is based. It is not only the predominant form of speech for official use in Mainland China and *Táiwān* but also one of the four official languages in Singapore and one of six used by the United Nations. On the Mainland, it has been referred to as *pǔtōnghuà* (普通话/普通話 'common speech'), a term coined during the language and script standardization efforts led by the People's Republic of China (PRC) government in the 1950s. In *Táiwān*, *guóyǔ* (国语/國語 'national language') remains to be the most common term. Yet another term, *huáyǔ* (华语/華語 'Chinese language'), is used in Singapore.

Historically, the need for a Chinese lingua franca (i.e., common speech) mostly existed within the circle of government officials, who were required to serve outside of their home regions and needed to be able to communicate with each other. The speech variety that arose to meet that need was usually that of the nation's capital, and therefore it changed over time as the capital of China changed locations. In the *Táng* (唐) dynasty (618–907), it was the local speech of *Cháng'ān* (长安/長安), today's *Xī'ān* (西安) in central China. By the Southern Song (1127–1276), this role had shifted to the language of then capital *Lín'ān* (临安/臨安), today's *Hángzhōu* (杭州) in Eastern China. During the last imperial dynasties, the *Míng* (明; 1403–1644) and the *Qīng* (清; 1644–1911), when the capital was located in Běijīng (called *Shùntiānfǔ* 顺天府/順天府 and later on *Jīngshī* 京师/京師) in the north, the mandarins, or public officials, communicated in a speech variety based on the northern dialects, hence the term "Mandarin" continuing in use today.

A national language for China, however, is a recent establishment. Up until the late 19th and early 20th centuries, most Chinese people spoke only their local dialects. The largely agrarian population at the time, living a land-bound life, had little need to communicate with those beyond their local areas. When the country was forced to open its doors to Western colonizers, the promotion of a standard form of speech became part of an urgent nationalist movement, and the concept of a "national language" emerged. It took decades for MSC to eventually become the common language of the Chinese in the real sense. Today, it is generally expected that young Chinese speak MSC in addition to their regional dialects (if they are significantly different from MSC), though many of the older generation may still only speak their local dialects.

Now let us take a closer look at some of the linguistic characteristics of Modern Standard Chinese. In the next chapter, we will discuss the writing of Chinese. Although, in theory, any kind of writing system may be used to write any language, the script that is most suitable or efficient for a given language is one that capitalizes on the structural features of the language. In this case, learning about the syllable structure, tonal system, and the role of homophony in MSC will be especially helpful for understanding the Chinese writing system.

Syllable structure

A **syllable** (represented by the Greek letter σ) is a timing unit in language that consists of, minimally, a vowel. The vowel is referred to as the **nucleus** of the syllable. A syllable may also include an **onset**, that is, one or more consonants that come before the nucleus, and/or a **coda**, that is, one or more consonants following the nucleus. The nucleus and the coda together are referred to as the **rhyme** of the syllable. In a language like Chinese, a syllable may also have an element that applies to its entirety, that is, a tone.

Let's look at an example of an English syllable in a diagram to get a more concrete sense of its structure. As shown in Figure 5.2, the monosyllabic word *feast* can be analyzed as consisting of the onset /f/, nucleus /i/, and coda /st/.

FIGURE 5.2 Structure of an English syllable: *feast* /fist/

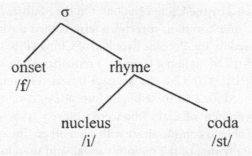

We can use a similar method to diagram the syllable structure of MSC. Traditional Chinese phonology divides the syllable into two parts, initial or *shēngmǔ* (声母/聲母), which is the syllable onset, and final or *yùnmǔ* (韵母/韻母), which corresponds to the rhyme. The onset can maximally be a single consonant and is optional. The rhyme is required and is minimally a single vowel, but it can also contain a sequence of two vowels (i.e., a **diphthong**). The rhyme may also have a **glide** (i.e., -i- /j/, -u- /w/, or -ü- /ɥ/)[3] in front of the nucleus and/or a coda nasal after it. The coda consonant must be one of two nasals, -n /n/ or -ing /ŋ/. Below is an example of the MSC syllable *biān* (Figure 5.3).

FIGURE 5.3 Structure of an MSC syllable: *biān*

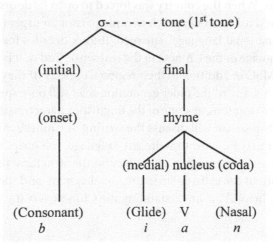

There are 1,840 possible MSC syllable shapes with tones, but only 1,359 (74%) are actually used. English has more distinct syllables, because consonant clusters are allowed both as the syllable onset and the coda. For example, the English word *sprints* has a sequence of three consonants (/s/, /p/, /r/) as its onset, and another three (/n/, /t/, /s/) as the coda. Indeed, compared to the 8,000+ syllable shapes in English, the MSC inventory is much smaller.[4]

THE STORY BEYOND

Biángbiáng noodles

Legitimate but unused MSC syllable shapes are sometimes employed for playful use online or in real life to represent onomatopoeic or dialectical pronunciation. One example is the name of a popular *Shǎnxī* noodle dish, *biángbiáng* noodles. *Biáng* conforms to the syllabic structure of MSC, but it is not associated with any morphemes in the language. That is, its meaning is unclear. Some say that the syllable mimics the sound the noodle-eaters make, and others speculate that it is in fact the sound of the chef slapping the dough to make the noodles. *Biángbiáng* noodles are usually handmade, broad and thick, and are consumed with a generous amount of hot red chili oil. Originally a poor man's meal in the country, it is now served in fashionable urban restaurants.

The popularity of *biángbiáng* noodles can partly be contributed to its playful name. Not only is the pronunciation not part of the standard MSC inventory, but the Chinese character that has been used to write *biáng* is also nonstandard and is not yet typable on the computer. What is more, with 57 strokes in its traditional form and 43 strokes simplified, it is one of the most complex Chinese characters ever invented.

Companion website

Exercise 5.1 MSC syllable structure

Tones

Modern Standard Chinese makes use of four contour tones and one so-called neutral tone[5] to distinguish lexical meaning, or word meaning. To be more exact, altering the tone of a Chinese morpheme changes it into a different morpheme. For words that contain only one morpheme, this means changing the meaning of the word. The classical example used to illustrate this, which you may recall from the *pīnyīn* tutorial (Chapter 4), is repeated in Table 5.2. The syllable *ma*, when realized with different tonal contours, results in different words.

It may be worthwhile to further clarify here the relationship between morphemes and words in MSC. Although mono-morphemic words are reasonably common, MSC words often consist of multiple morphemes. In most cases, a syllable with meaning constitutes a morpheme on its own; however, it may have to combine with at least one other morpheme to fully function as a word. For example, the morpheme *xiào* (校) is usually understood to mean "school," but it is rarely used independently to represent that meaning; rather, the di-morphemic word *xuéxiào* (学校/學校 'school'; 学/學 'to study') is preferred. There are many such examples in MSC.

As described in the *pīnyīn* tutorial, the contour tones are customarily referred to by their numerical names: first, second, third, or fourth tones. When pronounced in isolation in their full forms, the pitch contours of syllables bearing these tones can be represented using numbers indicating pitch level on a five-step scale. On this scale, 1 represents the lowest pitch, and 5 the highest, as shown in Figure 5.2 of the *pīnyīn* tutorial. In Table 5.2, the numbers in the parentheses after the tone names refer to such a notational system. For example, the pitch of the third tone, in its full form, starts out at mid-low (2), dips to low (1), and then rises to mid-high (4), and thus we can use 214 to represent the third tone.[6]

Homophony

One characteristic of MSC is the prevalence of **homophony**, the linguistic phenomenon of two or more different morphemes sharing the same pronunciation. You may be able to easily think of examples of homophony in English: *won, one; two, too, to; meet, meat; hear, here; their, there*; and *red, read*. Yet, you will probably find it challenging to compose a hundred-word passage all in the same syllable. With a stretch, we may come up with something like the below. Give it a try, and you may find that the size of a homophonous group of words is so small in English that you quickly run out of material.

Table 5.2 MSC tones

Tone name (pitch value)	*Pīnyīn*	Chinese characters	Meaning
First tone (55)	*mā*	妈/媽	'mother'
Second tone (35)	*má*	麻	'hemp'
Third tone (214)	*mǎ*	马/馬	'horse'
Fourth tone (51)	*mà*	骂/罵	'to revile'
Neutral tone	*ma*	吗/嗎	'(question marker)'

A: I stayed up till 1:58 last night.

B: I stayed up *to two to two, too*.

In Chinese, however, this may be easier. In fact, homophony is even more prominent in Classical Chinese than in MSC, so much so that the linguist Chao Yuen Ren (赵元任/趙元任, 1892–1982) proved it possible to compose a poem in the Classical Chinese style that tells a developed story, albeit a bizarre one, all using the same syllable. The poem consists of morphemes pronounced *shi* in various tones. Table 5.3 shows the poem in *pīnyīn* and in simplified characters. Note that although the poem is composed in the style of Classical Chinese, the *pīnyīn* representation is based on MSC pronunciation.

Chao made use of about 33 different morphemes in this poem.[8] The meaning of these morphemes and their MSC pronunciation are given in Table 5.4.

As the story goes:

> A poet named Shī lived in a stone den and liked to eat lions, and he vowed to eat ten of them. He used to go to the market in search of lions, and one day at ten o'clock, he chanced to see ten of them there. Shī killed the lions with arrows and picked up their bodies, carrying them back to his stone house. His house was dripping with water so he requested that his servants proceed to dry it. Then he began to try to eat the bodies of the ten lions. It was only then he realized that these were in fact ten lions made of stone. Try to explain this incident.[9]

Homophony exists in MSC to a lesser extent than in Classical Chinese. This is because many mono-morphemic words in Classical Chinese must be expressed in poly-morphemic (and therefore polysyllabic) words in MSC. For example, 誓 (*shì* 'to vow') and 狮/獅 (*shī* 'lions') become 发誓 (*fāshì* 'to vow') and 狮子/獅子 (*shīzi* 'lions') in MSC – no longer homophonous of each other. For this reason, it would have been more difficult to compose such a poem in MSC. Nonetheless, homophony remains an important feature of the language.

Table 5.3   "The story of a lion-eating poet," a single-syllable poem[7]

Shī Shì Shí Shī Shǐ	诗士食狮史
Shí shì shī shì Shī Shì, shì shī,	石室诗士施氏，嗜狮，
Shì shí shí shī.	誓食十狮。
Shī Shì shí shí shì shì shì shī.	施氏时时适市视狮。
Shí shí, shì shí shī shì shì.	十时，适十狮适市。
Shì shí, shì Shī Shì shì shì.	是时，适施氏适市。
Shī Shì shì shì shí shī, shì shǐ shì,	施氏视是十狮，恃矢势，
Shǐ shì shí shī shì shì.	使是十狮逝世。
Shī Shì shí shì shí shī shī, shì shí shì.	施氏拾是十狮尸，适石室。
Shí shì shī, Shī Shì shì shì shì shí shì,	石室湿，施氏使侍拭石室，
Shí shì shì, Shī Shì shǐ shì shí shì shí shī shī.	石室拭，施氏始试食是十狮尸。
Shí shí, shǐ shí shì shí shī shī shí shí shí shī shī.	食时，始识是十狮尸实十石狮尸。
Shì shì shì shì.	试释是事。

Table 5.4 Morphemes in the poem "The story of a lion-eating poet"

Chinese characters	Pīnyīn	Meaning
诗/詩	shī	'poetry, poem'
士	shì	'scholar'
食	shí	'to eat'
狮/獅	shī	'lion'
史	shǐ	'history, story'
石	shí	'stone'
室	shì	'room, den'
施	Shī	'(family name)'
氏	shì	'(affix to a specific family name to form a term of address)'
嗜	shì	'to enjoy very much; to be obsessed with'
誓	shì	'to vow'
十	shí	'ten'
时时/時時	shíshí	'oftentimes; frequently'
适/適	shì	(1) 'as it happens at the time' (2) 'to go to'
市	shì	'market'
视/視	shì	'to view, to examine'
时/時	shí	'o'clock' (here combined with the number ten to indicate a specific time of the day)
是	shì	(1) 'this, these' (2) 'to be'
恃	shì	'to take on (a particular pose)'
矢	shǐ	'arrow; to shoot arrows'
势/勢	shì	'pose'
使	shǐ	'to cause to'
逝世	shìshì	'to pass away'
拾	shí	'to pick up'
尸/屍	shī	'corpse'
湿/濕	shī	'wet'
侍	shì	'servant'
拭	shì	'to wipe'
始	shǐ	(1) 'to begin (doing something)' (2) 'not . . . until'
试/試	shì	'to try'
识/識	shí	'to recognize, to realize'
释/釋	shì	'to explain'
事	shì	'matter, thing'

Notes

1   The expressions "varieties," "speech varieties," and "language varieties" are used as neutral terms to refer to particular kinds of speech. This is to avoid confusion between such concepts as "languages" and "dialects," which are defined by relating speech varieties to each other, and are in this sense not neutral. As a rough analogy, "(speech/language) varieties" is a neutral term for "languages" and "dialects" just like "(speech) sounds" is a neutral term for "phonemes" or "allophones."

2   To avoid the confusion caused by the use of the term "dialect" to refer to distinct Chinese languages, linguist Victor Mair (1991) coined the term "topolect" as an English equivalent for the Chinese *fāngyán*. "Topo-" indicates "region" or "location" as a translation of *fāng* ('region, location') in *fāngyán* ("regional speech"). Because this term is not widely used in introductory materials on Chinese languages and dialects, this book does not adopt this term.

3   Pīnyīn followed by IPA is used here to represent the glides and later to represent the nasals.

4   According to DeFrancis (1977, p. 7), there are some 75 to 100 distinct syllables in Hawaiian, 100 to 300 in Japanese, 1,100 in Korean, 1,300 in Chinese, 4,800 for the Hanoi dialect of Vietnamese and 4,500 for the Saigon dialect, and 8,000 in English.

5   Neutral tones are so named because a syllable that bears such a tone is usually light and brief, and it can be perceived as "toneless" compared with syllables with full tones. However, it does not mean that a neutral-tone syllable does not have any pitch value. In fact, depending on the phonological context – usually the tonal value of the syllable immediately preceding it – a neutral tone can be realized as different pitches. It becomes a mid-register tone after a high-level (first) tone or a high-rising (second) tone, a mid-high tone after a low-dipping (third) tone, and a low tone after a falling (fourth) tone.

6   As noted in the *pīnyīn* tutorial, the full contour of the third tone is not generally realized in connected speech. When a third-tone syllable is immediately followed by at least one other syllable in the same utterance, it usually stops short as a low dipping tone (21). Speakers would sound highly stilted if they pronounced third-tone syllables in the full 214 contour in utterance-medial positions. When a third tone is utterance-final, however, it may be more fully realized.

7   Text adapted from Rogers (2005, p. 30).

8   In the Contemporary Chinese Dictionary, there are 85 *shi* morphemes represented by distinct characters.

9   Translation adapted from Rogers (2005, p. 30).

6 Written Chinese

CLASSICAL CHINESE WAS THE standard written form of Chinese for most of the imperial Chinese history. It still has a profound impact on the Chinese language today. In this chapter, we will take a brief look at this once dominant form of Chinese written language and how it relates to Chinese speech and writing today.

Classical Chinese as a written standard

When we discussed the relationship between writing and speech in Chapter 2, we had clarified the differences between a "written language" and a "writing system." Essentially, a written language is a language primarily used in writing, while a writing system is a set of symbols used to record and represent languages – spoken or written – in a graphic form. Classical Chinese was one of the examples we gave at that time for written languages. In fact, for more than two millennia and up till the early 20th century, Classical Chinese was the main form of written communication in China. Writing for official as well as personal purposes was done almost exclusively in Classical Chinese.

Educated Chinese wrote in the Classical style during that long period of time regardless of the variety of Chinese language they spoke. Their vernaculars were almost never mutually intelligible with Classical Chinese; in other words, they often spoke and wrote in different languages. Recall that, also in Chapter 2, we introduced the term **diglossia:**[1] the linguistic phenomenon of a speaker or writer using two different language varieties in divergent social contexts or to fulfill distinctive social functions. For most of the imperial Chinese history, an educated Chinese person typically spoke a local variety of Chinese and wrote in Classical Chinese, constituting a diglossic situation. Diglossia may also encompass the use of two speech varieties. For example, children of recent immigrants in the United States may speak English at school with their teachers and classmates and a different language, such as Mandarin or Spanish, at home with family and relatives. Diglossia also exists in modern China. After Classical Chinese ceased to be the written standard in the early 20th century, Modern Standard Chinese became the standard written (as well as spoken) language. Some Chinese also speak MSC (Mandarin), while many speak other dialects. Those who speak other dialects are diglossic. For example, students in Southeastern China may speak Mandarin in the classroom, Cantonese at home with family and friends, and write in Mandarin for both formal and informal communication.

Now, let's return to the topic of Classical Chinese. You may wonder: Has it always been a written language? Was it ever spoken? The answer may not be completely straightforward. **Classical Chinese**, also known as *wényán* (文言 'literary language'), in the strict sense refers to the written language of Classical literature created from the late Spring and Autumn period (early 5th century BCE) to the end of the *Hàn* dynasty (220 CE). The language spoken at the time was what is referred to today as "late Old Chinese." Although it is unclear if Classical Chinese can simply be understood as late Old Chinese rendered in writing, the common understanding is that they were very similar. After the *Hàn* dynasty and until the early 20th century, however, the similarity between the written language and the speech decreased as literary and formal writing continued to be done in the Classical style, while the spoken varieties of the Chinese language evolved.[2]

Used loosely, the term "Classical Chinese" may also incorporate writing done after the *Hàn* dynasty until the end of the imperial era in the Classical style, the standard style of writing for roughly 2,000 years. It is remarkable that Classical Chinese came to serve as the written standard for such a long period of time. How was it able to do so? The primary reason was that many important literary and philosophical works, for example, the canons of Confucius (孔子*Kǒngzǐ*; 551–479 BCE) and Mencius (孟子 *Mèngzǐ*; 372–289 BCE) were written in Classical Chinese. These works were so revered that later writers continued to write in their style. Another key factor that solidified Classical Chinese as the standard written style was the civil service system in imperial China, a meritocracy adopted to select able scholars to become ruling officials. Aspiring candidates were required to study the Confucian canons and write examinations in Classical Chinese in order to acquire a position in the ruling class. Being able to read and write in Classical Chinese thus enjoyed official, sanctioned prestige. The civil service examination system was established around the year 600 during the *Suí* (隋) dynasty, and it was not abolished until some 1,300 years later in 1905, shortly before the last dynasty ended. During this long period of time, although the spoken standard of Chinese continued to change, Classical Chinese remained the standard written language for official use and serious literature.

THE STORY BEYOND

The Standard style of Chinese calligraphy

The civil service examination system also had a profound impact on Chinese calligraphy. Candidates were required to write their examinations in the Standard style, referred to in Chinese as *kǎishū* (楷书/楷書 'model script'). In modern days, *kǎishū* continues to be the most common calligraphic style in which Chinese text is printed.

Classical Chinese, or *wényán*, was by no means the only written Chinese language before the 20th century. During the *Táng* (唐; 618–907) and *Sòng* (宋; 960–1279) dynasties, as the Chinese speech continued to diverge from the Classical written language, a new form of written Chinese emerged. By that time, the vernacular varieties of Chinese had become so distinct from Classical Chinese that understanding the latter would require dedicated education. The majority of the Chinese population was thus unable to read Classical text. The new written language approximated the vernacular varieties of speech and later came to be called *báihuà* (白话/白話), meaning "plain speech."[3] *Báihuà* gained wider popularity as time went on, and important literary works were written in *báihuà* during the *Míng* (明; 1368–1644) and

Qīng (清; 1644–1912) dynasties. With the last imperial dynasty coming to an end in the early 20th century, progressive intellectuals considered *wényán* an obstacle to mass education and literacy and condemned it as a "dead language." Instead, they advocated for writing in *báihuà*, a "living language" and "language of the people" that they refined and upheld as the national standard. *Báihuà* became the written language of the progressive education curriculum established since then, and it eventually replaced *wényán* as the official written language.

The impact of Classical Chinese on Modern Standard Chinese

Since the late 1920s, almost all writing in Chinese, public or private, official or personal, on paper or online, has been done in MSC, the national standard of Chinese speech. However, the register or style may vary significantly from informal to formal. The more formal the writing, the closer it is in style to Classical Chinese, and vice versa. This resemblance is primarily in morphology and lexicon – in how words are formed and in the choice of words. To understand the difference between formal and informal styles of writing in MSC, therefore, it will be helpful to compare the words in Classical Chinese and MSC. Let us look at one simple example. The following sentence in Classical Chinese is from *The Analects* of Confucius. Its *pīnyīn* annotation is based on MSC pronunciation, as how Classical Chinese is usually read today, for instance, in a classroom setting.

Classical Chinese:	子曰：“学而时习之，不亦悦乎？”
Pīnyīn:	*Zǐ yuē: "Xué ér shí xí zhī, bú yì yuè hu?"*
MSC:	孔子说：“学习而且时常复习，不也使人快乐吗？”[4]
Pīnyīn:	*Kǒngzǐ shuō: "Xuéxí érqiě shícháng fùxí, bù yě shǐ rén kuàilè ma?"*
Translation:	*Confucius says: "Study and often review – doesn't that also make one happy?"*

As is easy to notice, the MSC sentence is considerably longer. This is because monosyllabic words in Classical Chinese often (though not always) correspond to bi- or multisyllabic words in MSC. For this reason, Classical Chinese is in general terser than Chinese written in MSC. Table 6.1 gives a side-by-side comparison of the **content words** – nouns, verbs, adjectives, and adverbs – in the example.

Although Classical Chinese is no longer the standard written language, it still exerts its influence on writing in the Chinese language. Writers often incorporate Classical-style words or expressions not usually used in speech to make their writing sound more formal. Because of this practice, there may be a more significant difference between the written style and the spoken style in Chinese compared with English. The use of Classical-style, single-syllable content words where multisyllable alternatives are available may give a piece of writing a Classical flavor and thus makes it sound more proper or official. For example, in the written abstract of an academic article, to refer to the article itself, it would be more formal and often more appropriate to write 本文 (*běnwén*, 'this article') than 这篇文章/這篇文章 (*zhè piān wénzhāng*, 'this article'). While giving a presentation about the article,

Table 6.1 Correspondence between Classical Chinese and MSC content words

Classical Chinese (*pīnyīn*)	MSC (*pīnyīn*)	Meaning
子 (*Zǐ*)	孔子 (*Kǒngzǐ*)	'Confucius'
曰 (*yuē*)	说/說 (*shuō*)	'say'
学 /學(*xué*)	学习/學習(*xuéxí*)	'study'
而 (*ér*)	而且 (*érqiě*)	'and also'
时/時 (*shí*)	时常 /時常(*shícháng*)	'often'
习/習 (*xí*)	复习/複習 (*fùxí*)	'review'
不 (*bù*)	不 (*bù*)	'not'
亦 (*yì*)	也 (*yě*)	'also'
悦 (*yuè*)	使人快乐/使人快樂 (*shǐ rén kuàilè*)	'makes one happy'

however, the author may speak of it using the latter, longer expression to avoid sounding too bookish.

Such impact of Classical Chinese on Modern Standard Chinese is possible, as some have argued, because of the morphographic nature of the Chinese writing system.[5] Although the sounds of Chinese characters have changed, their meanings have remained by and large constant. This connection in character meaning makes Classical Chinese accessible to modern readers and writers. If Chinese had been written with a phonographic system like the Roman alphabet, then Classical Chinese words would have been spelled much differently than MSC words. This is because the phonology of MSC is drastically different from that of late Old Chinese, on which Classical Chinese is based. Classical Chinese pronounced in its Old Chinese sounds would be incomprehensible to MSC speakers, just as Old English would be incomprehensible to today's English users. If Chinese had been written with an alphabet as English is, Classical Chinese would have become much less accessible to modern readers and writers.

This is not to say, however, that an average Chinese reader today is able to understand a Classical Chinese text without much difficulty. Far from it – because MSC and Classical Chinese are greatly different in syntax and lexicon, it requires years of dedicated learning to be able to read Classical text with proficiency, and probably even more for composing a piece of writing in that style. The study of Classical Chinese is part of the standard curriculum from third grade through high school in Mainland China and is required for the college entrance exam, but even college students often hesitate to claim functional proficiency in Classical Chinese.

Notes

1   The term "triglossia" may be used when three language varieties are involved.
2   The written language used after the *Hàn* dynasty until the modern period is referred to as "Literary Chinese," although this term is often used interchangeably with "Classical Chinese." This book uses "Classical Chinese" as a cover term for both the pre-*Hàn* and post-*Hàn* periods. When "Literary Chinese" is used, it is considered interchangeable with "Classical Chinese."

3   The term "plain speech" may be misleading: *báihuà* is a written language and not speech. The language being written can be understood as Modern Standard Chinese or Mandarin.

4   The example is given in simplified characters in the main text. In the traditional script, the Classical Chinese version is "子曰：學而時習之，不亦悅乎？" The MSC version is "孔子說：學習而且時常復習，不也使人快樂嗎？"

5   See Hannas (1997, pp. 128–129).

7 The Chinese writing system

THE CHARACTER-BASED CHINESE SCRIPT is said to have the longest history of continuous use of all current writing systems.[1] Dating back to no later than the oracle-bone script (ca. 1250–1050 BCE) of the *Shāng* (商) dynasty,[2] it has remained the sole official writing system for Chinese for over 3,000 years. During the course of this long history, major changes took place: its overall inventory of characters grew, the shape of the characters evolved and underwent multiple reforms and standardizations, and most recently, the layout structure of Chinese text also altered. The nature of the writing system, however, remained the same.

To many Western readers first exposed to the Chinese writing system, two characteristics often stand out as vastly different from their native scripts: one, its drawing-like symbols, and two, the huge inventory of such symbols. Are Chinese characters indeed "little pictures"? How are they formed? How many of them are there? Are new ones created all the time? Are all the characters used? How many characters does one need to know? These are some of the questions we will address in this chapter.

▨ Nature of the Chinese script

Earlier in Chapter 3 we learned that the Chinese script is a **morphographic** writing system. With very few exceptions, each grapheme – in this case each Chinese character – represents a morpheme in the language. Recall that a morpheme is the smallest combined unit of sound and meaning. Thus a Chinese character not only represents speech sounds but also conveys certain meaning (or performs a certain grammatical function). For example, the character 人 is pronounced as *rén* and means "person, people." The character 了 is pronounced *le* and can indicate the completion of an action.

If you also remember from Chapter 3, we can be even more specific and say that the Chinese writing system is **morphosyllabic**. Almost all of the morphemes in Chinese are one syllable long. That is, a Chinese character almost always corresponds to one single syllable in representing speech sounds. In other words, there is a fairly consistent one-to-one relationship between a grapheme (i.e., a character), a syllable, and a morpheme for the Chinese writing system. Thus, the written characters 大人 represents a word containing two syllables, *dà* and *rén*,[3] and this word consists of two morphemes, *dà* meaning "big, large" and *rén* meaning "person, people." The meaning of the word, however, is not exactly "a big person" – the most common meaning of *dàrén* (大人) is "adult(s), grownup(s)." Indeed, the meaning of a Chinese word is often not simply the sum of its morphemes.

THE STORY BEYOND

Semantic transparency of Chinese

It is estimated that more than 70% of Chinese words are bi-morpheme compounds – that is, they contain two morphemes.[4] In writing, they are represented by two characters. Knowing the meaning or grammatical function of each character allows a reader to speculate the meaning of a new compound in reading. However, depending on the semantic transparency of the compound, such speculations may or may not be accurate. An often cited example of a semantically opaque word is 马虎 *mǎhu* 'careless, sloppy,' where 马 and 虎 each represents an animal as a stand-alone word: *mǎ* means "horse" and *hǔ* means "tiger."

You may have heard of the Chinese writing system being categorized as "logographic." What does this term mean? Is this an accurate characterization of the Chinese script? We in fact discussed this in Chapter 3 as a sidenote, and it may be worth revisiting it here. A **logographic** writing system is one in which a grapheme (in this case a **logograph** or **logogram**) represents a word or a phrase. Since in writing MSC, a Chinese character usually represents a morpheme, and because most of the MSC words consist of two or more morphemes, a morpheme in MSC is oftentimes a smaller unit than a word, and in writing, a character only represents part of a word. For this reason, it may not be accurate to classify the Chinese writing system as a logographic script in writing MSC. In comparison, the concept of a logographic script may be more applicable to Classical Chinese, in which single morphemes much more often function independently as words.

Formation of Chinese characters

As you know, the Chinese characters we see in daily use and in dictionaries today were created and standardized over a long period of time. Myriad factors came into play and determined what they now look like and how they should be arranged on the writing surface: political dominance, social change, cultural influence, aesthetic heritage, and so on. However, the kinds of linguistic processes by which the characters were formed are primarily three: pictography, extension, and differentiation.[5]

Pictography is the method to create new characters based on visual resemblance to the object or image represented. Characters created using this method are called **pictograms** or **pictographs**. Pictography is a method used from the very beginning of Chinese character construction, and pictograms are found in the earliest archeological evidence we have of Chinese writing, the oracle-bone inscriptions. Table 7.1 shows a few examples in the oracle-bone script and their contemporary forms.

As you see, although the modern characters have become significantly different from the oracle-bone forms, some may still exhibit visual traces of the physical objects or entities represented. The pictogram for "person," for example, depicts the profile of a standing person in the oracle-bone script, with the shorter stroke representing the arms and the longer one the torso and the legs. The modern character 人 suggests the image of a person with two equally long legs. It is not exactly the same image, but the picture-like quality, one may argue, is still there.

Table 7.1 Examples of pictograms

Oracle-bone script	Modern script (traditional)	Modern script (simplified)	Pīnyīn	Meaning
⊖	日	日	rì	'sun'
川	水	水	shuǐ	'water'
人	人	人	rén	'person'
馬	馬	马	mǎ	'horse'
女	女	女	nǚ	'female'

Other examples of modern pictograms may be less picture-like. The oracle-bone form for "sun" looks like a round object. The modern 日 (rì 'sun') character, however, is no longer round. If not informed of the connection between this form and its more circular ancestor, one may not be able to recognize it as a picture of the sun at all, and may think that it bears more resemblance to a window or a ladder.

Regardless, such changes in appearance have not altered the nature of the character, which was critically determined by the way the character was originally created. 日 (rì 'sun'), therefore, is still considered a pictogram. The existence of pictograms such as this one lends an element of truth to the popular belief that *some* Chinese characters are "little pictures."

Companion Website

Exercise 7.1 Abstract pictograms

However, it would be a gross exaggeration to make the blanket statement that Chinese characters are pictograms, because most of the characters in use today are not pictograms. Rather, the great majority is **semantic-phonetic compounds** that combine a meaning element and a sound element into a single character. For example, the left side of the character 妈/媽 (mā, 'mother') is 女 (nǚ, 'female, woman'), and the right side is 马/馬 (mǎ 'horse'). It is easy to see here that the 女 ('female') element serves as the meaning component of the character. In this case, its pronunciation as an independent character is irrelevant. 马/馬 (mǎ), on the other hand, serves as the sound element, and its meaning is irrelevant. Although the semantic element and the phonetic element in such a compound character may in themselves be pictograms when they stand alone as individual characters, as part of a semantic-phonetic compound, they lose that identity and together constitute a different type of character. This is because the linguistic process of forming a semantic-phonetic compound is categorically different from that of a pictogram, and the outcome is also categorically different.

How are semantic-phonetic compounds created? They usually are the result of two consecutive processes: extension and differentiation. **Extension** is the process by which an existing character is used to represent a morpheme that has a similar pronunciation (**phonetic extension**) or meaning (**semantic extension**). For example, 馬 (马) initially represents the morpheme *mǎ* 'horse' in Chinese. Later on, the same character is used to also write the morpheme *mā* 'mother,' because *mā* has a similar sound to *mǎ* 'horse.' Thus, by phonetic extension, the character 馬 (马) now is used to represent two unrelated meanings: "horse" and "mother." Here, the use of the symbol is extended purely for its sounds, and its meaning does not matter, so it is a case of phonetic extension.

The use of an existing symbol, such as a pictogram, to represent a similar-sounding morpheme unrelated in meaning is referred to in linguistics as the **rebus principle.** The rebus principle operates in phonetic extension. Many early writing systems used the rebus principle to represent abstract ideas with pictograms, as shown in the Chinese 馬 (马) example. For this principle to work, however, the symbols involved do not have to be pictograms. In modern-day texting, for example, "c u l8er" representing "see you later" contain three rebuses: "c" for "see," "u" for "you," and the number "8" for "ate" in "later."

Extension alone does not create new characters. Rather, it introduces new uses of existing characters. The creation of semantic-phonetic compounds is the result of a **differentiation** process following phonetic or semantic extension. In the case of 马/馬, representing two morphemes, *mǎ* 'horse' and *mā* 'mother,' with the same character eventually became confusing, and the need arose to be able to differentiate the morphemes from each other. Thus, a semantic component 女 'female' was added to 马/馬 to form a new compound character 妈/媽 *mā* 'mother.' As explained earlier, in the new compound, 马/馬 (*mǎ*) signifies the phonetic value only. After the differentiation process, the stand-alone character 马/馬 (*mǎ*) represents exclusively the morpheme *mǎ* 'horse,' and 妈/媽 *mā* represents 'mother.' So again, it is the differentiation following the extension that generates new characters, and these characters are semantic-phonetic compounds.

Table 7.2 shows different types of Chinese characters as percentages of the total character inventory over time. Before we look at the numbers in detail, take a look at the first row and note that Chinese characters are traditionally classified into four categories: pictograms (象形字 *xiàngxíng zì*), abstract pictograms (指事字 *zhǐshì zì*), semantic-phonetic compounds (形声字/形聲字 *xíngshēng zì*), and semantic-semantic compounds (会意字/會意字 *huìyì zì*). Today, however, not all of these categories are accepted as linguistically accurate. We know that pictograms and abstract pictograms are the product of pictography, and semantic-phonetic compounds result from the extension-differentiation process. The origin and status of semantic-semantic compounds, however, have been called into question. Some scholars consider it an "artificial, retrospective category,"[6] possibly the result of pedagogical inventions. They believe that the ostensibly semantic-semantic compounds may in fact be semantic-phonetic compounds, and because the phonetic components have undergone substantial phonological changes, their sound value is no longer apparent to MSC speakers. To make the characters easier to memorize, instructors may have created stories that reinterpret the meaning of the character as a sum of its components. Take the character 明 (*míng* 'bright') as an example:

日 (*rì* 'sun') + 月 (*yuè* 'moon') = 明 (*míng* 'bright')

Instructors may say something like "when the sun and the moon are put together, it is very bright." Over time, these mnemonic stories may have become popular beliefs about the origins of the characters.

Now, looking at the data in Table 7.2, what patterns do you observe? As you can see, along with the increase in the total number of characters, the percentages of pictograms, abstract pictograms, and semantic-semantic compounds decrease. On the other hand, the percentage of semantic-phonetic compounds dramatically increases. By the 2nd century CE that category became about four times as large as all the other categories combined. This trend continues. By the 18th century, semantic-phonetic compounds were estimated to constitute about 97% of characters in common use.[7]

Table 7.2 Different types of characters as percentage of total inventory over time

Period	Pictogram %	Abstract pictogram %	Semantic-semantic compound %	Semantic-phonetic compound %	Number of characters
12th–11th century BCE	23.9	1.7	34.3	28.9	1,155
2nd century CE	3.8	1.3	12.3	81.2	9,475
8th century CE	2.5	0.5	3.1	90.0	24,235

Source: Adapted from Rogers (2005, p. 45)

This tells us that, in creating new characters, semantic-phonetic compounding, or the extension-differentiation mechanism, is the most productive method. Pictography may have played a major role in the early stage, but it alone was far from being able to fully fulfill the linguistic demand of representing the language with written symbols in a systematic and specific manner. Recall that in Chapter 3 we discussed that writing, in essence, is making speech visible.[8] Speech sounds, therefore, are the critical link in connecting language to the written symbols. To fully, systematically, and reliably represent a language in writing, the written symbols must refer to the speech sounds of the language for it to work. Written symbols that directly represent meaning or ideas without referencing speech may only be able to represent language in a limited and unreliable manner. Therefore, it should come as no surprise that the absolute majority of Chinese characters are semantic-phonetic compounds, the only type of characters that contains a sound element. It is also in this critical sense that we say that the Chinese writing system represents sounds as well as meaning.

Companion Website

Exercise 7.2 Categories of Chinese character formation

The character inventory

One of the first impressions the Chinese writing system gives to non-native writers is likely its large number of characters. How many characters does the Chinese script have? There is probably no way to know for sure exactly how many characters have been created. Some characters dropped out of use over time. It was also not uncommon for characters to have alternative forms. Both of these factors complicate the answer to the question. However, one often cited source on this issue is the *Kāngxī* (康熙) *Dictionary* compiled between 1710 to 1716 on the order of the *Kāngxī* emperor of the *Qīng* (清) dynasty. It served as the standard dictionary for most of the 18th and 19th centuries in China. This dictionary contained more than 47,000 character entries. A later, supplemented version raised the total number of characters to nearly 50,000. Compared with the 26 symbols of the Roman alphabet – or 52 if including both lower and upper cases – these numbers are almost astronomical.

One cannot help but wonder: how many characters does a person need to know in order to achieve literacy? It is estimated that the knowledge of about 3,000–3,500 characters allows one to read the newspaper without major obstacles. Based on the curricular standards commonly adopted by elementary and middle schools in Mainland China,[9] students completing the second grade are expected to be able to read about 1,600 of the most frequently used characters and write about 800 of them. By fourth grade, they should know about 2,500 and to be able to write 2,000. When they finish elementary school (i.e., sixth grade), students will have learned to read 3,000 characters and write 2,500 of them. By ninth grade, or at the end of middle school, students should be able to read about 3,500 characters and write about 3,000. It is estimated that college students in contemporary China are generally able to read and write 4,000 to 6,000 characters.[10]

Changes in script style

By this point, you already know that the Chinese script did not always look like it does today. Over its long history, the appearance of its individual symbols changed a great deal. The shape of the strokes, the configuration and complexity of the characters, or the connectedness between strokes as well as between characters varied from one style to the next. Such changes are well documented, and we will take a close look when we learn about Chinese calligraphy later in this book. For now, it suffices to know what major script styles have existed.

Before we start, however, note that we refer to such changes as differences in the "style" of the script rather than in the script itself. This is because these changes are stylistic in nature, and they do not alter what kind of script the Chinese writing system is. Although the shapes of the strokes or the characters may have changed, the relationship between the written symbols and the language units they represent remains constant: each character almost always represents one morpheme. In other words, the script remains the same in nature despite the changes in its appearance. What may be confusing, however, is that the various styles are conventionally referred to in terms of "script": oracle-bone script, bronze script, clerical script, running script, cursive script, and standard script. We will also adopt these terms, but be aware that the "script" in these cases in fact refers to a particular "style" of the same Chinese script.

The most commonly seen style in both print and handwriting in modern China is the **standard script** (楷书/楷書 *kǎishū*). You may remember that the standard script became the standard because it was the style required by the civil service examination in imperial China. Another popular style in modern handwriting is the **running script** (行书/行書 *xíngshū*), in which the strokes are more fluid and have a tendency to connect. When the strokes become even more fluid and connected, and some characters are simplified, the style is known as the **cursive script** (草书/草書 *cǎoshū*). Standard, running, and cursive scripts developed at around the same time, in the 2nd--4th centuries BCE, and they were all derived from an earlier style called the **clerical script** (隶书/隸書 *lìshū*). The clerical style was designed to meet the demand for increased official documentation, and, indeed, it could be written much faster than its predecessors, the **seal scripts** (篆书 / 篆書 *zhuànshū*), including **great seal** (大篆 *dàzhuàn*) and **small seal** (小篆 *xiǎozhuàn*). The seal scripts received their names retrospectively when these styles were no longer used for mainstream writing and were mostly reserved for seal carving. Before the seal scripts, and, for a long time, the so-called **bronze script** (金文 *jīnwén*) was used. It was the style of inscriptions cast on bronze ceremonial vessels. The earliest archeological evidence we have so far for Chinese writing is carving of characters on ox bones or turtle under-shells used for divination some 3,000–3,500 years ago. These characters are collectively referred to as the **oracle-bone script** (甲骨文 *jiǎgǔwén*). Figure 7.1 shows a few examples of the various script styles.

FIGURE 7.1   Changes in script style

	Oracle bone	Bronze	Great seal	Small seal	Clerical	Running	Cursive	Standard

Structure of the Chinese writing system

Ordering characters

Unlike letters in an alphabet, Chinese characters do not follow a linear order predetermined by convention, such as a, b, c, . . . z. How can Chinese characters be ordered or categorized then? Given the large number of symbols in the Chinese writing system, this may be a particularly intriguing question.

One major principle for classifying Chinese characters is to group them by their common components. If you have some knowledge about Chinese characters, you may understand that there are basically two types in terms of their structural composition: one is composed of a single graphic element, such as 马/馬 (*mǎ* 'horse') and 女 (*nǚ* 'female'), and the other contains more than one element, such as 妈/媽 (*mā* 'mother'). Characters of the second type often have a component that reoccurs in a number of other characters. In the case of 妈/媽, for example, the 女 element is also a part of 姐 (*jiě* 'older sister'), 妹 (*mèi* 'younger sister'), 好 (*hǎo* 'good'), 姓 (*xìng* 'surname'), 婴/嬰 (*yīng* 'infant'), 婪 (*lán* 'greedy'), and hundreds of other characters. It seems natural, therefore, to group these characters together under their shared component 女.

In fact, this is how most Chinese dictionaries index the characters. A modern print dictionary typically contains a character index divided into some 200 sections, each headed by the graphic element that characters in that section share. Such elements, therefore, are referred to as **section headers** (部首 *bùshǒu*). Another term for section headers is **radicals**, probably because they are seen as graphic roots for generating characters. Characters with the same radical are grouped in the same section in the character index, as shown in Table 7.3.

Table 7.3 A section of the character index in a Chinese dictionary

氵 部		污	2017		...
二画		江	958	五画	
汁	2455	汛	2188	沫	1319
汀	1910	...		浅	940
汇	865	四画		法	525
...		沣	584	...	
三画		汪	1979	十八画以上	
汗	761	沅	2358	灏	780

Within the same section, characters are arranged by the number of strokes they have, from the fewest to the greatest. Sections of characters are then arranged based on the number of strokes of their headers or radicals, also from the fewest to the greatest. The radical system developed for the *Kāngxī Dictionary* contained 214 radicals. It has served as a de facto standard for Chinese dictionaries compiled thereafter. Contemporary dictionaries typically make use of 180–200 radicals, which is usually the *Kāngxī* radicals minus one or two dozen that form characters no longer in common use.

Kāngxī, however, was not the first dictionary that had made use of radicals to organize Chinese characters. This practice dates back some 1,600 years before to a dictionary called *Shuōwén Jiězì* (说文解字/說文解字 *lit.* 'explaining graphs and analyzing characters') compiled by Xǔ Shèn (许慎/許慎 58–148 CE). Completed in 100 CE during the Eastern *Hàn* dynasty, Xǔ Shèn's dictionary was not the earliest in China, but it was the first to analyze the structure of Chinese characters in order to provide a rationale behind their organization. It is regarded as "a major conceptual innovation in the understanding of the Chinese writing system,"[11] and the radical system made it much easier to look up characters. Most of the radicals in *Shuōwén Jiězì* indicate the meaning of the characters, but some represent the pronunciation.

THE STORY BEYOND

Cosmology in *Shuōwén Jiězì*

Xǔ Shèn's dictionary contained 540 radicals (and 9,353 character entries plus 1,163 graphic variants) – more than twice the number of radicals in the later *Kāngxī Dictionary*. It contained radicals that are not considered such today. Thirty-four radicals headed empty sections, and 159 had only one character under them. Obviously, Xǔ Shèn did not aim to maximize the number of characters in each section as modern dictionaries do. Rather, the 540 sections were the result of his desire to represent cosmology in the organization of the characters. Five hundred and forty is not a random number; it is equal to six times nine times ten ($6 \times 9 \times 10$). Six and nine represent *yīn* (阴/陰) and *yáng* (阳/陽), respectively, and ten is the number of the "heavenly stems" (天干 *tiāngān*) in the ancient Chinese time-reckoning system.

Looking up a word in a Chinese dictionary may be somewhat more complicated than in a Western dictionary, depending on what type of information is already known. If one knows the pronunciation of a character, then locating it is not much different from finding a word in an English dictionary. This is because, besides the section-header system, contemporary dictionaries also make use of *pīnyīn* to organize character and word entries. In fact, it typically contains three parts: (1) a radical index, which is a list of all the radicals or section headers that the dictionary uses; (2) a character index, which groups characters by radical or section header; and (3) the main body, which consists of character and word entries arranged by pronunciation coded in *pīnyīn* following the alphabetical order. Thus, if one knows the pronunciation of the character and are familiar with the *pīnyīn* system, one may simply turn to the pages that have the desired *pīnyīn* representation.[12]

However, if the pronunciation of the character is unknown and the only available information is its graphic form, as it often happens in reading, then the process becomes more involved. To look up a character, one starts by identifying its radical. For instance, the character 柏 has the radical 木. This obviously requires some familiarity with character radicals; otherwise, one may simply not know. The second step is to find the radical 木 in the radical index, in which the section headers are arranged by stroke count. Knowing that 木 has four strokes, we can find it by going to the part of the radical index marked as four strokes. This gives us the page number for the 木 section of the character index. The third step is to find the character 柏 in the character index. In the 木 section of the character index, characters are arranged by the stroke count of only a part of the character – the part that is not the radical. In our case, 白 (i.e., 柏 minus the radical 木) has five strokes. We can find the 柏 character in the five-stroke subsection of the 木 section in the character index. This gives us the page number of the 柏 character in the main body of the dictionary. Turn to that page, and we see that 柏 is pronounced as *bǎi* and means "cypress."

Companion Website

Exercise 7.3 Ordering characters

Layout conventions

The page layout of Chinese text changed in recent history. Up until the early 20th century, Chinese had typically been written in columns from right to left on a page as a matter of convention. Pages in a book were also arranged to be read from right to left. Thus, the front cover of a book opened on the left, and the reader turned the pages from left to right as she read on. Now modern books usually follow the Western convention, with text written horizontally from left to right on a page and the front covers opening on the right. However, the old format is sometimes used to invoke a sense of tradition, especially on books about historical subjects, as a style choice or a marketing device.

Native English speakers learning Chinese may find it challenging to read and write Chinese text because of how characters are arranged on a page. Whether they are written or printed in rows or in columns, Chinese characters are placed in imaginary squares. In other words, each character is roughly the same size in a square shape. Schoolchildren in China typically practice writing on grid paper, fitting each character in one square cell, as shown in the top row of Table 7.4. Beginning students of Chinese who are native English speakers sometimes make the assumption that characters in the same words need to be written closer together, and may produce something like what is in the bottom row when they are expected to write as shown in the top row. Unlike writing in English, however, word boundaries are not marked in Chinese. Characters are written next to each other with even spacing regardless of whether they are part of the same word.

Table 7.4 Chinese characters written in imaginary squares

Translation: 今天 *jīntiān* 'today'; 天气/天氣 *tiānqi* 'weather'; 很 *hěn* 'very'; 舒服 *shūfu* 'comfortable'.
"The weather today is very comfortable."

THE STORY BEYOND

Where does one word end and another begin?

You may wonder if it becomes confusing for Chinese native readers to comprehend rows (or columns) of characters strung together without much indication of word boundaries. The reading process is indeed a little different from most Western languages, for which word boundaries are usually marked by spaces between words.

Instead of word boundaries, proficient readers of Chinese rely on lexical knowledge to parse words, that is, to determine where one word ends and the next one begins. Parsing strung-together Chinese characters may be easier than parsing strung-together English letters, however, for at least two reasons. First, Chinese characters represent meaningful units of the language (i.e., morphemes). Although word boundaries are not marked, characters naturally mark morpheme boundaries. Proficient readers are familiar with how morphemes combine to form words, so delineating word boundaries mentally as they read may not be very difficult. In writing English, however, letters are not meaningful units, and morpheme boundaries are not consistently marked, so visually there are no clear units of meaning. This reality may interfere and confuse the reader when she tries to make use of her lexical knowledge to parse the text. For example, identifying words in the following string of letters may produce *the*, *rear*, *ear*, *spa*, *aces*, *cat*, *ate*, *or*, and *aries*, none of which is in the intended text "there are no spaces to indicate word boundaries." As the text gets longer, it gets even more confusing.

therearenospacestoindicatewordboundaries

A second reason is that the Chinese script contains a much greater variety of symbols. In a lengthy text, Chinese characters can be much more easily distinguished from each other than Roman letters. This also aids the reader in making out the words to comprehend the text.

Notes

1 This view is generally accepted. However, disagreement exists among scholars. For example, see the blog post here: http://languagelog.ldc.upenn.edu/nll/?p=3954.
2 The oracle bones are the earliest archeological evidence for Chinese writing that has been officially recognized. Inscriptions on artifacts of an even earlier period were discovered between 2003 and 2006 in excavations of the Neolithic-era *Liángzhǔ* (良渚) relic site near Shanghai. These symbols are etched on more than 200 fragments of ceramic, stone, jade, wood, ivory, and bone, and are dated some 1,500 years before the oracle-bone script. Scholars still debate as to whether these markings should be considered writing in the strict sense. See Tang (2013) for more information.
3 In the word *dàren* (大人, 'adult'), the morpheme *rén* (人, 'person, people') is typically pronounced in a neutral tone in MSC. This is why *ren* does not carry a tone mark.
4 Wang, Hsu, Tien, and Pomplun (2014)
5 This framework is based on Rogers (2005).
6 Boltz (1996, p. 197); quoted by Rogers (2005, p. 37).
7 DeFrancis (1989, p. 99).
8 Ibid.
9 These standards refer to the *National Standards for Chinese Language Courses of Full-time Compulsory Education* (全日制义务教育语文课程标准), published in 2011.
10 Hue and Hu (2003).
11 Boltz (1993, p. 431).
12 Homophones are ordered by their tonal value in the order of first, second, third, fourth, and neutral tones.

8

Demythifying the Chinese script

ALTHOUGH THE CHINESE LANGUAGE (speech) is not necessarily more complex than any other natural language, it has been commonly perceived as one of the most difficult to comprehend. An interesting illustration of this point is a "map of incomprehensibility," created by linguist and professor Mark Lieberman based on sayings equivalent to the English "it's Greek to me" in a variety of languages. If the language thought to be prohibitively incomprehensible to English speakers is Greek, then what is it to the Greeks? You guessed right – it is Chinese. The Greeks are not alone, however. It turns out that native speakers of Dutch, French, Hebrew, Hungarian, Latvian, Lithuanian, Polish, Portuguese, Russian, and Spanish all point to Chinese when they find that a language is difficult to understand. On the map of incomprehensibility, although not all arrows are directed to Chinese, Chinese apparently stands out for being on the receiving end of far more of them than any other language. Now, the question is, what do the Chinese say when they encounter a language impossible to understand? Well, instead of pointing to another language, the Chinese look upward at the sky – they say "it's heavenly script (天书/天書 *tiānshū*) to me." Perhaps even the Chinese themselves cannot find another worldly script that is more difficult than their own.[1] Indeed, probably thanks to its complex writing system, Chinese has been perceived as one of the most difficult languages.

Whether the Chinese script is the most difficult to comprehend can be a matter of debate. There have been, however, a number of popular myths surrounding the writing system. In fact, Victor Mair once commented, "there is probably no subject on earth concerning which more misinformation is purveyed and more misunderstandings circulated than Chinese characters (漢字, Chinese *hanzi*, Japanese *kanji*, Korean *hanja*) or sinograms."[2] What are these misunderstandings? If you recall, we have in fact talked about a few of them earlier in this book: the ideas that Chinese characters are pictures, each Chinese character tells a story, or speakers of mutually unintelligible Chinese languages can read and understand the same newspaper. John DeFrancis summarized such misconceptions into six myths: the ideographic myth, the universality myth, the emulatability myth, the monosyllabic myth, the indispensability myth, and the successfulness myth.[3] In this chapter, we will focus on the first two: the ideographic myth and the universality myth, because they are more closely related to the topics in Parts II and III of this book.

The ideographic myth

The "ideographic myth" is possibly the most widespread misconception about the Chinese writing system. Chances are you have heard some version of it. The most straightforward may simply be referring to Chinese characters as "ideographs." An **ideograph** or **ideogram** is a symbol in a system of writing that directly represents one or more ideas without referencing any language or speech. In other words, an ideograph represents only meaning and not speech sounds. Based on this notion, one would be able to understand the meaning of an ideograph simply by looking at it and does not have to know the language behind it – that is, what particular segment of speech it represents in the language being written. If Chinese characters were ideographs, therefore, one would be able to know the meaning of Chinese characters without knowing the Chinese language. This idea may seem absurd. After all, if you have not studied Chinese, when presented with a passage written in Chinese characters, you surely would not be able to comprehend very much of it, if at all. Before discrediting the ideographic myth right away, however, let's think about what may have led to its creation and wide spread, and this will help us further understand why this ideographic conception is not accurate.

First of all, Chinese characters or character components with a pictographic origin may have created an impression that the script could be understood directly without referencing the Chinese language (speech). Because pictographs, in their proto-form, mimic the physical shape of the objects they denote – for example, you may remember that the character for "sun" in the oracle-bone script is composed of a circle with a dot in the center – they create the impression that reading and understanding Chinese characters may rely solely on what the characters look like. However, pictographic characters make up a very small portion of the character inventory. In today's Chinese script, they account for less than 5% of the characters in a commonly used dictionary.[4] The overwhelming majority are compound characters that consist of both a sound component and a meaning element, that is, semantic-phonetic compounds. Granted that the semantic components of the compounds are often pictographic – for example, 晴 (qíng 'sunny'), 昨 (zuó 'yesterday'), 晚 (wǎn 'late, evening'), 旱 (hàn 'drought'), 景 (jǐng 'scenery, view'), and 智 (zhì 'intelligence, wisdom') are a few commonly used characters that contain the radical 日 (rì 'sun') – but as these examples illustrate, the semantic elements only vaguely suggest the meaning of the characters, if at all. One must know the speech sounds that a character represents in order to know its full meaning. Indeed, without the knowledge of the Chinese language behind the characters, even stand-alone pictographs may not be readily comprehensible. We will come back to this last point later in this chapter.

The idea that Chinese characters are ideographs may also have to do with the fact that the characters indeed represent "ideas" or meaning. Almost all characters are associated with specific concepts, be they concrete or abstract, or with some kind of grammatical functions. The Chinese writing system is morphographic. That is, a single grapheme, in this case a Chinese character, corresponds to a morpheme in the language. Since a morpheme is the smallest combination of sound and meaning, a Chinese character represents a meaningful syllable in speech. A phonographic script such as the Roman alphabet is different: each grapheme, that is, each letter, represents a meaningless speech sound. From the perspective of the alphabet users, therefore, the fact that Chinese characters have meaning may be the distinctive feature that sets it apart from more familiar scripts. As a result, possibly, this feature might have received far more attention than the fact that Chinese characters also represent speech sounds.

Indeed, before John DeFrancis proposed "the diverse oneness of writing,"[5] there appeared to have been an almost exclusive focus among scholars and educators on the difference between the Chinese script and Western writing. DeFrancis cogently argued that the Chinese writing system, like any other full system of writing, was in essence visual representation of speech sounds. This is because, just like any other script, the Chinese writing system is a systematic set of symbols designed to make speech visible. It cannot bypass the language (speech) it writes to convey meaning and still do so in a fully functional manner. Perhaps because Sinitic characters have been one of the most salient visual symbols of East Asia and have long embodied the Western fascination with the mysterious Far East, this insight had evaded specialists and amateurs alike for centuries in the West. On the other hand, Chinese scholars have contributed to the dissemination of the ideographic myth as well. It is not rare even till this day to see the semantic dimension of the characters emphasized in scholarly publications in Chinese, for example, by labeling the writing system a *biaˇ o yì wénzì* (表意文字), a "meaning-representing script," as if the characters have little to do with speech sounds. The difference between the morpheme-based Chinese writing system and Western phoneme-based alphabets have been accentuated to such an extent that the Chinese writing system has come to be perceived as almost the complete opposite of the alphabetic script.

Yet in fact, the notion of an ideographic writing system is in itself a myth. That is, no fully functioning scripts consist primarily of visual symbols that represent meaning without referencing speech. To further understand this point, let's take a step back and think about a larger question: how do languages represent meaning? Languages work through mutual agreement among members of their speech communities. People who speak the same language and wish to communicate in that language with each other must agree on how it works. At the morphological level, this means they must agree on the meaning of the individual morphemes. For example, English speakers must accept that the word *books* is composed of the morpheme *book* that means "book" and the morpheme *-s* that indicate the plural form of a noun. At the syntactic level, members of the same speech community must agree on how morphemes combine to make meaningful sentences. For example, in English one must say *I have books* instead of *I books have*. Now, it is crucial to understand that such agreements are almost always arbitrary. That is, there is little inherent to the speech sounds /book/ that decides that its meaning should be "book." As a result, such agreements are subject to change over time. The morpheme *book*, for example, came from the Proto-Germanic word **bōk*, which meant "beech," referring to the beechwood tablets or beech trees on which runic symbols were inscribed. Although a historical connection exits between the two meanings, "beech" and "book," the connection has become a covert one and, more to the point, modern English speakers would not need to know it in order to effectively use the word *book*. The same can be said about Chinese characters, including the very small portion of pictographs and abstract pictographs. The character 目 (*mù*), for example, was derived from the image of an eye. The angular shape of the modern character, however, makes that visual connection rather tenuous and ambiguous: Does it represent a window? A ladder? Or perhaps a highly abstract plow? What is the basis for choosing one possibility over another? As it turns out, modern readers simply rely on learning the arbitrary linguistic connection between the character and the morpheme it represents. That is, they learn that the speech sounds /mù/ in Chinese can mean "eye," and that when they mean "eye" they are conventionally represented in writing by the grapheme 目 They learn to use the character without having to know anything about the visual connection between the earlier form of the character and the physical object on which that form was based. That knowledge is more likely acquired after they have already learned the character. In this sense, Chinese characters convey meaning by referring to the Chinese language, and therefore they ideographs.

The universality myth

The universality myth refers to the notion that Chinese characters enable people speaking in mutually unintelligible ways to communicate with each other in writing. One commonly cited example of such a notion is the belief that although people in China may speak drastically different dialects or languages, they can all read the same newspaper. Chinese characters are thus seen as a unifying force over the vast territory of diverse speakers. Indeed, the character-based script has once been credited as one of "the two great institutions that have held the Chinese state together."[6]

This belief, however, is not entirely sound. If you think about it carefully, you will see that the idea is in fact an extension of the ideographic myth: because Chinese characters represented ideas without referring to speech, they were able to convey meaning across a variety of languages or speech. That is, the same characters could carry the same meaning and were simply pronounced differently in different languages. Granted, there appears to be an abundance of such cases. Speakers of various Chinese languages often do not need to look far for a written word that they can say in their regional pronunciation. For example, the characters 上海 'Shànghǎi (city name)' in Mandarin are pronounced as /shanghai/. In Wú (Shanghainese) they are pronounced /zã.hɛ/,[7] where /ã/ represents a sound similar to the pīnyīn /ang/ and /ɛ/ a vowel as in the English word head. In Cantonese, the same characters may be pronounced as /soenghoi/.[8] Therefore, according to this understanding, even though speakers of various Chinese dialects may not be able to understand each other in oral communication, they could just write things down. In the written form, the meaning would carry across and allow the parties involved to understand each other.

It all sounds plausible. But is this how it really works? One important assumption on which the universality myth rests is that Sinitic languages such as Mandarin, Wú, and Cantonese are very much the same in every aspect other than their phonology. That is, they have more or less the same set of words, these words are combined in more or less the same way to form sentences, and the only major difference between them are in how the words are pronounced. This is, however, rather far from the truth. Chinese languages are generally estimated to be about 20% different in syntax, 40% in vocabulary, and 80% in pronunciation.[9] Although sound difference is the most pronounced, the distinction in vocabulary and syntax is substantial as well, and that can make it rather difficult for the speaker of one Chinese language to read and understand the written form of another, even if the same script is used.

Let's look at an example comparing Mandarin and Cantonese: the sentence "please give me his book." As shown in Table 8.1, the top section is the Mandarin sentence written in simplified and traditional characters, annotated in pīnyīn, and glossed in English. The bottom section is Cantonese represented in the traditional script, annotated in Jyut6ping3 Romanization,[10] and glossed in English.

Table 8.1 "Please give me his book" in Mandarin and Cantonese[11]

Mandarin	**Simplified script**	请 给 我 他 的 书。
	Traditional script	請 給 我 他 的 書
	Pīnyīn	*Qǐng gěi wǒ tā de shū.*
	English gloss	please give I/me he *possessive* book

(Continued)

Table 8.1   Continued

Cantonese	Traditional script	唔該 畀 佢 本 書 我。
	Jyut6ping3 Romanization	*M4goi1 bei2 keoi5 bun2 syu1 ngo5.*
	English gloss	please give he *measure* book I/me

As you can see, pronunciation only accounts for part of the differences between the Mandarin and the Cantonese sentences. They also use different words, including grammatical particles, and different word orders. The morpheme "please" in Mandarin is a single syllable represented in a single character 请 (*qǐng*), while in Cantonese it is bi-syllabic and written with two characters 唔該 (*m4goi1*). In Mandarin, the possessive marker *de* (的) indicates possession ('his') when placed immediately after the pronoun *tā* (他 'he'), while in Cantonese this role is fulfilled by the measure word *bun2* (本). What may throw the reader off the most is that the Mandarin word order is "verb – indirect object – direct object," while in the Cantonese sentence it is "verb – direct object – indirect object." This example shows that for the speakers of one Chinese language to be able to fully and accurately comprehend the written text of another, lexical and syntactic knowledge will be crucial as well as the ability to read and understand the written characters. In other words, one must know the language behind the writing.

Yet it is indeed a common observation that many Cantonese speakers do read the same newspapers as the Mandarin speakers. They can even read out loud, character by character, text in the newspaper in the Cantonese pronunciation. How do we understand that? At least two factors may have contributed to this phenomenon. First of all, educated speakers of Cantonese are generally speakers of Mandarin as well. Mandarin or *Pǔtōnghuà* (普通话/普通話 'common speech') is the official language of the People's Republic of China. Since the 1950s, the PRC government has made sustained efforts in promoting the common speech throughout China. Teachers must be certified in Mandarin proficiency and students of non-Mandarin regions are required to learn to speak, read, and write Mandarin in schools and universities. In addition, official broadcasting and publications, especially those at the national level, are done in Mandarin in almost the entirety of China today. Aside from school education, speakers of non-Mandarin Chinese are regularly exposed to Mandarin programming on television, the Internet, and other venues of social communications. As a result, they become proficient Mandarin readers and writers essentially by learning it as an additional language. It is no surprise that they are able to read the newspapers when the great majority of newspapers published in China are written in Mandarin.

Another factor at play is the existence of cognates among the various Chinese languages. **Cognates** are words in related languages that have been derived from the same ancestral form. They are typically similar in meaning but are pronounced somewhat differently. For instance, *gratitude* in English and *gratitud* in Spanish are a pair of cognates. In fact, there are many cognates between English and other Indo-European languages. The English *beer* and the German *Bier* are another example. Based on the estimates mentioned earlier, the Sinitic languages share between them on average about 60% of the vocabulary, which may be understood as composed of cognates. In the example we looked at earlier, for instance, *shū* 'book' in Mandarin and *syu1* 'book' in Cantonese are such a pair. The existence of many cognates allows Cantonese speakers to articulate words written in Chinese characters in the pronunciation of Cantonese, even though it is really Mandarin that has been written. The result of such rendering, however, is something of a cross between Mandarin lexicon and syntax and Cantonese pronunciation. It may sound Cantonese to non-Cantonese speakers and is probably intelligible to Cantonese speakers educated in Mandarin, but it is far from being idiomatic Cantonese speech. Native Cantonese speakers may tell you that it sounds strangely formal and no one would actually speak like that.

This is not to say, however, that the character-based Chinese script cannot be successfully used to write varieties of Chinese other than Mandarin – or languages not related to Chinese, for that matter. In fact, Cantonese has been recorded in characters since the late *Míng* dynasty, and today written Cantonese is widely used in publishing newspapers, magazines, and in advertising in the Cantonese-speaking region.[12] In Part III of the book, we will also see how the Chinese writing system has been used to write Korean, Japanese, and Vietnamese. Some adaptations may be made for the script to meet the need of the particular language. In the case of Cantonese, among other strategies, a number of new characters have been created partly to represent morphemes that do not have easily identifiable counterparts in Mandarin. A well-known example is the character 冇 (*mou5* 'to have not') which is a single morpheme in Cantonese. In Mandarin, however, one has to use two morphemes 没有 (*méiyǒu* 'not have') to jointly express the same meaning. The new character 冇 is cleverly derived from 有 by taking out the two strokes inside it. There are hundreds of Cantonese-specific characters, and Table 8.2 offers a few more examples.

Table 8.2   Examples of Cantonese-specific characters

Cantonese character	*Jyut6ping3* Romanization	Meaning
係	hai6	'to be'
睇	tai2	'to look'
咗	zo2	'already'
攰	gui6	'tired, exhausted'
奀	ngan1	'small, skinny'
呫	tam3	'cajole, sweet-talk'
瘰	mak6	'a mole (on the skin)'
煠	zaau3	'to fry in oil'

By this point, we see that sharing the character-based Chinese script as a common writing system does not in itself enable fully functional communication between speakers of mutually unintelligible languages. But may a morphographic writing system like the Chinese fare better, still, than a phonemic script like the Roman alphabet, in potentially serving as a universal script? When we think of the languages written in the Roman alphabet in addition to English – Afrikaans, Estonian, Icelandic, and Turkish, to name just a few – and how little we may be able to read the text written in these languages if we have not studied them, it may not be difficult to appreciate the futility of a universal script that is alphabetical. Indeed, its phonemic nature means that differences in the sounds of the languages are inevitably captured and reflected in the spelling of the words. This is not the case with Chinese characters. Although they represent speech sounds just like any other writing system does in the sense that they make speech visible, the connections between the sounds and the symbols are largely opaque, and, to a great extent, one must learn these connections by memory. This opaqueness, however, is the very property that makes it possible to link a character to sounds (morphemes) from different languages. For instance, the character 海 ('sea, ocean') in 上海 (*Shànghǎi*) may not only be read as /hai/ in Mandarin, /hɛ/ in *Wú*, and /hoi/ in Cantonese, but also /umi/ in Japanese, /hae/ in Korean, /biển/ in Vietnamese, /sea/ in English, /mar/ in Spanish, and so on. This idea was perhaps what gave rise to the thought of using the Chinese writing system as a universal script in the first place. Enticing as it is, we should keep in mind that, as we have seen in the case of Cantonese and Mandarin, a shared script even between closely related languages may not work that well.

Notes

1 Be aware that this example confuses "language" and "script," two distinct linguistic concepts. Although the Chinese writing system may be significantly more complex than other scripts, the Chinese language (speech) is not necessarily so compared to other languages.

2 See the foreword to the book *Ideogram* by J. Marshall Unger (2004).

3 DeFrancis (1984).

4 Refer to Rogers (2005, p. 45).

5 DeFrancis (1989).

6 John K. Fairbank, quoted by Kraus (1991) on p. 6. The other one of "the two great institutions" in this quote is the ruling elite.

7 These are IPA symbols.

8 Tone marks are omitted in these examples to reduce complexity, but Mandarin, *Wú*, and Cantonese have different tonal systems.

9 DeFrancis (1984, p. 63).

10 *Jyut6ping3* is a Romanization system for Cantonese designed by the Linguistic Society of Hong Kong in 1993. The numerals mark tones.

11 This example is adapted from an example in the "List of diglossic regions" entry on Wikipedia, http://en.wikipedia.org/wiki/List_of_diglossic_regions.

12 See Snow (2004).

PART III

Borrowing the Chinese writing system

9

Chinese characters in Asia

An overview

I T IS WELL KNOWN that the Chinese script, or *hànzì* (汉字/漢字 'Chinese characters,' Japanese *kanji*, Korean *hanja*, Vietnamese *hán tự*), has been used not only for representing the Chinese language but also for writing Korean, Japanese, and Vietnamese. Until recent history and for thousands of years, the character-based script had been the primary writing system throughout East Asia. This shared script, along with a common written language in Classical Chinese (aka Literary Chinese) style and a shared lexicon in historic and modern forms of the languages, served as the foundation for a prevailing East Asian textual culture among the neighboring cultures of Korea, Japan, Vietnam, and China. While maintaining its diverse identities,[1] the region was also distinguished by a shared heritage in Confucian teachings and values, Mahayana Buddhist beliefs and practices, as well as Chinese legal codes.[2] Perhaps due to the visual distinctiveness of *hànzì*, this region was sometimes referred to as the "Chinese characters cultural sphere (汉字文化圈/漢字文化圈 *hànzì wénhuà quān*)."[3] In this chapter, we take a broad overview at the role of the Chinese writing system in China's neighboring cultures, and we will more closely examine how the Chinese script was borrowed to write Korean, Japanese, and Vietnamese in Chapters 10–12.

From shared borders to common vocabularies

The historic geography of what we now call China, Korea, Japan, and Vietnam, as you can imagine, was not exactly the same as today's map. As shown in the map of East Asia at the beginning of the 3rd century CE (Figure 9.1), for example, China and Japan's territories were significantly smaller some 1,800 years ago. Korea was not yet a unified nation, and what is now northern Vietnam was politically part of China. Of course, the borderlines between China, Korea, and Vietnam as nation-states continued to shift well into modern times. Therefore, it would be good to keep in mind that when we speak of these familiar country names we do not refer to the modern nation-states; rather, our focus is on the geocultural entities consisting of people speaking different languages (or groups of languages) – Chinese, Korean, Japanese, and Vietnamese – as well as their cultural beliefs and practices. That said, the geographical proximity of historic Korea, Japan, and Vietnam to China, as the map reminds us, was no doubt a crucial condition for the spread of the Chinese writing system to these areas. With its vast territory, advanced technology, and sophisticated culture, China was held in high prestige for most of its pre-modern history and exerted particularly important impact on its neighboring cultures.

FIGURE 9.1   Map of East Asia at the beginning of the 3rd century CE

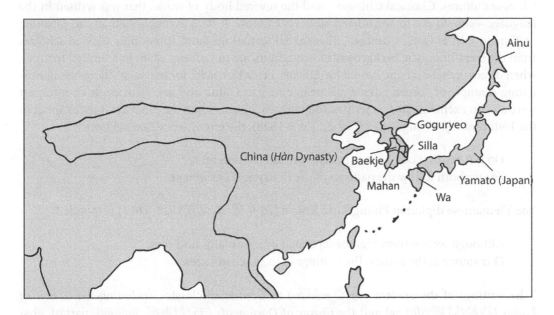

The Chinese writing system spread to Korea and Japan via the dissemination of literature written in Classical Chinese, including the Confucian classics and Buddhist sutras. Koreans became aware of Chinese writing before the 2nd century BCE[4] – possibly the earliest outside of China. In the 4th century CE, Confucian classics were taught in Korea and Koreans were also writing Buddhist scriptures in *hanja*. Sometime later in the 4th or the 5th century, Korean scholars went to Japan to teach Classical Chinese text to the Japanese, further spreading the use of the Chinese script.[5] By this point, speakers of Korean and Japanese were learning to read and write Literary Chinese in Chinese characters. In doing so, they might have read and recited out loud the Classical Chinese texts following local conventions in pronunciation. In ordinary speech, of course, they used their native languages. Neither the Koreans nor the Japanese, however, wrote down their native languages before their exposure to Chinese texts. For a long time, becoming a learned scholar meant learning to read Classical Chinese and to compose literature in that style using the Chinese script. Classical Chinese, much like Latin in the European context, served as the common literary language of East Asia.

The situation in Vietnam was somewhat different. Northern Vietnam was ruled by China for more than a thousand years, from 111 BCE to 939 CE, and Classical Chinese was introduced there in as early as 186 CE as the written language used by the governing Chinese officials.[6] The Vietnamese language, on the other hand, was not written on a large scale until after Vietnam gained independence from China. A Vietnamese script based on Chinese characters was then developed to represent the Vietnamese vernacular. For official writing purposes, however, Literary Chinese represented in the Chinese script continued to dominate until the late 19th century.

Having served as the written language for China, Korea, Japan, and Vietnam for millennia, Classical Chinese encoded in Chinese characters became the foundation of a common textual tradition in East Asia. As some scholars argue, from the perspective of the non-Chinese cultures, Classical Chinese – and the revered body of works that was written in the language – should not be considered uniquely Chinese. It "was as much Vietnamese, Japanese or Korean as it is [was] Chinese."[7] This shared textual medium sometimes allowed scholars from different linguistic backgrounds to communicate in writing, albeit in a limited manner, when direct verbal exchange could be difficult. Peter Kornicki, for instance, offers one illuminating example of "brush talks":[8] a Korean envoy to China and his Vietnamese counterpart were able to exchange poems written in Literary Chinese when they met at China's capital in the 16th century. Yi Sugwang (李睟光, 1563–1628), the envoy from Korea, wrote:

> Do not say that our garments, caps, or rites are different,
> For we both follow the patterns of the *Poetry* and *Documents*.

The Vietnamese diplomat Phùng Khắc Khoan (冯克宽/馮克寬1528–1613) responded:

> Although we are from regions separated by mountains and seas,
> Our source is the same – the writings of the ancient sages.

"The writings of the ancient sages" referred to Confucian classics, including the *Classic of Poetry* (诗经/詩經 *Shījīng*) and the *Classic of Documents* (书经/書經 *Shūjīng*), part of what formed a shared literary and philosophical canon among the East Asian societies.

The linguistic and textual tradition of East Asia was institutionally sustained through the imperial examination system, the civil service examinations (科举/科舉, Chinese *kējǔ*, Korean *gwageo*, Vietnamese *khoa-cử*) established in China (605–1905 CE) and adopted in Korea (788–1894 CE) and Vietnam (1075–1913 CE).[9] The examinations functioned as a theoretically egalitarian system to select able adult males to the ruling class regardless of their social status or family pedigree and was considered a progressive meritocracy for most of its history. To compete in the exams, candidates had to be well-versed in Confucian classics, be able to compose in the style of Classical Chinese essays and sometimes poetry, and be masters of calligraphy in at least the standard script (楷书/楷書 *kǎishū*). Under the examination system, literacy in Literary Chinese was a basic educational requirement throughout the area.

Owing to the shared literary and philosophical traditions rooted in Confucian and Buddhist texts and the use of the same script, a large number of Chinese words were borrowed into Korean, Japanese, and Vietnamese (KJV). To prepare for the civil service exams, candidates mastered Chinese words through reciting the texts and composing prose and verses in Classical Chinese, so it is hardly surprising that they gradually added Chinese vocabulary to their native lexicon. In today's terms, these borrowed words are referred to as Sino-Korean, Sino-Japanese, and Sino-Vietnamese words, where the prefix "Sino-" refers to China. However, they have long been integrated into the vocabulary of the KJV languages so that native speakers may be oblivious of their Sinitic origin.

There are several sources for Sino-KJV lexical items. Among them, non-Chinese learners importing words and expressions from Classical Chinese into their native languages may be the earliest and most important one. Interestingly, for the same target language this process took place multiple times at different points in history. In the case of Vietnamese, for example, specialists distinguish at least two layers of Sinitic loanwords: the Old-Sino-Vietnamese

(OSV) layer borrowed during the Eastern *Hàn* dynasty (25–190 CE) and the more recent Sino-Vietnamese (SV) layer borrowed during the *Táng* dynasty (618–907 CE).[10] Thus, the same word may have been borrowed more than once and end up with multiple pronunciations due to sound change in both the Chinese and the Vietnamese languages. For example, the morpheme for "shoe," represented by the character 鞋, was borrowed first as *giày* from the Old Chinese **gre*[11] and then again as *hài* from the Middle Chinese *hɛ*. Similarly, the morpheme for "(for a female) to marry to someone," written as 嫁, first came into OSV as *gả* from the Old Chinese **kras* and then from the Middle Chinese *kæH* into SV as *giá*.[12]

Another important source of Sino-KJV vocabulary is creation of new words based on the Classical Chinese model. Some of these words were coined in classical times. They often represented native concepts that had no counterparts in Chinese: for example, *maccha* (抹茶 'powdered green tea'), *jūdō* (柔道 *lit*. 'gentle way,' a sport of unarmed combat), and *haiku* (俳 句 a traditional form of Japanese poetry) in Japanese. Sometimes, they represented concepts that did also exist in Chinese, such as *jujeonja* (酒煎子 'kettle, teakettle') or *pyeonji* (便紙 'letter') in Korean.

Many Classical-Chinese-style new words were created in the modern era to translate Western concepts that were not available in either Chinese or the native language. For instance, *linh mục* (靈牧 'pastor') in Vietnamese was coined by combining the morphemes for "soul (靈)" and "shepherd (牧)." Creation of this kind was particularly prolific during the Meiji period (1868–1912) in Japanese, and, interestingly, many compounds coined at that time were not much later back-borrowed and thoroughly integrated into Modern Standard Chinese. Examples included *diànhuà* (电话/電話 'telephone': 'electric' + 'speech') from the Japanese *denwa*, *kēxué* (科学/科學 'science': 'classification' + 'study') from *kagaku*, and *shèhuì* (社会/社會 'society': 'community' + 'meet') from *shakai*. Some were imported into Korean, for instance, *yeonghwa* (映畫 'movie': 'shine' + 'picture') from Japanese *eiga* (映画[13]) and *gongjang* (工場 'factory') from *kōjō* (工場), or into Vietnamese. The Chinese themselves also translated Western works and created new words in the process, some of which were then borrowed into the other languages. For example, the word *dàishùxué* (代数学/代數學 'algebra': 'replace' + 'number' + 'study') invented by a Chinese mathematician became *dai sūgaku* in Japanese, *dae suhak* in Korean, and *đại số học* in Vietnamese.[14]

As you can see, the creation and borrowing of Chinese or Chinese-style words among the East Asian cultures were dynamic and multi-directional. Often multiple compounds were created around the same time for the same concept and would coexist until a winner emerged. Though sometimes the winner differed between languages,[15] often the same form prevailed. As a result of the cross-borrowing, a substantial (though limited) common lexicon may be observed in the modern forms of the languages. It is estimated that about 60% of Korean words are considered Sino-Korean.[16] Similarly in Japanese about 60% of the words in a typical modern dictionary are Chinese in origin.[17] Sino-Vietnamese words may account for about one-third of the Vietnamese vocabulary when the register is informal, and in formal text, that percentage goes up to also about 60%.[18] Table 9.1 shows a few examples from Chinese, Korean, and Japanese. It is remarkable that a shared vocabulary, limited as it is, could exist on such a scale among four languages that are, as we will discuss further in this chapter, not genetically related. A shared written language encoded in a common writing system may have made it possible.

Table 9.1   Chinese, Sino-Korean, and Sino-Japanese words

Chinese	Korean	Japanese
新聞 *xīnwén* 'news'	신문 *sinmun* 'newspaper'	新聞 *shinbun* 'newspaper'
介紹 *jièshào* 'to introduce'	소개 *sogae* 'to introduce'	紹介 *shōkai* 'to introduce'
空港 *kōnggǎng* 'airport'	공항 *gonghang* 'airport	空港 *kūkō* 'airport'

THE STORY BEYOND

Sino-Korean/Japanese words vs. native Korean/Japanese words

Although Korean words are usually not written in *hanja* anymore and are instead represented using the Korean alphabet *hangeul*, you can still sense the connection between the Korean words and their Chinese counterparts based on their pronunciation. To an educated native Korean speaker, the distinction between Sino-Korean and native Korean words is fairly clear. Words loaned from Chinese usually have one syllable for one meaningful unit (morpheme), while native Korean words tend to be polysyllabic. The same may be said for Sino-Japanese vs. native Japanese words, as native Japanese morphemes also often contain more than one syllable. Sino-Korean or Sino-Japanese words are generally more formal and are associated with erudition and tradition in the perception of their users. By contrast, native Korean or Japanese words are often informal and may suggest familiarity, closeness, and warmth.

Why borrow?

You may wonder why the people speaking Korean, Japanese, and Vietnamese borrowed a writing system to record their language instead of creating their own script. To begin with, the borrowing of writing systems is very common, and inventing a writing system from scratch is, in fact, quite rare. Writing was invented independently only about three times in history: some 5,000 years ago by the Sumerians, about 3,500 years ago by the Chinese, and more than 2,000 years ago by the Mayans. Since ancient times, as cultures came into contact, the idea of writing also spread, and more and more languages came to be written. In almost all cases, however, an existing writing system or a derived form was adopted to record the new language.[19] The Roman or Latin alphabet, for example, was the outcome of a series of borrowings: the Romans borrowed it from the Etruscans in Italy, who borrowed their script from the Greeks. The Greek alphabet came from the Semitic writing system of the Egyptians, which was inspired by the script of the Sumerians in Mesopotamia.[20] Chinese may be the only modern language the writing of which did not involve borrowing from a pre-existing script to some extent.[21]

Another factor that led to the adoption of the Chinese script in writing other East Asia languages was the perceived prestige of the Chinese culture. When Korea and Japan came into contact with China and for the 1,500 years after that, the powerful and sophisticated Middle Kingdom (中国/中國 *Zhōngguó* 'China': 中 'center, middle'; 国/國 'country, kingdom') was regarded the center of the world and was held in absolute high esteem. Educated Koreans, Japanese, and Vietnamese absorbed Classical Chinese texts and wrote in that style using Chinese characters before their native languages were written down. Therefore, when the time came to write their own languages, the Chinese script was adopted as a natural choice.

As we discussed in Chapter 3, theoretically speaking, any language can be written using any writing system. That is, a language is not inherently associated with a particular (type) of writing system. The pairing between a language and its conventional script is precisely that – conventional. This is because, unlike language, for which "native speakers" exist, a writing system does not exactly have "native writers" (when we used this term, we used it to mean writers who were native speakers). Language (speech) is naturally acquired and the acquisition outcome is biologically conditioned. Beyond the first dozen years or so – termed by linguists as **the critical period** – it becomes very difficult for humans to achieve full proficiency in a new language. But learning to write is a different matter. A learners' potential proficiency is not critically conditioned by age, and anyone with reasonable general competence should be able to fully learn a new script given the appropriate amount of time and effort.

This is not to say, however, that the conventions we have for writing various languages are insignificant; quite the contrary, as we will see later in this book, the choice of one writing system over another often carries with it hefty cultural meaning and may signify the sociopolitical identity of an institution or the writers. In this sense, we may feel that the conventional writing system of a language is more "native" than other alternatives. It is also in this sense that we use the term "native script" to refer to the writing system customarily employed to write a language.

General borrowing strategies

What happens when we borrow a script? We may need to adapt the script so that it adequately represents the necessary linguistic information for the writing to be readable. Such adaptions may involve a variety of approaches. Here, we focus on three common strategies that we know have actually been used in borrowing the Chinese script to write Korean, Japanese, and Vietnamese, shown in Table 9.2. Historically, the borrowing of the Chinese script was intertwined with importing elements of the Chinese speech – sound, meaning, or both – into the target language.

Table 9.2 Common strategies for borrowing Chinese characters to write Korean, Japanese, or Vietnamese[22]

Strategy	Examples	
	Source (Chinese)	Target (K/J/V)
(1) Sound-only borrowing	[C] 五 wǔ 'five'	[K] 五 o '(a verb ending)'
(2) Meaning-only borrowing	[C] 春 chūn 'spring'	[K] 春 pom 'spring'
	[C] 心 xīn 'heart'	[J] 心 kokoro 'heart'
	[C] 海 hǎi 'sea'	[J] 海 umi 'sea'
(3) Sound-meaning borrowing	[C] 春 chīn 'spring'	[K] 春 ch'un 'spring'
	[C] 心 xīn 'heart'	[J] 心 shīn 'heart'
	[C] 海 hǎi 'sea'	[J] 海 kai 'sea'

Sound-only borrowing disregards the meaning of the characters in Chinese and focuses on their Chinese pronunciation instead to represent morphemes that have similar pronunciations in the target language. In the Korean example, the character 五's meaning in Chinese is irrelevant. The reason why it was chosen to represent the Korean grammatical marker is because its pronunciation is close to the Korean morpheme. Meaning-only borrowing uses Chinese characters to represent native morphemes of the same or similar meaning. The pronunciation of the character follows that of the native morpheme, which is usually very different from the Chinese pronunciation and may even have different numbers of syllables. The Chinese morphemes are monosyllabic, while the Korean or Japanese counterparts are often multisyllabic. For instance, written as 海, the Chinese 'sea,' *hǎi*, has only one syllable, while the Japanese morpheme *umi* has two syllables. Finally, for sound-meaning borrowing, essentially an entire Chinese morpheme is imported into the native or target language. For example, the morpheme 'heart' in Chinese is pronounced as *xīn* in Modern Standard Chinese and written as 心. This morpheme is borrowed into Japanese, pronounced as *shin*, and written as the same character.

Now let's learn a couple of new terms. They will be important for us to know before we continue the discussion of borrowing strategies. You may have noticed that, as the result of borrowing from the source language (Chinese), the same character may have multiple pronunciations, or "readings," in the target language (Korean, Japanese, or Vietnamese). This is because the same character may represent multiple morphemes: the Chinese morpheme that has been borrowed into the target language and the native morpheme that has the same or similar meaning. When the character is read as the Chinese morpheme (e.g., 心 as *shin* in Japanese), it is referred to as **on** (音 'sound') reading. When it is read as the native morpheme (e.g., 心 as *kokoro*), it is called **kun** (訓 'meaning, interpretation') reading. These terms are used in Japanese linguistics to talk about the various readings of *kanji*. Here we borrow them to discuss the strategies used in adopting the Chinese script to write Korean and Vietnamese as well.

More specifically, the three strategies outlined in Table 9.2 may be referred to in these terms. First of all, we can call the sound-only borrowing **phonetic on**. Since the sound is borrowed from Chinese, and the character is read based on its pronunciation in Chinese, the reading is considered *on* reading (instead of *kun* reading). The character 五 as a verb ending in Japanese is pronounced as *o*, similar to the Chinese pronunciation of this character. Although the pronunciation of this character in Chinese has changed, one can still detect the similarity between the modern Japanese reading *o* and the modern Chinese pronunciation *wǔ*. Then why do we refer to this kind of borrowing as "phonetic" *on*? This is because only the sound is borrowed in this case and the meaning is not. When the meaning is borrowed together with the sound, we use a different term: **semantic on** refers to sound-meaning borrowing. In this case, both the pronunciation and the meaning of the Chinese morpheme are borrowed into the target language. As an example, the character 春 'spring' in Korean can be read as *ch'un*, a pronunciation based on Chinese. It is in fact very similar to the modern Chinese pronunciation of the same character, *chūn* (春 'spring'). Thus, this borrowing of 春 'spring' from Chinese into Korean constitutes a semantic *on*. The difference between phonetic *on* vs. semantic *on* is in whether the character is borrowed purely for its phonetic value (phonetic *on*, sound-only borrowing) or whether the meaning of the morpheme is imported as well (semantic *on*, sound-meaning borrowing). The third strategy, meaning-only borrowing, may be referred to as a **semantic kun**. In this case, the character is read not in its Chinese or source pronunciation, but in its native or target pronunciation. Its meaning is consistent with the character's meaning in Chinese. For instance, 海 'sea' in Japanese, as a semantic *kun*, is pronounced as *umi*, a native Japanese morpheme that is very different in sound from the Chinese morpheme *hǎi* ('sea').

Is there also **phonetic *kun***, you may ask? Yes, there is. A phonetic *kun* involves a character borrowed to represent a morpheme in the target language that is not apparently connected to the source language in either sound or meaning. This is usually the accumulative effect of two or more borrowing processes. For example, the character 加 in Modern Standard Chinese is pronounced as *jiā* and has the meaning "to add" or "more." The character was first borrowed into Korean via semantic *on* and was read as *ka* with the same meaning. Then it was used to represent the native morpheme *do* 'more,' making it a semantic *kun*, losing its Chinese sound. After that its usage extended again to writing the verb ending *-hadoni* 'do so and' due to sound similarity, shedding its Chinese meaning. At this point, 加 has transformed into a phonetic *kun* and no longer has any apparent connection to the Chinese original in either sound or meaning.[23]

If all this may seem a little too abstract, let us take a step back and do an exercise with English. Our task, let us assume, is to write the English utterance /the flowers are pretty/ using Chinese characters. We use // to indicate that it is the speech that is being represented. So, what is it like to record this utterance using Chinese characters? There may be a range of possibilities.

First of all, we can use the first strategy (i.e., sound-only borrowing) to write the entire sentence. To do this, we just need to choose characters that have similar sounds in Chinese and use them to represent the English. This should be relatively straightforward. Because many characters have the same pronunciation, here we choose characters that are neutral or positive in meaning, as is generally the practice representing English proper nouns in Chinese. The pronunciation of the English utterance remains exactly the same, but now it is written in Chinese characters. These characters are read as phonetic *on*, because their pronunciation in writing this sentence is close to their original Chinese pronunciation. The meaning of the characters is irrelevant. This is the first approach.

Written as:	仄	福拉沃兹	阿	普里帝
Pronounced as:	/the/	/flowers/	/are/	/pretty/
Chinese sounds:	*ze*	*fulawozi*	*a*	*pulidi*[24]
English meaning:	'the	flowers	are	pretty'

Another approach is to write the English words, where possible, through meaning-only borrowing of Chinese characters. This is not difficult to do for /flowers/ and /pretty/, where we can simply use the Chinese equivalents: 花 (*huā* 'flowers') and 漂亮 (*piàoliang* 'pretty'). So, instead of writing four characters 福拉沃兹 for /flowers/ we now only need one character 花, but we keep the pronunciation of /flowers/. So now we've imported the character and its meaning but changed its pronunciation to accord with the spoken English word /flowers/. Similarly, /pretty/ is now written as 漂亮. However, there are no equivalents of the words /the/ or /are/ in Chinese, so we cannot use this strategy on these words, and they will have to be written phonetically. So we have:

Written as:	仄	花	阿	漂亮
Pronounced as:	/the/	/flowers/	/are/	/pretty/
Chinese sounds:	*ze*	*hua*	*a*	*piaoliang*
English meaning:	'the	flowers	are	pretty'

Now let us take it one step further: we can borrow both the meaning and the pronunciation of Chinese characters. This requires importing whole words from Chinese into English. This concept is probably familiar to you, because there are a good number of Chinese loanwords in English that you likely know well. For example, *wonton, fengshui,* and *ginseng* come from Cantonese, Mandarin, and Southern *Mǐn*,[25] respectively. These words are borrowed into English so that their meaning and pronunciation in English are the same as or are close approximations of their meaning and pronunciation in Chinese. The difference in the current task is that, since we are borrowing the Chinese writing system to write English, we will also write the words in Chinese characters, i.e. 云吞/雲吞 (*wonton*), 风水/風水 (*fengshui*), and 人参/人參 (*ginseng*), and read them as, respectively, /wonton/, /fengshui/, and /ginseng/. Let's try applying this strategy to /flower/: /huā/ (花 'flower') and write it using the same character as we do for Chinese and pronounce it more or less similar to what we do in Mandarin. Since English does not use tones, we will drop the tones.

Written as:	仄	花	阿	漂亮
Pronounced as:	/the/	/hua/	/are/	/pretty/
Chinese sounds:	*ze*	*hua*	*a*	*piaoliang*
English meaning:	'the	flowers	are	pretty'

Now we have incorporated all three strategies in the same sentence. 花 (/hua/ 'flowers') is a semantic *on* because we've borrowed both the sound and the meaning of the character. 漂亮 (/pretty/ 'pretty') is a semantic *kun*, because we've borrowed only the meaning and kept the English pronunciation. Finally, 仄 (/the/ 'the') and 阿 (/are/ 'are') are both phonetic *on*, because we've borrowed only the pronunciation and not the original meaning.[26]

Again, because Chinese does not have equivalents of the words /the/ and /are/, we cannot borrow them from Chinese. In fact, foreign loanwords in a language are almost never words like /the/ or /are/. These words are what we refer to as **function words** – words that serve certain grammatical functions – a category that includes articles (e.g., *the*), pronouns (e.g., *she, he,* or *they*), and auxiliary verbs (e.g., *are*).[27] Loanwords are almost always words like /flower/ and /pretty/, or **content words** – words with concrete meaning, such as nouns, main verbs, adjectives, and adverbs. This is because function words are a closed class. New function words are almost never created, so there is little "room" for importing words into this category. On the other hand, new members of content words are frequently added to a language.

Companion Website

Exercise 9.1 Knowledge of the source language

Exercise 9.2 Borrowing a writing system

Variations and parallels

Perhaps because Chinese characters were once used to write Korean, Japanese, and Vietnamese, and their native speakers are in geographically connected regions, a common misconception is that these languages are all related to Chinese. We know that, as previously discussed, this understanding is far from the truth. Chinese and Vietnamese are not related to each other or from the same language family. Chinese is part of the Sino-Tibetan family, which includes Tibetan, Burmese, and more than 450 other languages. Vietnamese is in the Austroasiatic family together with over 1,200 other languages such as Khmer and Mon. The genetic relations of Korean and Japanese are more controversial, but most linguists today consider them unrelated to each other[28] or to Chinese.

Not being genetically related, however, does not mean that the languages do not share any structural or functional features. Indeed, it may be difficult to imagine two languages that are completely different from each other, given the limited typological variations shared among the vast number of languages. In the case of Korean, Japanese, Vietnamese, and Chinese, there are important common linguistic features between them as well as significant differences. In adapting the Chinese script to representing the speech of the other languages, therefore, both divergences and parallels may be observed. Linguistic challenges exist in all of these cases, but some of the challenges are similar and others are not. Here we will focus on three linguistic aspects that matter a great deal in the consideration of writing: word order, verb form, and morpheme shape. We will see that in all three aspects, Chinese and Vietnamese resemble each other, and Korean and Japanese are similar to each other yet both different from Chinese. This means that using the Chinese writing system to record Vietnamese is a relatively more straightforward process than adapting it to writing Korean and Japanese, while between the latter cases there are significant parallels in the kinds of strategies employed to make the writing work.

First of all, in terms of word order, Chinese and Vietnamese are largely SVO[29] (subject-verb-object) while Korean and Japanese are SOV. In the beginning of their contact with China, the Koreans and the Japanese studied Chinese text and learned to read and write Classical Chinese in Chinese characters, much like today's students learning to read and write in a foreign language. For a long period of time, all writing was done in Classical Chinese following the Chinese word order, and the native languages were not recorded in writing. Chinese texts composed in Literary Chinese in China were brought to Korea and Japan and carefully studied by scholars. To facilitate this learning, auxiliary written symbols were added to the original texts so that an educated Korean and Japanese scholar would be able to read them as Korean or Japanese. This kind of marking system in Korean is called *gugyeol* (口訣) 'oral formulae' and its Japanese counterpart is called *kanbun* (漢文) 'Chinese text'. Gradually, the Chinese script was adapted to writing the native languages as well, and writing in Chinese characters shifted into the SOV word order. In Korea, this kind of writing was called *idu* 'clerical reading', and for Japanese, it occurred when *man'yōgana* (万葉仮名 *Man'yō* 'ten thousand leaves', the name of an ancient Japanese poetry anthology written using *man'yōgana*; *-gana* 'borrowed names'), the script that first used Chinese characters to write Japanese, was adopted. We will take a closer look at each of the above scripts when we talk about writing Korean and writing Japanese in the next two chapters.

When it comes to how verbs change form, the four languages also divide into two camps: Chinese and Vietnamese are the so-called **isolating languages**. Their verbs and nouns generally do not change forms. That is, they do not inflect or take on grammatical affixes to indicate grammatical functions such as tense (past, present, future), number (singular vs. plural), or case (normative when a noun is the subject, accusative when the noun is the direct object, etc.). By contrast, Korean and Japanese are **agglutinative languages**, in which words are formed by attaching suffixes to stems. The suffixes are meaningful units, or morphemes, that indicate grammatical functions. Thus, a word in Korean or Japanese may contain a significantly greater number of morphemes than in Chinese and Vietnamese. While this was not a challenge that writers of Vietnamese needed to deal with, those who used Chinese characters to write Korean or Japanese must come up with ways to represent the grammatical suffixes that did not exist in Chinese. In both languages, these elements were first represented by full Chinese characters used as phonetic symbols, then by simplified forms of the characters, and eventually by symbols of scripts later designed to write specifically Korean or Japanese. For Korean historically and Japanese until this day, a mixed script has been used in which the verb stem is often written in *hanja* (Korean) or *kanji* (Japanese), and the inflectional suffixes are in the Korean *hangeul* letters or the Japanese *kana* symbols.

Another linguistic distinction that deserves our attention is in the shape or size of the morpheme in terms of the number of syllables. Chinese and Vietnamese morphemes are generally single syllables or **monosyllabic**, but the native morphemes of Korean and Japanese are usually **polysyllabic**. In writing Chinese, as we learned in Part II, the majority of characters represent monosyllabic morphemes. This one-character-one-syllable relation translated easily into Vietnamese. For writing Korean or Japanese, however, the difference in morpheme shape introduced additional complexity. Chinese characters sometimes represented Chinese morphemes imported into the language, which were almost always monosyllabic, while other times they represented native morphemes, which were typically polysyllabic. As a result, there was no consistent symbol-syllable relation as there was for Chinese and Vietnamese. In the case of Korean, when a mixed script was later adopted in which Sino-Korean words were written in *hanja* and native Korean words were rendered in *hangeul*, a one-character-one-syllable relationship emerged for *hanja* characters. For Japanese, however, *kanji* continued to represent both Sino-Japanese and native Japanese words when *kana* was incorporated to form a mixed script, so there continues to be varied relationships between *kanji* characters and the number of syllables they may represent.

Interestingly, the one-on-one relationship between character and syllable had a lasting impact on Vietnamese and Korean writing even after the Chinese script had been completely abandoned in writing these languages. Since the 1940s, Vietnamese has used the Roman alphabet as its official script just like English or French. Unlike English or French, however, Vietnamese is written morpheme by morpheme – much as Chinese characters used to be written – rather than word by word. Words are segmented into syllables (morphemes) and spaces are placed between syllables (morphemes) even if they belong to the same word. In the case of Korean, this one-on-one symbol-syllable correspondence is in a sense maintained as well. *Hangeul* letters are written in syllable blocks resembling Chinese characters instead of being arranged linearly as in writing English. Each syllable block occupies a squarish space and may contain multiple letters arranged along both the horizontal and the vertical dimensions. Unlike writing Vietnamese in the Roman alphabet, however, Korean written in *hangeul* does mark word boundaries with spaces or punctuation marks.

Today, Chinese characters have been largely disused in the writing of the other languages. Although they are still used in the mixed Japanese script, their numbers have been significantly limited. In writing Vietnamese, the Chinese script has been completely replaced by the Roman alphabet. The use of *hanja* in North Korea has been abolished since 1949, while in South Korea *hanja* has been by and large abandoned in day-to-day writing since the 1970s.

Nonetheless, it is both interesting and instructional to learn about the borrowing of the Chinese script in writing these languages. Building on the overview presented in this chapter, the following chapters will delve into this topic in more detail.

Notes

1 Kornicki (2018, pp. 15–17).
2 Xiong (2006, p. 302).
3 The coinage of the term is credited to Sadao Nishijima (西嶋定生, 1919–1998), a Japanese historian of China.
4 King (1996), cited by Rogers (2005, p. 68); also see Taylor and Taylor (2014, p. 172).
5 Taylor and Taylor (2014, p. 172).
6 Fisher (2001, p. 186).
7 In Keith Taylor's book cited by Kornicki in the section "Chinese and other languages."
8 Kornicki (2018, p. 18).
9 Although Japan adopted the governing structure and the laws of *Táng* China, the Chinese-style civil service examinations never took root there.
10 Alves (2001, pp. 222–223).
11 The asterisk indicates that this is a reconstructed form rather than a historically attested form.
12 Alves (2009, p. 625).
13 Notice that the character for "picture" is different in Korean (畫) and Japanese (画) because the Japanese form has been simplified. The same simplified form is used for Chinese after the script reform of the 1950s–1980s.
14 Wilkinson (2015, p. 42).
15 Ibid., p. 43.
16 Sohn (2011, pp. 44–55).
17 Shibatani (1990) notes that this percentage is as of 1859 (p. 142). This means it does not include the new compounds created based on Chinese characters during modernization in the *Meiji* period (1868–1912).
18 DeFrancis (1977, p. 8).
19 Only ancient cuneiform, Egyptian hieroglyphs, Chinese characters, and the much later Korean *hangul* are original creations and most scripts used today are derived from one of the three ancient scripts (Taylor & Taylor, 2014, p. 272).
20 Rogers (2005, p. 4).
21 Ibid., p. 4.
22 The Japanese examples are from Seeley (1991, p. 1). Korean examples are from Taylor and Taylor (2014, pp. 173–174). Pronunciations given in the "Source" column are Modern Standard Chinese. The actual borrowings took place based on earlier versions of Chinese that most likely had different pronunciations.
23 Taylor and Taylor (2014, p. 174).
24 Tones are not marked because they are not relevant here.
25 Southern *Mǐn* is also referred to as Hokkien, Fujianese, or Taiwanese. Originating in Southern Fujian Province in China, it is a group of mutually intelligible Chinese dialects spoken throughout Southeast Asia, *Táiwān*, and by some overseas Chinese.
26 仄 (zè) in Chinese refers to oblique tones (as opposed to level tones), a term used in classical Chinese poetry. 阿(ā) may represent a prefix to names of people, as in the name of the character 阿 Q in Lǔ Xùn's well-known novella, *The True Story of Ah Q*.

27 The verb BE is an auxiliary verb and should be regarded as a function word.

28 See Song (2005, p. 15) and Campbell and Mixco (2007, pp. 7, 90–91) for Korean and Vovin (2014) and Kindaichi (2017) for Japanese.

29 It is worth noting that Vietnamese and Chinese differ when it comes to the relative positions between a noun and its adjective modifier. In Chinese, the adjective usually precedes the noun; while in Vietnamese it is the other way around.

10 Writing Korean

AS WE LEARNED IN the previous chapter, Korean was the first non-Chinese language that the Chinese writing system was adapted to write. It is likely that Koreans were exposed to Chinese writing as early as the 2nd century BCE,[1] and by the 3rd to the 4th centuries CE educated elites were already using the Chinese script to write Korean.[2] Since then and until the *Joseon* dynasty (朝鮮1393–1897), Chinese characters, or *hanja* (漢字), had been used in a variety of ways in traditional Korea, both to write the Korean language, as in the *idu*[3] (吏讀, 'clerical reading') script and the *hyangchal* (鄉札 'vernacular letters') script, and to annotate Classical Chinese texts using a system called *gugyeol* (口訣 'oral formulae'). The Korean alphabet, *hangeul* (한글*han* 'great,' *geul* 'writing'), was created in the 15th century, but Chinese characters continued to dominate the written culture for hundreds of years after that. A mixed script of *hanja* and *hangeul* emerged in the modern era. After a gradual transition since the mid- to late 20th century, today's Korean writing is almost exclusively done in *hangeul*. In this chapter, we will take a closer look at each of the ways of writing mentioned above following roughly their order of historical occurrence.

THE STORY BEYOND

Hanja, *hancha* or *hanca*? A note on Romanization

Perhaps because the official Korean script, *hangeul*, is in itself an alphabetical writing system, Romanization, to most native speakers, is not an important issue. Unlike Chinese students on the Mainland, who study *pīnyīn* in elementary school and use it to facilitate the learning of Chinese characters and input Chinese text on computers, Korean students usually do not learn any Romanization systems.[4] The Korean script serves all purposes.

To linguists and learners of Korean as a foreign language, however, Romanization is important. There are at least three or four methods generally accepted for Romanizing Korean: the Revised Romanization (RR, 2000); the Ministry of Education system (1984), which is based on and sometimes referred to as McCune-Reischauer (MR, 1937); and Yale (1942). RR, which is adopted in this book (unless otherwise noted), is the official Romanization system sponsored by the South Korean government. Unlike MR, RR does not use any diacritics or apostrophes. It also differs in the spelling of certain sounds and is believed by Koreans to better represent the Korean pronunciation than MR and therefore help foreign learners more accurately pronounce Korean words.[5] Since its establishment in 2000, public signage, online maps, and so on in South Korea have mostly been updated to RR. Yale has been the established standard among linguists, because it most accurately represents Korean at the abstract, phonemic level (but less so at the phonetic level that conveys how sounds are actually pronounced). To non-native speakers or those not trained in the Korean language or phonology, the Yale system may be more challenging as a tool for approximating Korean pronunciation.

Below are how 한글 'Korean writing' and 한자 'Chinese characters' are Romanized in the various systems:

RR: *hangeul, hanja*
MR: *han'gŭl, hancha*
Yale: *hankul, hanca*

It is worth noting that the *han* in *hangeul* is unrelated to the *han* in *hanja*. The former is a native Korean morpheme that means 'great, right' or represents the Korean identity, while the latter is from the Chinese morpheme 漢 (MSC: *hàn*) meaning "China" or "Chinese."

THE STORY BEYOND

The *Gwanggaeto* Stele

The earliest evidence so far discovered of writing in the Korean language is the inscription on the *Gwanggaeto* (廣開土) Stele,[6] erected in 414 CE. It was a memorial created by King *Jangsu* of *Goguryeo* (高句麗; aka *Goryeo* 高麗; 37 BCE–668 CE) for his deceased father, King *Gwanggaeto* the Great. The text inscribed on the stele is written in Classical Chinese[7] and is composed of as many as 1,802 characters, making it a prime example of the early stage of writing in Korea.

Idu 'clerical reading'

Idu (吏讀,[8] 'clerical reading') was an all-*hanja* script created during the Three Kingdoms period (57 BCE–668 CE).[9] The script was used most widely for writing official documents in the Korean language, and was the method of writing for the Korean civil service from its formation in 958 CE to its termination in 1894.[10] In this type of writing, the basic words were usually of Chinese origin and were written in Chinese characters read as semantic *on*.[11] That is, they represented Chinese loanwords pronounced in approximately the same way as in Chinese. Korean grammatical morphemes were also represented in Chinese characters in the *idu* script. Such characters were often used purely for their phonetic values (phonetic *on*), each representing a Korean syllable.

Let us look at an example. Following is an excerpt from a Korean translation of the *Míng* dynasty Chinese legal code (in Chinese *Dàmíng Lǜ* 大明律 'Great *Ming* Laws') in 1395.[12] In this example, native Korean words and suffixes are underlined and followed by Romanization in parentheses. Their English gloss is italicized. Characters that are not underlined are Sino-Korean loanwords.

必于 (*pilok*)　　　　　七出乙 (*ul*)　　　　　犯爲去乃 (*hɔ-ke-na*)
although　　　　　　 7-expel-*AC*　　　　 violate-*do-but*

三不出有去乙 (*is-ke-nul*)　　黜送爲去乙良 (*hɔ-ke-nul-lang*)
3-not-expel-exist-*therefore*　　expel-*do-if*

減二等遣 (*ko*)　　　　婦女還本夫齊　　(*cey*)
reduce-2-grades-*and*　　woman-return-original-husband-*DC*

'Even though a woman breaks the law of the seven valid reasons for divorce, there exist three exceptions. If one expels his wife despite the exceptional cases, he will be demoted by two grades and his wife will be sent to her husband.'

To a Chinese reader, the Sino-Korean words are readily recognizable based on the English translation: for example, 犯 'violate,' 三 'three,' 不 'not,' 減 'to reduce,' and 婦女 'woman' all carry the same basic meaning as in Modern Standard Chinese. These words have become part of the Korean lexicon.

However, the text as a whole may not be easily comprehensible to the Chinese reader. There are a few reasons for this difficulty. First, as you can tell from this example, *idu* writing was in the Korean word order. The object of a verb precedes the verb rather than following it as in Chinese: for example, "woman-return" means "return (the) woman." Second, besides the Sino-Korean words, the text also contains native Korean words and grammatical suffixes. If the Chinese reader is unversed in the Korean language, she or he may not be able to understand the meaning or the function of these elements, even if they are written in Chinese characters. The characters are used purely for their phonetic values, and their Chinese meaning is irrelevant to the meaning of the text. For instance, the Chinese meanings of 必 (in Chinese: *bì* 'must') and 于 (*yú* 'at') may not add up to the meaning of the word 必于 in *idu* (*pilok* 'although'). Such characters may confuse a Chinese reader interpreting them as meaningful graphs.

■ *Hyangchal* 'vernacular letters'

Hyangchal (鄉札 'vernacular letters' or 'local letters') is an all-*hanja writing* system used to transcribe native Korean poetry called *hyangka* (鄉歌 'vernacular poetry, local poetry'). The name *hyangka* suggests that such poetry is native Korean literature rather than Chinese literature. *Hyangka* poems often deal with themes such as love and loss. Some are Buddhist in nature and authored by Buddhist monks. About 25 *hyangka* poems have survived, dating from the 7th to the 10th centuries.[13]

The characteristics of the *hyangchal* script reflect the nature of *hyangka*, the language being written. First of all, *hyangchal* follows the Korean word order. Second, because *hyangka* uses almost exclusively native Korean words, the Chinese characters are almost never read as semantic *on* as in the case of Sino-Korean loanwords written in the *idu* script. Rather, they are either used as semantic *kun* or, very commonly in this kind of writing, phonetic *on*. In fact, the native Korean content words in *hyangchal* are often written in two characters with the first one being a semantic *kun*, indicating the meaning of the whole word, and the second a phonetic *on* indicating the pronunciation of the last syllable of the word. This configuration is almost reminiscent of the Chinese semantic-phonetic compounds.

As an example, here is the first line of an 8th-century poem *Henhwaka*[14] (獻花歌 'song of presenting flowers').[15]

紫布	岩乎	过希
tolpwoy	*pahwoy*	*kus-oy*
azalea-[*bu*]	rock-[*hu*]	side-LOC
'by the side of the azalea crag'		

The second row in the example provides Romanization based on the Korean spoken at the time. For Chinese characters used as phonetic *on*, their pronunciation in Modern Standard Chinese ([*bu*] and [*hu*]) is given in the third row as a reference. The first two characters (紫布) represent the bi-syllabic native Korean noun *tolpwoy* 'azelea.' Each syllable is represented by one character. The first character (紫, in MSC: *zǐ* 'purple, violet') is related in meaning to 'azelea' and is read in the native Korean sound *tolp*. The second character (布, in MSC: *bù* 'cloth') is used to represent the second syllable of the word by phonetic similarity to the Korean syllable *woy*, and its meaning in Chinese ('cloth') is irrelevant. The same pattern applies to the second noun *pahwoy* ('crag'). Such "semantic *kun* + phonetic *on*" combinations are a salient feature of how Chinese characters are used in writing *hyangka*.[16]

◼ *Gugyeol* 'oral formulae'

Unlike *idu* and *hyangchal*, which were used to write the Korean language, *gugyeol* (口訣 'oral formulae') is an annotation system designed to make Classical Chinese text easier to understand to Korean readers. Dating back to the early Goryeo dynasty (918–1392), *gugyeol* was mainly used in the *Joseon* dynasty (1392–1897) when studying Confucian classics and Buddhist works became increasingly important. While the original form of the text in Chinese is preserved – and thus the writing is in the Chinese word order – the purpose of *gugyeol* is to make the Chinese text readable as Korean. This is accomplished primarily by inserting certain *hanja* graphs in appropriate locations to represent grammatical morphemes present in Korean but not in Chinese. Below is an example.[17] The text is the first sentence of a children's primer on moral rules written in 1670. *Gugyeol* characters are underlined and their pronunciation is given in square brackets.

天	地	之間	萬物	之中	厓
heaven	earth	between	all things	among	at [*ey*]
唯	人	伊	最	貴	爲尼
only	man	SUBJ. [*i*]	most	noble	does, and so... [*honi*]
所	貴乎	人	者	隱	
what is	noble	man	TOPIC	TOPIC [*nun*]	
以	其	有	五倫	也	羅
because of	his	have	Five Human Relationships	EMPHATIC	is [*la*]

'In the multitude of the myriad things midst heaven and earth (at that place), man (he) is the most noble (and so): What is noble in man (it) is his possession of the Five Human Relationships (it is).'

The *gugyeol* characters are phonetic *on* borrowed for their sound values. If we take these characters away, the text will be no different from the original Chinese text. Based on such markings, however, proficient *gugyeol* readers would be able to render the annotated text into grammatical Korean. This practice resembled the Japanese *kanbun* (漢文 'Chinese writing') tradition that we will discuss in the next chapter.

As this practice developed, some 30 frequently used *gugyeol* characters evolved into simplified graphs that were either fragments or shorthand shapes of the original characters.[18]

For example, the character 厓 is simplified into 厂, 伊 into 亻, 爲 into ㆚, and 尼 into ヒ. The simpler forms allow the graphs to be written in a size smaller than the original text, making it easier to differentiate the Chinese words and the Korean grammatical morphemes. Below are the first two lines of the example above written in this manner.

天地之間萬物之中厂 唯人亻 最貴㆚ヒ

The simplified *gugyeol* is similar in form and function to *katakana* in Japanese, which also represent grammatical morphemes amidst Chinese characters, a role later taken over by *hiragana*. These are not the only parallels between Korean and Japanese in how they have adapted Chinese characters to fulfill their writing needs. We will see a few more in the next chapter when we discuss the Japanese scripts in detail.

Hangeul

Hangeul (한글 *han* 'great,' *geul* 'writing') is the official script used to write Korean today in both North Korea, where the script is referred to as *josongul* (조선글 'Korean writing'), and South Korea. The creation of *hangeul* is attributed to King Sejong the Great (世宗大王 1397–1450), who ruled as the fourth monarch of the *Joseon* dynasty (reign 1418–1450). *Hangeul* is an alphabetic writing system designed with careful attention to the sound system of the Korean language at the time. Consisting of no more than 40 letters,[19] it is much easier to learn and use than the Chinese script or its Korean adaptations. During King Sejong's time, only elite members of the society could afford an education to learn *hanja*, the Chinese-character script. It is said that the king invented the script so that all his people would be able to easily and accurately read and write the Korean language. The work to design *hangeul* was completed in 1443,[20] and in 1446, King Sejong introduced the alphabetical script in a publication titled *Hunminjeongeum* (訓民正音), *The correct sounds for the instruction of the people*. Its preface reads:

> Because the speech of this country is different from that of China, it [the spoken language] does not match the [Chinese] characters. Therefore, even if the ignorant want to communicate, many of them in the end cannot state their concerns. Saddened by this, I have [had] 28 letters newly made. It is my wish that all the people may easily learn these letters and that [they] be convenient for daily use.

However, the alphabet met with strong objections from the educated elite. To them, writing simple letters was for women and children, the uneducated of the population. Some even went so far as to claim that only "barbarians like Japanese and Mongolians possess their own scripts," and for Koreans, there was no need for such a "mean, vulgar, useless" script.[21] Despite King Sejong's efforts to popularize *hangeul*, it took almost 500 years for it to eventually replace *hanja* as the predominant script in actual use. During that time, *hangeul* was primarily used by women and authors of popular fiction. Writing for official purposes was done almost exclusively in Chinese characters and remained so until the early 20th century, and until that time *hanja*, and along with it the Chinese culture, maintained its high status in Korea.[22]

THE STORY BEYOND

Korean Alphabet Day

Today, the Korean alphabet is commonly seen as a valued cultural asset, a symbol of Korean identity, and a source of national pride. The proclamation of the script is even celebrated as a public holiday. In South Korea, *Hangeul* Day is on October 9 of each year, and in North Korea, *Josongul* Day is on January 15. If you visit Seoul, South Korea, you will see a bronze statue of King Sejong in *Gwanghwamun* Square. The statue was unveiled in 2009 in celebration of the *Hangeul* Day.

Although *hangeul* appears to have been inspired by other writing systems, including the *Phags-pa* script used to write Mongolian (as well as Chinese) and the Chinese seal script, it is different from both of them in fundamental ways and is generally considered an original creation. The design of the *hangeul* alphabet is based on a sophisticated understanding of 15th-century Korean phonology.[23] If you recall, in traditional Chinese phonology, a syllable is divided into two parts, an initial (consonant) and a final (e.g., vowel, vowel plus nasal). By contrast, King Sejong's analysis divided a Korean syllable into three parts: an initial consonant, a medial vowel, and a final consonant. This analytical approach to understanding the Korean syllable structure paved the way for the creation of an alphabet. Furthermore, what makes *hangeul* an interesting alphabet is that the design of its consonant and vowel letters follows certain scientific or philosophical rationales. Let us take a closer look.

The consonant graphemes are not a collection of discrete letters but form a system built upon five basic letters. These basic symbols are shaped in such a way to suggest the articulatory configurations in the speaker's mouth (Figure 10.1). The bilabial /m/ is written with ㅁ, which looks like a mouth with two lips. ㅅ, a supposedly tooth-like character, represents /s/, a dental consonant that involves the front of the tongue approximating the upper teeth. The pronunciation of /n/ requires that the tip of the tongue touch the bony protruding structure right behind the upper teeth, a gesture represented with the letter ㄴ. The /g/ sound involves the back of the tongue raised to touch the back portion of the roof of the mouth, and the letter ㄱ supposedly represents this gesture. The consonant /ng/ is written with a circle depicting the open throat. This symbol is now also used to indicate the lack of an initial consonant in a syllable.

FIGURE 10.1   Five basic *hangeul* consonant shapes suggesting phonetic rationale

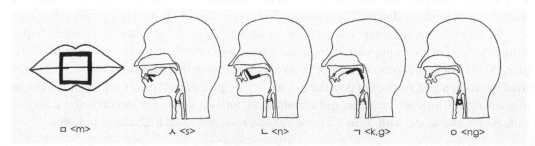

ㅁ <m>   ㅅ <s>   ㄴ <n>   ㄱ <k,g>   ㅇ <ng>

On the basis of these five symbols, strokes are added to derive additional consonant letters. For example, adding one stroke above ㄴ <n> generates the letter ㄷ <d>. The consonants /n/ and /d/ are closely related to each other because they are pronounced at the same place of articulation involving the same gesture of the tongue. Then adding another stroke gives us the letter ㅌ <t>, representing the aspirated version of the /d/ sound. Doubling the ㄷ symbol produces ㄸ <dd>, the letter for the tense version of the /d/ sound. Such derivative relationships between consonant letters are shown in Table 10.1.

Table 10.1   *Hangeul* consonant letters[24]

Basic	Stops	Aspirated	Tense
ㄱ <g>		ㅋ <k>	ㄲ <gg>
ㄴ <n>	ㄷ <d>	ㅌ <t>	ㄸ <dd>
ㅁ <m>	ㅂ <b>	ㅍ <p>	ㅃ <bb>
ㅅ <s>	ㅈ <j>	ㅊ <ch>	ㅆ <ss>, ㅉ <jj>
ㅇ <ng>		ㅎ <h>	

Hangeul vowels are said to have been designed based on a set of neo-Confucian notions – heaven, earth, and man – that were understood as the three "great powers of the universe or the three germinants of Chinese philosophy."[25] The horizontal line represents earth, the essence of *yīn* (阴/陰 'shade, overt, negative, opposite of *yang*'), the point (or short horizontal or vertical line) represents the sun in heaven, the essence of *yáng* (阳/陽 'sun, overt, positive, opposite of *yīn*'), and the vertical stroke symbolizes human beings who are mediators between heaven and earth.

Like the consonant letters, vowel letters also form a system. The six basic vowel letters are created by adding a short horizontal or vertical line to a long horizontal or vertical line, as shown below:

ㅏ <a>; ㅓ <eo>; ㅗ <o>; ㅜ <u>; ㅡ <eu>; ㅣ <i>

Then, two or more basic vowel letters combine to form compound vowel letters. For example, adding a short horizontal or vertical line changes ㅏ <a> to ㅑ <ya>, ㅓ <eo> to ㅕ <yeo>, ㅜ <u> to ㅠ <yu>, and ㅗ <o> to ㅛ <yo>.

An important feature of *hangeul*, as mentioned previously, is that it is written in syllable blocks and is probably the only alphabetical script written this way. Instead of being written linearly as they are in English, *hangeul* letters are arranged in a square, two-dimensional space to form a combination of letters that represents a syllable. The letters within the same syllable block are read left to right and top to bottom. For example, the word *hangeul* (한글) has two syllables and is thus written in two syllable blocks. The results of such arrangement are squarish letter combinations reminiscent of Chinese characters, each of which also corresponds to a syllable. The visual resemblance between *hangeul* and *hànzì* (the Chinese script) is indeed prominent. Make no mistake, however – they are not the same kind of writing system. *Hangeul* is phonemic, as is by definition for all alphabetic scripts, and, as you may recall from Part

II, *hànzì* is morphemic (or morphographic). Each *hangeul* letter corresponds to a Korean phoneme, while each Chinese character represents a morpheme in writing Chinese. It is the basic linguistic unit a grapheme represents, not the spatial arrangement of graphemes, that determines the nature of a script.

Syllables, however, are the units in which proficient *hangeul* users read and write. Korean syllables may be in the shape of V, CV, CVC or CVCC. ("V" represents "vowel" and "C" represents "consonant.") Each *hangeul* syllable block consists of at least a C and a V. When the vowel is not preceded by a consonant in speech, in writing the letter ㅇ /ng/ is used to stand in as a null consonant. See Table 10.2 for a few examples of Korean syllable shapes. The Korean syllable structure is more complex than that of Modern Standard Chinese, which makes use of about 1,359 different syllable shapes, and even more so than Japanese, which has only 113 distinct morae. (Recall that in Chapter 1 we learned that a **mora** is similar to but not the same as a syllable. It is a phonological unit intermediate between a phoneme and a syllable, and it is the basic unit for the Japanese *kana*: each *kana* symbol represents one mora.) There are 3,000 to 4,000 distinctive Korean syllables.[26]

Table 10.2 Korean syllable shapes and *hangeul* syllable blocks

Syllable shape	Hangeul	Romanization
V	아	a
CV	다	da
CVC	달	dal
CVCC	닭	dalg

Beginning writers, including Korean elementary-school students, start with learning 140 basic CV syllables formed by combining the 14 basic consonants and the 10 basic vowels (Table 10.3). The composition of the syllable blocks follows a regular pattern: if the vowel contains a vertical stroke, the consonant appears on its left; if the vowel has a horizontal stroke, then the consonant comes on top.

Table 10.3 140 basic Korean syllables[27]

	ㅏ a	ㅑ ya	ㅓ eo	ㅕ yeo	ㅗ o	ㅛ yo	ㅜ u	ㅠ yu	─ eu	ㅣ i
ㄱ g	가	갸	거	겨	고	교	구	규	그	기
ㄴ n	나	냐	너	녀	노	뇨	누	뉴	느	니
ㄷ d	다	댜	더	뎌	도	됴	두	듀	드	디
ㄹ r/l	라	랴	러	려	로	료	루	류	르	리
ㅁ m	마	먀	머	며	모	묘	무	뮤	므	미
ㅂ b	바	뱌	버	벼	보	뵤	부	뷰	브	비
ㅅ s	사	샤	서	셔	소	쇼	수	슈	스	시
ㅇ (null)	아	야	어	여	오	요	우	유	으	이
ㅈ j	자	쟈	저	져	조	죠	주	쥬	즈	지
ㅊ ch	차	챠	처	쳐	초	쵸	추	츄	츠	치

(*Continued*)

Table 10.3   Continued

	ㅏ a	ㅑ ya	ㅓ eo	ㅕ yeo	ㅗ o	ㅛ yo	ㅜ u	ㅠ yu	ㅡ eu	ㅣ i
ㅋ k	카	캬	커	켜	코	쿄	쿠	큐	크	키
ㅌ t	타	탸	터	텨	토	툐	투	튜	트	티
ㅍ p	파	퍄	퍼	펴	포	표	푸	퓨	프	피
ㅎ h	하	햐	허	혀	호	효	후	휴	흐	히

Hangeul's status has risen since the mid- to late 19th century as Korea underwent reforms in favor of Western-style modernization. Gradually, a mixed script emerged with *hanja* representing Sino-Korean words and *hangeul* representing native Korean words and grammatical morphemes. This pattern was very similar to, though not as complex as, the modern-day mixed script of Japanese, which we will discuss in the next chapter. *Hangeul* is now the predominant script used in both Koreas. In North Korea, *hangeul* became the sole script for official writing when *hanja* was abolished in 1949. The use of *hanja* in South Korea, although not completely abandoned, has declined dramatically since the 1950s and, by the 1980s, *hanja* practically disappeared from public media such as newspapers. In both Koreas, however, a limited number of *hanja* is still taught in schools. For example, high school students in South Korea are generally expected to learn about 1,800 characters before they graduate. Some linguists argue that *hanja* should continue to be taught and used for the variety of advantages it offers to learning and communication.[28] It will be interesting to see if *hanja* will rise again as elements in the Korean script in the foreseeable future.

THE STORY BEYOND

Hangeul-only script vs. mixed script

In South Korea, the debate over the use of a *hangeul*-exclusive script vs. a mixed script of *hangeul* and *hanja* has ebbed and flowed for decades. A recent policy that once again set off arguments from both sides was the Ministry of Education's decision in September of 2014 to include 400–500 characters (for writing roughly 300 words) in elementary-school textbooks starting in 2018.[29] Based on this policy, the *hanja* characters would be used to annotate and disambiguate words. Although they would be part of the text, they would not be required for any exams so that students would not be required to memorize them. Those who argued for the inclusion of *hanja* characters pointed out that the abundance of homophones—different words with identical pronunciation—in the Korean language meant that words that appeared the same in *hangeul* might often have very different meanings. For example, the Korean expression *sam yeon pae* could both mean "to lose three times in a row" and "to win three times in a row."[30] Although it might be possible to determine the intended meaning based on context, without knowing the *hanja* behind the different meanings, such knowledge, as some argued, was not complete. For this reason, the *hangeul*-exclusive script has been accused of resulting in "functional illiteracy" despite the high rate of basic literacy.[31] Proponents of the all-*hangeul* script, however, insisted that the use of *hanja* would weaken the Korean identity.[32] Most Korean school teachers appeared to be against the new policy, worried that it would put additional strains on elementary-school students, who were already carrying a heavy academic burden.

Notes

1 See Taylor and Taylor (2014, p. 172).
2 Ibid.
3 The term *idu*, when used in a broad sense, encompasses *hyangchal* and *gugyeol*. In this book, it is used in its narrow sense to refer only to *idu* proper.
4 The situation is similar in *Táiwān*, where students learn *bopomofo* (ㄅㄆㄇㄈ) instead of a Romanization system to annotate the pronunciation of characters or input Chinese text on computers.
5 Chung (2008).
6 A stele is a tall stone slab erected as a monument in ancient times.
7 Notably, in the inscription Korean names are written phonetically using *hanja* in the *idu* script.
8 The term *idu* is written variously in Chinese characters as 吏讀, 吏頭, 吏吐, 吏道, or 吏套.
9 See Sohn (2001, p. 124). In addition, according to Rogers (2005), the earliest surviving piece of writing in *idu* was from 754 CE (see p. 69).
10 Rogers (2005, p. 69).
11 See Chapter 9 for what constitutes a semantic *on*.
12 This example is taken from Sohn (2001, p. 127). Note that the Romanization of native Korean morphemes may be based on the Yale system, but this does not affect our understanding of the example.
13 Brown and Yeon (2015, p. 428).
14 The Romanization used here is MR.
15 Example adapted from Brown and Yeon (2015, p. 428).
16 Ibid., p. 428.
17 Adapted from Lee and Ramsey (2000, p. 52).
18 Taylor and Taylor (2014, p. 175).
19 According to Taylor and Taylor (2014), the number of letters is counted differently in North Korea and South Korea: 24 in the North and 40 in the South. This difference exists because, in addition to the 14 basic consonant letters and 10 basic vowels, South Korea also considers the 5 double consonants and 11 compound vowels part of the alphabet. (p. 184)
20 Some scholars say 1444, which is also considered correct. This is because, based on historical records, the script was completed in the 25th year of King Sejong's rule according to the lunar calendar. This lunar year was for the most part in 1443 but also extended into 1444.
21 Taylor and Taylor (2014, p. 181).
22 King (1996, p. 218).
23 See Taylor and Taylor (2014) and Rogers (2005).
24 Adapted from Taylor and Taylor (2014, p. 183), Table 11–1.
25 Ibid., p. 183; also see Rogers (2005, p. 71).
26 Lee and Ramsey (2000, p. 67).
27 Adapted from Taylor and Taylor (2014, p. 187), Table 11–4.
28 Ibid., Chapter 13, "Why should hancha be kept?"
29 See for example Kim (2015) and Jeon (2015).
30 Kim (2017).
31 Jeon (2015).
32 Lee and Shim (2015).

11 Writing Japanese

W**HEN JAPAN CAME INTO** contact with China, the Japanese language was generally not recorded in writing. In around the early 4th century,[1] Chinese written text – and along with it the idea of writing – was first introduced via Korea to Japan. The Japanese first learned to read and write in Chinese, then adapted the Chinese writing system to recording their own language, and eventually created additional systems of writing to supplement, facilitate, and in certain cases replace the use of Chinese characters. Today, Japanese writing makes use of a mixture of four scripts: *kanji* (漢字[2] 'Chinese characters'), *hiragana* (平仮名 'simple borrowed characters'), *katakana* (片仮名 'partial borrowed characters'), and *rōmaji* (Roman letters)[3] and is considered one of the most complex in the world. In this chapter, we will look at how Japanese writing came to be the way it is.

THE STORY BEYOND

A Note on Japanese Romanization

Before we proceed further, it will be good to learn about how we represent Japanese in Roman letters. There are a number of systems, and two of the most common ones are Hepburn and *kunrei* (訓令). This book uses the Hepburn system, because it is the most widely used and is also the system adopted by the Library of Congress. Compared to *kunrei*, it is closer to Japanese pronunciation from the perspective of English speakers.

The Hepburn system was popularized by James Curtis Hepburn (1815–1911), an American physician and missionary who lived and worked in Japan from 1859 to 1892. In 1867, he published the first modern Japanese–English dictionary. In the third edition of this dictionary, he adopted a new Romanization system devised by the Society for the Romanization of the Japanese Alphabet (*Rōmajikai*). It came to be known as the Hepburn system, because it was Hepburn's dictionary, which quickly became the standard reference book for Japanese language learners, that popularized the script.

The *kunrei* system was promulgated by the Japanese government in 1937 and revised in 1954, and it is considered the official Romanization system in Japan. It shows phonological details more consistently for conjugation, so that the stem form remains visually constant, even though it changes phonetically. It is good for pedagogy and is the system taught to Japanese children in elementary school.

The chart below lists the main differences in spelling between the Hepburn and *kunrei* systems. Note that long vowels in Hepburn are marked with the macro "‾" while in *kunrei* they are marked with the caret "^."

Hepburn	Kunrei	Hepburn	Kunrei	Hepburn	Kunrei
shi	*si*	*sho*	*syo*	*ā*	*â*
chi	*ti*	*cha*	*tya*	*ē*	*ê*
tsu	*tu*	*chu*	*tyu*	*ī*	*î*
fu	*hu*	*cho*	*tyo*	*ō*	*ô*
ji	*zi*	*ja*	*zya*	*ū*	*û*
sha	*sya*	*ju*	*zyu*		
shu	*syu*	*jo*	*zyo*		

Kanbun

To further understand how the Japanese language came to be written in Chinese characters, it is useful to learn about **kanbun** (漢文 'Chinese text/literature/writing'), Classical Chinese text annotated to facilitate Japanese speakers' reading of the text as Japanese. Although initially a method to help Japanese speakers understand Classical Chinese material, *kanbun* also became a style of writing in Classical Japanese using Chinese characters. Educated Japanese not only studied literature brought in from China but also composed poetry and wrote official documents in Classical Chinese in the *kanbun* style. A great amount of Japanese literature was written in *kanbun* over thousands of years until as recently as the 20th century.

How does reading *kanbun* work? Let us look at an example. In Table 11.1, the *kanbun* text is written vertically on the right. Because Chinese text was traditionally arranged in vertical columns read from right to left, *kanbun* also used this arrangement. To facilitate the reading process, an annotation system consisting of *kaeriten* (返り点 'return marks') was developed. These were symbols added to the text to indicate the order in which the characters should be read. The *kaeriten* were written to the lower left of the characters *in a size smaller than the main text*. The text in this example is the first sentence of a story from the book *Hán Fēizǐ* (韩非子/韓非子) of the Warring States Period (mid-3rd century BCE). In English, this sentence means, "there was a *Chǔ* person selling shields and spears." *Chǔ* (楚) was the name of one of the seven major Warring States before China was united in 221 BCE.

Table 11.1 Reading *kanbun*

Chinese	楚	人	有	鬻	盾	與	矛	者	楚
Romanization	Chǔ	rén	yǒu	yù	dùn	yǔ	máo	zhě	人
Meaning	Chǔ	person	there exists	sell	shield	and	spear	(nominal-izer)	有 下
									鬻
									二
Japanese	楚	人	盾	矛	與	鬻	者	有	盾 與
Romanization	So	jin	jun	mu	yo	iku	sha	yū	一
Meaning	Chǔ	person	shield	spear	and	sell	(nominalizer)	there exists	レ 矛 者 上

On the surface, the text appears no different from ordinary Classical Chinese text. In order to read it as Japanese, the reader must make adjustments to account for the difference in word order between Chinese and Japanese. In highly simplified terms, word order in a Chinese sentence is typically subject – verb – object, while in Japanese it is usually subject – object – verb. The reader would rearrange the characters into the Japanese order, read them in Japanese pronunciation, and add grammatical suffixes where needed. The outcome would essentially be a translation of the Classical Chinese text in Classical Japanese with a certain *kanbun* flavor.

Let us try to read the *kanbun* text in the example. We start from the very top, 楚人 (*So jin*, '*Chǔ* person'). There is no marking of any kind for these two characters, so we simply read them and move on. The next character 有 (*yū*, 'there exists') is marked with a 下 (*ge*, 'down, bottom'). This tells us that we will need to move this character to below where the mark 上 (*jō*, 'up, top') is, in this case at the very end of the sentence. So, we skip 有 and move on to the next character 鬻 (*iku*, 'to sell'). This character has a number 二 (*ni*, 'two') attached to it, which means it cannot be read until the character marked with the number 一 (*ichi*, 'one') has been read. So, we skip 鬻 as well. The character following it, 盾 (*jun*, 'shield'), is unmarked, so we go ahead and read this one. After that, 與 (*yo*, 'and') is marked again. レ (*re*, 'reverse mark') indicates that the two characters adjacent to it switch positions with each other. Therefore, we read 矛 (*mu*, 'spear') next, and then go back to 與. After 與 we bring in 鬻, as this is the position marked with the number 一. Then we read 者 (*sha*, 'nominalizer'), and finally the verb 有 (*yū*, 'there exists'). There. As you see, it is quite a laborious process. But at the same time it is also quite fascinating.

Companion Website

Exercise 11.1 Reading *kanbun*

The existence of *kanbun* shows us that, in the case of Japanese, the borrowing of a writing system, as we have seen, is not merely a matter of linguistic encoding of the native speech in a "non-native" script. In fact, the importing of the Chinese script took place amidst extensive and deep learning of the Chinese culture, including its language, literature, philosophy, and so on.[4] Thus, the borrowing of the Chinese script was a by-product of the sustained contact between cultures and it facilitated rigorous integration of one culture into another.

Kanji

The use of Chinese characters, or *kanji*, in writing Japanese traces its origin to as early as the 4th century CE. Between the 4th and the 7th centuries, a large number of Koreans and Chinese emigrated to Japan. Besides introducing Chinese text to Japan, including Confucian classics and Buddhist writing, the scholars among them also tutored the Japanese people in the arts, science, and technology of China. By the 7th to the 8th centuries, Japan's educated elites, including aristocrats, officials, and Buddhist monks, had integrated many aspects of the Chinese culture into Japanese life, including the use of Chinese characters. For instance, one of the early examples of writing in *kanji* was a 17-article constitution drafted by Prince Shōtoku (574–622 CE) in the year 604.[5] For hundreds of years since the initial use of *kanji* and until *kana* was created in the 9th century, the character-based writing system had remained the sole script for Japanese, and it still serves an important role in Japanese writing today.[6]

How many *kanji* are used in writing Japanese? Up until the Meiji period (1868–1912), although the *kana* scripts had been in existence for centuries, official and scholarly writing was almost exclusively done in *kanji*. Since then, government-sponsored script reforms have transformed Japanese writing from an all-*kanji* script to a mixed script. From 1879 to 1968, the percentage of *kanji* used in newspapers declined from 90% to 60% of all written graphs.[7] Based on data collected between 1941 and 1981, the number of different *kanji* ranged around 3,000 for magazines and newspapers and around 5,000 for Japanese literature.[8] In general, the 2,000 most frequently used *kanji* account for about 99% of all *kanji* occurrences, and up to another 3,000 account for the remaining 1%.[9] Table 11.2 and Table 11.3 offer information from various official lists of *kanji* decreed for common use and elementary school instruction from the end of World War II to the beginning of the 21st century. On one hand, the Japanese government made efforts to limit the use of *kanji*. On the other hand, as these tables show, the number of *kanji* officially sanctioned for basic literacy has somewhat increased.

Table 11.2   *Kanji* for common use[10]

Number of *kanji*	Year	Name of list
1,850	1946	Temporary *kanji*
1,945	1981	Common *kanji*
2,136	2010	Common *kanji*

Table 11.3   *Kanji* for primary school[11]

Number of *kanji*	Year
881	1948
996	1970
1,006	1989

Chinese characters in Japanese may have multiple pronunciations. This is because the same *kanji* may represent both the borrowed Chinese morpheme and the indigenous Japanese counterpart. Official documents in Japan were written in the *kanbun* style for thousands of years, from the late Heian period (794–1185) until after World War II. Not surprisingly, it made a lasting impact on the Japanese language. As discussed in the overview, a large number of Chinese words were borrowed into the Japanese lexicon – it has been estimated that about 60% of Japanese vocabulary is Chinese in origin.[12] Oftentimes, the Chinese loanword and the native Japanese word are both preserved in the language and associated with the same *kanji*. In other words, the same character may represent multiple morphemes and have multiple pronunciations. However, their uses are usually not interchangeable. The reader must know which to use given a specific context. The Chinese reading typically appears in a compound, while the Japanese reading usually occurs on its own. For example, 山 (in Chinese: *shān* 'mountain') is read as *san* as part of the proper noun 富士山 *Fujisan* 'Mount Fuji' and the names of other mountains that are well known. But it is read as the native word *yama* when referring to a generic mountain.

山 'mountain' (1) *san*, (2) *yama*
富士山は日本で一番高い山です。
Fujisan wa Nihon de ichiban takayi yamadesu.
'Mount Fuji is the highest mountain in Japan.'

Recall that in the overview chapter we have learned a pair of linguistic terms to help us talk about the different readings of *kanji*. When the character is read with pronunciation in its source language (Chinese), it is called ***on*-reading** (音読み *onyomi* 'sound reading'). If it is read with the pronunciation in the target language (e.g., Japanese), it is called ***kun*-reading** (訓読み *kunyomi* 'meaning reading'). Furthermore, depending on whether the original meaning of the character is kept or not, the reading can be regarded as either semantic or phonetic. Taken together, there can be four different types of readings: semantic *on*, semantic *kun*, phonetic *on*, and phonetic *kun*. We already looked at a few examples for these concepts in the overview chapter. Let us review them with a few additional examples:

Semantic *on*: e.g., 着 *chaku* 'start' in 着手 *chakushu* 'start'
Semantic *kun*: e.g., 着 *ki* 'to wear' in 着物 *kimono* 'clothing'
Phonetic *on*: e.g., 天 *ten* 'sky' in 天火 *tempi* 'oven'
Phonetic *kun*: e.g., 張 *haru* 'to strech' for *haru* 'spring'[13]

First, **semantic *on*** is when the whole Chinese morpheme – both the meaning and the sound – has been borrowed into Japanese. For example, the word 着手 (着 'to put'; 手 'hand') means "to start" in both Chinese and Japanese. Its pronunciation in modern Japanese, *chakushu*, is reminiscent of how it sounds in modern Chinese, *zhuóshǒu*. The similarity in both meaning and sound is a clue that the entire word was borrowed from Chinese into Japanese. Thus, the 着 in the Japanese word 着手 has a semantic *on* reading.

When only the meaning is borrowed but the *kanji* is read with its native Japanese pronunciation, this reading is referred to as **semantic *kun***. The character 着 (*ki* 'to wear') in the second example 着物 (*kimono* 'clothing'; 物 *mono* 'thing') has a semantic *kun* reading. On one hand, its Chinese meaning has been preserved in Japanese: 着 (*zhuó*) in Chinese means "to wear" as well. On the other hand, the character's Chinese pronunciation is not adopted in Japanese, and it is pronounced as the native Japanese morpheme *ki*.

Phonetic *on* refers to the reading of *kanji* based on its Chinese pronunciation when the meaning of the character in Chinese is irrelevant to its meaning in Japanese. In the third example, the character 天 in Japanese is pronounced as *ten*, akin to its modern Chinese pronunciation *tiān*. Yet its Japanese meaning "oven" has little to do with its Chinese meaning "sky." Apparently, in this case, the character 天 was borrowed purely for its phonetic value to represent a native Japanese morpheme.

Finally, a Chinese character may be used in Japanese to represent a morpheme irrelevant to its Chinese original in either meaning or sound. In this case, the reading is referred to as **phonetic *kun***. In the last example, the *kanji* 張 (*haru* 'spring season') appears to be unrelated to the character in Chinese in either pronunciation (MSC *zhāng*) or meaning ('to stretch'). How did it come to be used this way? It was likely a two-step process. First, 張 ('stretch') was used to represent the synonymous morpheme *haru* ('stretch') in Japanese. At that point, it was a case of semantic *kun*. Then, the character was used to represent the Japanese morpheme *haru* 'spring (season)' that happened to have the same pronunciation. The new meaning it took on was no longer related to its original meaning in Chinese. As a result, the character lost its connection to the Chinese original both in sound and in meaning and came to be read as a phonetic *kun*.

As we have seen, the appropriate reading of a *kanji* is determined by context. The same *kanji* may be read in its Chinese pronunciation or its Japanese pronunciation. This makes reading *kanji* sometimes a very complex matter.

To make matters worse, Chinese words were borrowed into Japanese not all at once, but during different historical periods and from varied dialectal sources. This resulted in three major types of *on*-readings: *Go'on* (呉音 'sound of the Chinese state *Wú*'), *Kan'on* (漢音 'sound of Chinese'), and *Tō-Sòon* (唐宋音 'sound of *Táng* and *Sòng* dynasties'). *Go'on* borrowing occurred during the 5th and the 6th centuries from a Southern dialect of China's Six Dynasties period, when Buddhist works were introduced to Japan via Korea. *Kan'on* was brought to Japan during the 7th and the 8th centuries and reflected the pronunciations of Chinese in the cities *Cháng'ān* (長安) and *Luòyáng* (洛阳/洛陽) of the *Táng* dynasty. Finally, *Tō-Sòon* came to Japanese from southern China along with Zen Buddhism during the 14th century, when China was in the *Yuán* or *Míng* dynasty.

As a result of this complicated borrowing history, although most *kanji* have just one *on*-reading, some may have as many as three. For example, the character 明 in today's Mandarin is pronounced as *míng* and has several meanings: (1) 'bright, light, clear'; (2) 'immediately following this year/day'; (3) 'as in *Míng* dynasty.' In Japanese, the *kanji* 明 may be read in its *Go'on*, *Kan'on* or *Tō-Sòon* depending on what word it is in, as shown in Table 11.4.

Table 11.4 The *on*-readings of the *kanji* 明 in Modern Japanese

	Type of on-reading	*Katakana*	Romanization	Example (*kanji*, Romanization, meaning)
(1)	Go	ミョウ	*myou*	明日 *myounichi* 'tomorrow'
(2)	Kan	メイ	*mei*	文明 *bunmei* 'civilization'
(3)	Tō-Sō	ミン	*min*	明朝 *minchou* '*Míng* dynasty'

In addition, the same *kanji* may also have a number of *kun*-readings, that is, read with its Japanese pronunciations. *On*-readings often occur in compounds, while *kun*-readings are usually stand-alone morphemes or words. What distinguishes *kun*-readings in writing is the addition of some type of inflectional ending written in *hiragana*. Let's look at the *kanji* 明 again as an example (Table 11.5).

Table 11.5 The *kun*-readings of the *kanji* 明 in Modern Japanese

	Kanji with inflectional ending in hiragana	*Hiragana*	Romanization	Meaning
(1)	明かり	あかり	*akari*	'light' as in 'sunlight'
(2)	明かり	あかり	*akari*	'bright' or 'cheerful'

	Kanji with inflectional ending in *hiragana*	*Hiragana*	Romanization	Meaning
(3)	明るい	あかるい	akarui	'to get bright (as in dawn)'
(4)	明るむ	あかるむ	akarumu	(uncommon, same as (3))
(5)	明らむ	あからむ	akaramu	'clear' or 'obvious'
(6)	明らか	あきらか	akiraka	'to become a new day/year'
(7)	明ける	あける	akeru	'to become a new day/year'
(8)	明く	あく	aku	'to open' (restricted to certain expressions)
(9)	明くる	あくる	akuru	'the next or following (year)'
(10)	明かす	あかす	akasu	'to disclose or explain'

The reading of the *kanji* 明, at least superficially, may correspond to *a-* (1, 2, 7, 8, 9, 10), *aka-* (3, 4, 5), or *aki-* (6). There is much morpheme-specific information the reader or writer must know in order to pronounce or write the morpheme correctly.

Companion Website

Exercise 11.2 Reading *kanji*

Man'yōgana

The Japanese term **kana** (仮名) refers to the moraic scripts[14] used to write the Japanese language historically and in modern times. *Kana* comes from *karina*, in which *na* means "names, letters," while *kari* may have a range of meanings including "borrowed," "fake," "temporary," "unofficial," and "irregular."[15] Thus, *kana* may mean "borrowed names," because in the earliest *kana* script, *kanji* or Chinese characters were "borrowed" as sound symbols to represent the Japanese speech. *Kana* may also mean "fake names," or "unofficial letters" as opposed to the *kanji* script that was already in place and deemed the authentic and official system of writing for Japanese at the time.

Man'yōgana (万葉仮名) was considered the earliest method of writing that made use of *kanji* as sound graphs to represent Japanese. *Man'yō* literally means "ten thousand leaves." This poetic name was derived from the *Man'yōshū* (万葉集), *Collection of Ten Thousand Leaves*, the famous anthology of approximately 4,500 Japanese poems composed during the Nara period (710–794 CE). It is the earliest known anthology of Japanese poetry. The poems in this collection were recorded in writing using a complex combination of methods. In many instances, Chinese characters were used for their phonetic values regardless of their meaning. For example, the character 天 (*t'ien* in Middle Chinese) were used to represent the Old Japanese mora *te*, and 安 (*ân* in MC) for *a*.[16] This kind of writing came to be known as *mun'yōgana* (*Man'yō* + *kana*). Some scholars believe that the Korean *hyangchal*, which also used Chinese characters primarily as sound symbols, had an impact on *man'yōgana*.[17]

When *man'yōgana* was in use, it was up to the writers to choose which *kanji* to pick to represent a given mora. Since different characters could be pronounced the same, multiple characters might be used to represent the same mora. By the end of the 8th century, more than 970 *kanji* characters were in use to write the fewer than 90 morae of the Japanese language at the time.[18] For example, over 40 different kanji were used to represent the mora *shi* and over 30 characters were used for *ka*.[19] Gradually, however, each mora came to be written with a preferred Chinese character, and over time these preferred characters became simplified.

Man'yōgana was the linguistic precursor for both *hiragana* and *katakana*. As the practice of using Chinese characters to represent Japanese morae became more common, the character forms also became increasingly simplified. Simplification took two directions: *hiragana* symbols were derived from the cursive forms of their source *man'yōgana* characters, and *katakana* symbols were formed by taking pieces from the source characters, which were often but not always the same characters as the source of the corresponding *hiragana* symbols. For example, the five vowels below are usually the first five morae represented in a *kana* chart of a modern Japanese textbook. The source characters for *u* and *o* are the same for the *hiragana* and the *katakana* symbols; for *a*, *i*, and *e*, however, they are different characters. In fact, the *hiragana* and *katakana* signs were not standardized until the year 1900, when Japan's Ministry of Education enacted regulations on *kana* forms and usage.[20]

Table 11.6   Derivation of *hiragana* and *katakana* from *man'yōgana*

Rōmaji	a	i	u	e	o
Hiragana (*man'yōgana*)	あ (安)	い (以)	う (宇)	え (衣)	お (於)
Katakana (*man'yōgana*)	ア (阿)	イ (伊)	ウ (宇)	エ (江)	オ (於)

▮ *Hiragana* and *katakana*

Modern *kana* consist of two parallel sets of graphs, *hiragana* and *katakana*. As you can see in Table 11.7, the *kana* scripts are different from each other in appearance. *Hiragana* symbols, having derived from a cursive style of Chinese characters (see Table 11.8 for a few examples), have strokes that are curvy and fluid, giving it a feminine look. *Katakana*, on the other hand, makes use of straight and angular lines as in the standard style of Chinese characters and thus looks more masculine. Most of the *katakana* symbols came from fragments of Chinese characters (Table 11.8). Interestingly, the gender difference in the appearance of the *kana* graphs corresponds with the historical use of the two scripts. *Hiragana* was primarily used by female authors for personal writing, such as letters, poems, and diaries, and it was thus referred to as "women's hand (女手 *onnade*)." Notably, female authors also used *hiragana* to write novels. One of the masterpieces in classical Japanese literature, *The Tale of Genji* (源氏物語 *Genji Monogatari*) was written almost entirely in *hiragana* by the noblewoman Murasaki Shikibu in the early 11th century. *Katakana*, on the other hand, in its early history was mostly used by men in official writing.[21]

Table 11.7   Japanese *kana*

Hiragana	あ	い	う	え	お	か	き	く	け	こ	さ	し	す	せ	そ
Katakana	ア	イ	ウ	エ	オ	カ	キ	ク	ケ	コ	サ	シ	ス	セ	ソ

Table 11.7 Continued

Rōmaji	*a*	*i*	*u*	*e*	*o*	*ka*	*ki*	*ku*	*ke*	*ko*	*sa*	*shi*	*su*	*se*	*so*
Hiragana	た	ち	つ	て	と	な	に	ぬ	ね	の	は	ひ	ふ	へ	ほ
Katakana	タ	チ	ツ	テ	ト	ナ	ニ	ヌ	ネ	ノ	ハ	ヒ	フ	ヘ	ホ
Rōmaji	*ta*	*chi*	*tsu*	*te*	*to*	*na*	*ni*	*nu*	*ne*	*no*	*ha*	*hi*	*fu*	*he*	*ho*
Hiragana	ま	み	む	め	も	や		ゆ		よ	ら	り	る	れ	ろ
Katakana	マ	ミ	ム	メ	モ	ヤ		ユ		ヨ	ラ	リ	ル	レ	ロ
Rōmaji	*ma*	*mi*	*mu*	*me*	*mo*	*ya*		*yu*		*yo*	*ra*	*ri*	*ru*	*re*	*ro*
Hiragana	わ			を	ん										
Katakana	ワ			ヲ	ン										
Rōmaji	*wa*			*wo*	*n*										

Table 11.8 *Kanji* origins of *kana*

Rōmaji	Kanji	Hiragana	Kanji	Katakana
i	以	い	伊	イ
na	奈	な	奈	ナ
so	曾	そ	曾	ソ
me	女	め	女	メ
ru	留	る	流	ル

The nature of the *kana* scripts may need some clarification. *Hiragana* and *katakana* are often referred to as Japanese syllabaries, but this categorization is not entirely accurate. In Chapter 3 of this book we learned that a **syllabary** is a writing system in which a grapheme consistently represents a syllable. In *kana*, however, a grapheme does not always correspond to a syllable. One obvious example we can see in Table 11.7 is ん or ン representing a single consonant /n/, which does not fully constitute a syllable. We will see more examples shortly for how one *kana* symbol may not correspond with one Japanese syllable. To more accurately understand the nature of the *kana* scripts, we will need to reintroduce the concept "mora" that we touched on in Chapter 3. If you recall, a **mora** is a phonological unit intermediate between a phoneme and a syllable. In Japanese, it is most of the times a syllable, but it can also be a phoneme (i.e., a single sound).

What exactly constitutes a mora in Japanese? To answer this question, let us first look at the phonemic inventory of Japanese – what consonants and vowels the Japanese language uses. Japanese makes use of five vowels /a, i, u, e, o/ and 14 consonants /p, t, k, b, d, g, s, h, z, j, r, m, n, w/. In addition, there are two kinds of consonants usually represented with the capital letters /N/ and /Q/. /N/ is a nasal sound that usually occurs at the end of a syllable. Depending on what comes after it, the phonetic value of /N/ is different: it is [n] before /n, t, d/, [m] before

/m, p, b/, and [ŋ] (sounds like the English *ng*) before /k, g/. /Q/ is used to represent the first segment of a double consonant, which includes *kk, tt, ss*, and *pp*. Vowels in Japanese can be either short or long, sometimes affecting the meaning of the word, for example *kite* ('Come!') vs. *kīte* ('Listen!'), and sometimes not, for instance *sayonara or sayōnara* ('goodbye').[22] A long vowel can also be called a **geminate vowel**. These consonants and vowels combine to form Japanese syllables.

To understand Japanese morae, we will also need to understand the syllable structure of the Japanese language. The vowels and consonants cannot randomly combine to form syllables and must follow certain patterns. For example, the 14 regular consonants can only occur at the beginning of a syllable and not at the end. /N/ and /Q/, however, occur at the end of a syllable. Consonant clusters, such as *pl, dw, str* that we use in English, are not allowed in Japanese. These restrictions mean that the Japanese syllable structure is relatively simple. We can summarize its possibilities in Table 11.9, which also offers examples. First of all, a syllable in Japanese can be any of the five single vowels, short (V) or long (VV), or a combination of vowels (V_1V_2) called **diphthongs**. It can also be any of these varieties of vowels preceded by a consonant (CV, CVV, CV_1V_2), sometimes with a [y][23] sound in between (CyV, CyVV). Furthermore, it can be a short vowel followed by a /N/ or a /Q/ without a consonant preceding it (VN, VQ), with a consonant preceding it (CVN, CVQ), or with a Cy sequence preceding it (CyVN, CyVQ).

Table 11.9   Japanese syllables

Syllable shape	Morae	*Rōmaji*	*Hiragana*	*Katakana*
V	V	*a*	あ	ア
VV	V-V	*ē*	ええ	エエ
V_1V_2	V_1-V_2	*ai*	あい	アイ
CV	CV	*de*	で	デ
CVV	CV-V	*kō*	こお	コオ
CV_1V_2	CV_1-V_2	*tai*	たい	タイ
CyV	CyV	*kyo*	きょ	キョ
CyVV	CyV-V	*ryoo*	りよお	リヨオ
VN	V-N	*an*	あん	アン
VQ	V-Q	*it(ta)*	いつ(た)	イッ(タ)
CVN	CV-N	*pan*	ぱん	パン
CVQ	CV-Q	*kit(te)*	きつ(て)	キッテ
CyVN	CyV-N	*syon*	しょん	ション
CyVQ	CyV-Q	*tyot(to)*	ちょつ(と)	チョッ(ト)

Now we are ready to come back to our question of what constitutes a mora – a **mora** is a timing unit equivalent to the time required to pronounce a short syllable in Japanese speech. It can be any of the following: V (note that VV or V_1V_2 counts as two morae), CV, CyV, or a syllable-final N or Q. Notably here, N or Q each counts as a mora. Therefore, unlike a syllable, which requires minimally a vowel, a mora can correspond to just one consonant. All the above segments or combinations receive one mora in speech. That is to say that pronouncing them psychologically takes about the same amount of time in Japanese, which can be thought of as one beat. For example, the word /nippon/ ('Japan') has two syllables and four morae. The word /ichi/ ('one') also has two syllables, but it only has two morae. (Syllable boundaries are indicated using dots, and mora boundaries are marked with dashes.) Although these two words have the same number of syllables (and thus take about the same amount of time to say in English), it takes significantly more time to say /nippon/, which receives four beats, than /ichi/, which has two beats, in Japanese.[24]

/nippon/ 'Japan' /ichi/ 'one'

Two syllables: /nip.pon/ Two syllables: /i.chi/

Four morae: /ni-p-po-n/ Two morae: /i-chi/

Companion Website

Exercise 11.3 Syllables and morae

Mora is an important concept not only for describing the timing of Japanese speech but also for characterizing the nature of the *kana* scripts. You may have noticed that, in Table 11.9, although all examples are one syllable long, they are not all written in one *kana* symbol, and some require two or more *kana* graphs. This is because every *kana* graph does not correspond to one syllable – it basically represents one mora. (Note that a smaller よ / ヤ (*yo*) is used when the [y] sound occurs between a C and a V, but it does not receive a mora on its own. A smaller つ / ツ (*tsu*) is used to represent the first segment of a geminate consonant, that is, a silent beat, which does take up one mora.) Let us look at two more examples below.

/okaasan/ 'mother' /kinoo/ 'yesterday'

/o-ka-a-sa-n/ /ki-no-o/

おかあさん きのう

オカアサン キノウ

Okāsan has five morae and is written with five *kana* graphs. *Kinō* has three morae and is written with three *kana* symbols. If they were written using a syllabic script, then because *o.kaa.san* has three syllables, it would be represented with three graphemes, and by the same token, *ki.noo* would be represented by two graphemes. In sum, the *kana* scripts are more accurately described as moraic rather than syllabic writing systems.

A mixed script

Using Chinese characters to write Japanese requires overcoming substantial linguistic challenges. We already touched upon some of the major differences between Japanese and

Chinese in Chapters 1 and 9. Here we will examine them in a little more detail. The two languages differ in how words and sentences are formed. Japanese verbs conjugate depending on whether it is in the polite form, negative form, perfective form, and so forth. Chinese verbs, however, generally occur in the same form. Japanese also makes use of a variety of particles that do not have counterparts in Chinese. Some of them may be attached to nouns to indicate their grammatical role: whether they are the topic (-*wa* は) or the subject (-*ga* が) of the sentence, or whether they are the direct object (-*o* を), the indirect object (-*ni* に), the location (-*de* で), or the direction of the action (-*ni* に), and so on. Others can be attached to sentences to form questions (-*ka* か) or to soften the tone of a request (-*ne* ね), and so forth. Another major difference is in sentential word order, as you may recall from the overview chapter. For these reasons, writing Japanese using the Chinese script is not always a straightforward process.

Let's look at two examples to get a better sense of the syntactic differences between Chinese and Japanese and to see how the mixed script works. To express "go to the library to meet with Xiao Wang," the word order in Chinese is largely the same as in English, while in Japanese, the object comes before the verb, and the verb comes last. The same difference can be observed for the second example, "I do not eat fish." In both examples, nouns, pronouns, and verb stems are written in *kanji*, while particles and verbal suffixes are in *hiragana*.

(1) 'go to the library to see Xiao Wang'

Chinese (simplified characters):	去	图书馆	见	小王
Chinese (traditional characters):	去	圖書館	見	小王
	qù	*túshūguǎn*	*jiàn*	*Xiǎo Wáng*
	go	library	see	Xiao Wang
Japanese:	図書館で		小王に	会います
	toshokan de		*Xiao Wang ni*	*aimasu*
	library-*location*		Xiao Wang-*indirect obj.*	*meet-sent.end*

(2) 'I do not eat fish.'

Chinese (simplified characters):	我	不	吃	鱼。
Chinese (traditional characters):	我	不	吃	魚。
	Wǒ	*bù*	*chī*	*yú.*
	I	not	eat	fish
Japanese:	私は[25]		魚を	食べません。
	Watashi wa		*sakana o*	*tabemasen.*
	I-*topic*		fish-*direct obj.*	*eat-not*

Writing in the Chinese script was adapted to the Japanese language over time, and changes were made to accommodate the major differences between Japanese and Chinese. First, the Japanese spoken word order was gradually adopted into Japanese writing, and eventually, additional scripts were created to make writing and reading easier. To write the suffixes and particles that did not exist in Chinese, early on, Chinese characters were borrowed purely for their phonetic value. These characters were usually written smaller and were added to the main characters of the text. Today, Chinese characters are no longer used in this capacity. In their place, *hiragana* is used instead, as shown in the examples above.

In the mixed script today, *kanji*, *hiragana*, and *katakana* usually play different roles. Although the number of *kanji* is officially limited to a little over 2,000, *kanji* is still an indispensable and arguably most important component.[26] *Hiragana* and *katakana* are used for different purposes and functionalities. *Hiragana* is used to write grammatical particles, inflectional endings, and sometimes whole words. It is also often used to indicate the pronunciation of *kanji* in publications such as newspapers and magazines. *Katakana* was formerly the script for representing grammatical particles and suffixes. Today, it is used for non-Chinese loanwords, specialized vocabulary, emphasis, and onomatopoeia. Aside from these linguistic factors that regulate – to a great extent – the choice of script, there are also socio-cultural stereotypes that predisposes native Japanese writers to using one script over another. We will discuss this point in detail in Chapter 20. For now, the story below may serve to illustrate how script choice is deeply rooted in convention. Switching to a new script may indicate a change in the connotation of a word even though the literal meaning remains intact.

THE STORY BEYOND

Fukushima

The *Tōhoku* earthquake and tsunami on March 11, 2011, led to a nuclear disaster in the *Fukushima* I Nuclear Power Plant in Japan that involved hydrogen-air chemical explosions, nuclear meltdowns, and the release of radioactive material. *Fukushima*, the name of the coastal prefecture (located to the north of Tokyo on the island of *Honshu*) or the name of the prefecture's capital city, is customarily written in *kanji* as 福島. Since the nuclear accident, it was sometimes written in *katakana*, フクシマ, to distinguish it as the site of a disaster instead of a prefecture or a city.

   This practice had its historical precedence. After the August 1945 nuclear bombings, "*Hiroshima* (広島, ヒロシマ)" and "*Nagasaki* (長崎, ナガサキ)" were written in *katakana* instead of *kanji* when referred to as the bombing sites[27] or used to represent "nuclear victimhood."[28]

   Furthermore, the word *hibakusha* may serve as an example for script flexibility that allowed associations to be made between nuclear contamination in *Fukushima* and nuclear victimhood in *Hiroshima* and *Nagasaki*. The term *hibakusha* (被爆者) originally referred to survivors of the World War II atomic explosions. Written in *katakana*, it ambiguously represented 被爆者 'atomic bomb victims' and 被曝者 'people exposed to radiation.' The two words were pronounced exactly the same, as *baku* could either mean 爆 'explosion' or 曝 'exposure.'[29] In March 2012, the first anniversary of the *Fukushima* disaster, about 2,000 protesters gathered in *Hiroshima*. In their slogan "No More *Hiroshimas*, No More *Fukushimas*, No More *Hibakushas*," Hiroshima, Fukushima, and *hibakusha* were all written in *katakana*, precisely with the intention to bring together victims of the atomic bombs and those of the nuclear plant accident.[30]

   Although useful as means to distinguish the locations as sites of disastrous events from names of cities or prefectures in their normal sense, such *katakana* rendering might also come to be associated with the fear, shame, and anxiety people experienced in the aftermath of the disasters. Perhaps for this reason, a year after the nuclear plant accident, voices on the Internet called for the abolishment of using *katakana* to write "*Fukushima*."[31] To Japanese readers and writers, restoring the writing of the name to its original *kanji* script might represent a successful and complete restoration of the contaminated place to its original, pristine condition.

Notes

1 This time period is based on Rogers (2005, p. 56), but it varies depending on the sources. For example, Taylor and Taylor (2014) dates the introduction of Chinese writing to Japan to after the late 4th century, because according to them the Koreans did not begin to use Chinese characters until in

the 3rd century (p. 273). Yamada (1991) suggests that *kanji* was first introduced to Japan in the 5th century (p. 141), and Gottlieb (1995) dates it to the 6th century (p. 3).

2   Here the characters 漢字 are Japanese *kanji*, so the simplified Chinese characters used in China do not apply. Although some *kanji* characters are also simplified, they may not be the same as the simplified characters in China.

3   Or, at least three scripts – *kanji* and the two *kana* – are required. The use of *rōmaji* is comparatively marginal. Some scholars (e.g., Taylor and Taylor (1995)) also consider Arabic numerals as a fifth script. Since its use is mostly limited to representing numbers and is not normally used to write non-numerical speech, it is not considered a full script in this book.

4   Taylor and Taylor (2014, p. 272).

5   Ibid., pp. 272–273.

6   Ibid., p. 274.

7   Kaiho and Nomura (1983), quoted by Taylor and Taylor (2014) on p. 274.

8   See Taylor and Taylor (2014, p. 274).

9   Ibid.

10 Adapted from ibid., p. 275, Table 16–2.

11 Ibid.

12 Shibatani (1990) notes that this percentage is as of 1859 (p. 142). This means it does not include the new compounds created based on Chinese characters during modernization in the *Meiji* period (1868–1912).

13 Poem 529 of the *Man'yōshū*. Seeley (1991, p. 50).

14 See Chapter 3 for the definition of mora and moraic writing system.

15 Taylor and Taylor (2014, p. 285).

16 These examples are taken from Seeley (1991, p. 50). Transcriptions follow what is in this book: Middle Chinese uses the reconstruction given in B. Karlgren's *Grammata Serica Recensa*, and Old Japanese uses the modern Hepburn Romanization.

17 For example, King (1996, p. 218).

18 Joshi and Aaron (2006, p. 483).

19 Taylor and Taylor (2014, p. 285).

20 Smith (1996, p. 212).

21 Sugimoto and Levin (2000, p. 137).

22 This example is taken from Taylor and Taylor (2014, p. 258).

23 Here, the *y* is not an IPA symbol, but an English letter, representing the sound /j/ in IPA. Note that in IPA, the letter *y* is also used, and /y/ represents a vowel.

24 Theoretically a word with four morae takes about twice as much time to say as a word with two morae. A native speaker of Japanese I interviewed, however, reported that for her, -*n* would take about half the time as a CV mora and C(C) would take about one third of the time as a CV mora. By this calculation, *Ni-p-po-n* is about 2.8 times the length of a CV mora and *i-chi* is twice as long. Thus, although *Nippon* is significantly longer than *ichi*, it is not quite twice as long.

25 Usually speakers leave out the topic unless it is unclear. It is kept here for comparison purposes.

26 Taylor and Taylor (2014) say that "*kanji* is the most complex and at the same time the most important" (p. 272).

27 Brannigan (2015, p. 156).

28 Seaton (2016, p. 347).

29 Ibid.

30 Penney (2012).

31 Tahara (2012).

12 Writing Vietnamese

LIKE KOREAN AND JAPANESE, the writing of Vietnamese has had a fascinating history. It involves at least three different scripts: *chữ nho* (𡨸儒 'Confucian script') refers to the Chinese writing system, *chữ nôm* (𡨸喃 'southern script') contains Vietnamese characters created based on the Chinese script, and *quốc ngữ* (國語 'national script') is an adaptation of the Roman alphabet. Among the languages of the Chinese-character cultural sphere, Vietnamese is the only one that has completely abandoned the Sinitic script to be written with the Roman alphabet in modern times. In this chapter, we will look at how Vietnamese writing transitioned from one script to another with a focus on the contexts of these transitions. We will see that, linguistic factors aside, the changes in writing were closely intertwined with the political history of Vietnam and the national identity of the Vietnamese.

▇ *Chữ nho* 'Confucian script'

Although there is much uncertainty about the languages of the early inhabitants in the Vietnamese territory, we know that a spectrum of Vietnamese languages was spoken. However, none of them was written before the arrival of the Chinese, and the recorded history of Vietnam began with its rule by China. For more than 1,000 years – that is, from 111 BCE to 939 CE – the northern Vietnamese territory was governed by the Chinese empire as its protectorate. The area was known to the Chinese as *Nányuè* (南越, 'Southern Viet') during the *Hàn* dynasty (206 BCE–220 CE) and as *Ānnán* (安南 'Peaceful South') during the *Táng* (618–906). The millennium-long dominance of China had a profound impact on Vietnam's cultural and linguistic history. In particular, over a period of 30 to 40 generations, speakers of *Hàn-Táng* Chinese, members of the ruling class in Vietnam, accumulated in the area of modern Hanoi.[1] Classical Chinese became the language of administration, as was in the rest of the Chinese empire, and writing, be it for a Chinese or a Vietnamese audience, was solely done in Classical Chinese encoded in Chinese characters.

This type of writing is known as *chữ nho* (𡨸儒 'Confucian script') in Vietnamese. This term may be misleading, because *chữ nho* was not just a script or a set of characters but should be more accurately understood as a written language, that is, Classical Chinese, encoded in the Chinese script. *chữ nho* texts are practically indistinguishable from compositions in Classical Chinese by Chinese authors of the same time period. However, it was composed specifically in the Vietnamese context, so when read aloud, it was rendered in the Vietnamese pronunciation. Another term for the *chữ nho* script is *chữ Hán* (𡨸漢), meaning 'Chinese script', but this term is less frequently used. Some scholars suggest that this was because the Vietnamese were willing to acknowledge their indebtedness to Confucius but were unwilling to do so to the Chinese.[2]

The use of the Chinese writing system persisted in Vietnam even after its independence from China. The Chinese rule in Vietnam ended in 939 CE, soon after the collapse of the *Táng* dynasty. During more than 700 years of self-rule and until Vietnam was taken under colonial governance by France in the mid-19th century, Classical Chinese remained the administrative and scholarly language. *Chữ nho* was eventually made the official writing of Vietnam in 1174 CE. As in the Chinese tradition, Vietnamese scholars recorded history and composed poetry using *chữ nho*. In addition, *chữ nho* was employed to write a wide range of popular literature, including oral tales of myths and legends and stories concerning everyday life.[3]

The sustained use of *chữ nho* was testimony to the further flourishing of the Confucian culture in independent Vietnam. Although no longer subjugated to Chinese control in political terms, the cultural influence of China took root and continued to develop, and Vietnam continued to look to China for models of governance. For example, an examination system similar to the Chinese civil service examination was established for selecting officials. In 1075, the first examination on Confucian learning was held. By the 15th century, Confucian culture had gradually spread into southern Vietnam. The use of Chinese characters further expanded to writing for such mundane purposes as billing and invoicing in commercial transactions. By this point, however, *chữ nho* was no longer the sole written language and script. A modified script based on the Chinese writing system came into existence and began to be used to write the Vietnamese language.

■ *Chữ nôm* 'southern script'

The *chữ nôm* script refers to the system of writing created based on the Chinese script to record the Vietnamese language. The name of the script can be written in a number of ways, because *nôm* characters (characters that belong to the *chữ nôm* script) were never standardized. The first character may be written as 𡨸, 宁, 字, or 宁, and it means "writing" or "script." The second character can be written as 喃 or 諵. It is derived from the Chinese character 南 and has the same meaning, "south, southern."

The writing of Vietnamese using modified Chinese characters was developed after Vietnam had become independent from China[4] and was used for at least seven centuries, from the 13th to the beginning of the 20th century.[5] Although the earliest piece of writing we can find in *chữ nôm* was from the 13th centuries, its development clearly started a few centuries before.[6] One impetus for the development of the *nôm* script was the rich tradition of oral literature in Vietnam. As in illiterate cultures elsewhere, stories, songs, and sayings had been orally transmitted from generation to generation and constituted an integral component of the Vietnamese cultural life. Those who became literate in the Chinese script eventually sought to write down such oral creations and to express themselves in writing in their native language. By this time, the Vietnamese language has integrated a large number of Chinese words and even some sentence structures. It had become so similar to Chinese that it seemed only natural to use symbols that looked like Chinese characters to transcribe the Vietnamese language.

Chữ nôm is in fact a mixed script that evolved from simply borrowing Chinese characters to creating new characters.[7] It is a complex system of writing containing characters that looked Chinese in appearance but were not Chinese. Characters borrowed from the Chinese script were used to write Vietnamese words in at least two different ways. On one hand, they could be straight borrowings from Chinese to represent similar-sounding morphemes that were Chinese in origin. For example, the character 才 (*cái* 'talent') was used to write the Vietnamese morpheme *tài* with the same meaning.[8] This was a case of semantic *on*. On the other hand, a borrowed character might be used as a sound symbol for a Vietnamese morpheme that had a different meaning. An example is the character 半 (in MSC: *bàn*), which in Chinese meant 'half,' used for the Vietnamese morpheme *bán* 'to sell.' Another example is the use of the Chinese characters 布 (*bù* 'cloth') and 盖 (*gài* 'cover') together for the archaic Vietnamese term *bố cái* 'father and mother.'[9] The sounds come from Chinese yet the meaning is irrelevant. Thus, these were cases of phonetic *on* and were similar to uses of Chinese characters in the Korean *idu* ('clerical reading') and *hyangchal* ('vernacular letters') scripts and the Japanese *man'yōgana*.

The idea of using Chinese characters as phonetic symbols in representing another language was likely not new to Vietnamese speakers. As Buddhism spread to Vietnam from the 2nd century CE, speakers of Vietnamese had been exposed to Buddhist scriptures encoded in Chinese characters. The Sinitic symbols were used as phonetic representations for words with origin in Sanskrit and other foreign languages, so the idea of using Chinese-like characters to transcribe speech had not been a strange one. This might have been another factor that contributed to the creation of *nôm* characters.

Fascinatingly, however, a large number of new characters – both modified Chinese symbols and newly invented characters – were employed to phonetically transcribe native Vietnamese words. Based on their method of creation, invented *nôm* characters consisted of two major types: one, composite creations that combined two Chinese symbols into single characters, and, two, partial or simplified Chinese characters that functioned as independent *nôm* characters. Among the first type, the most numerous subtype was semantic-phonetic compounds created following the Chinese principle of character formation, with one component taken from Chinese for its semantic value and the other component representing the pronunciation. For example, the character 至,典 represented the Vietnamese word *đến* 'to arrive (at).' It contained on the left-hand side a Chinese character 至 (*zhì*), meaning "to arrive (at)" (its pronunciation is irrelevant), and on the right-hand side the character 典 (*diǎn*), representing the pronunciation (its meaning is irrelevant). Another example was the character 媄, pronounced as *mẹ* for "mother" in Vietnamese. This pronunciation was represented by the component on the right, 美, which in Chinese had a similar pronunciation, and it is pronounced *měi* in Modern Standard Chinese. The meaning of this component in Chinese ('beautiful') was irrelevant. The part on the left, 女 (in Chinese: *nǚ*, 'female'), indicated the meaning of the whole character.[10]

A smaller group was semantic-semantic composite characters. The *nôm* character 圣 contained in the upper part a Chinese character 天, meaning "heaven," and in the lower part a Chinese character 上, meaning "above." The combination represented the Vietnamese word *trời*, meaning "heaven," but there was no hint of the pronunciation in the formation of the character. Another example was the composite character 㐲 that represented *mất* 'to lose' in Vietnamese. It was composed of two Chinese characters, 亡 (*wáng*) and 失 (*shī*), both with the same meaning, "to lose," in Chinese.[11]

There were also phonetic-phonetic compounds composed of two sound components. In fact, one reason Vietnamese speakers created new compound characters was because consonant clusters – strings of two or more consonants (e.g., /str/ in /strong/) – existed in the Vietnamese language at the time. For example, the characters 巴 and 賴 are put together with 巴 (/ba/) on top of 賴 (/lái/) to represent the morpheme /blái/ 'fruit,' and 巨 (/cụ/) above 朗 (/lăng/) to write the morpheme /klăng/ 'silence.'[12]

A second type of new character created as part of the *chữ nôm* script was simplified Chinese symbols. Often only parts of the original characters were preserved. For example, the top component of the Chinese character 爲 (*wéi*, 'to do'), that is, 爫, was taken on its own to represent the Vietnamese morpheme *làm* 'to do, to make.' The bottom portion of the Chinese character 衣 (*yī* 'clothing'), i.e., 衣, was used to represent *ây* 'that, those.' Another possibility was that the *nôm* character changed the original character by deleting some strokes while adding others at the same time. For instance, the character for *lạ* 'strange' came from the Chinese character 羅 *luó* 'net.'[13]

FIGURE 12.1 Vietnamese character lạ 'strange'

Although promotion of the *chữ nôm* script was limited for most of its history, it received support from several Vietnamese emperors. One of them was Trần Nhân Tông (1258–1308), who used *chữ nôm* during his reign (1279–1293) to explain his ordinances to the people.[14] Another royal supporter of *chữ nôm* writing was Hồ Quý Ly (胡季犛, 1336–1407). When he was the emperor (1400–1407), he endorsed efforts to replace *chữ nho* with *chữ nôm* as the official writing of Vietnam.[15] Unfortunately, the reform did not take off, because Chinese forces of the *Míng* dynasty invaded in 1407 and ended his rule. Despite the promotion of *chữ nôm* by some among the ruling elites, the script never gained enough prestige to replace *chữ nho* as the script for formal writing except during very brief periods. That role continued to be fulfilled by *chữ nho*, as it remained the script of choice for official and scholarly purposes until the beginning of the 20th century.

THE STORY BEYOND

First piece of literary writing recorded in *chữ nôm*

In 1282, Nguyễn Thuyên (阮詮), the Minister of Justice at the time, composed what is considered to be the first piece of literary writing in *chữ nôm*. It was a charm he wrote in verse thrown in the Red River to drive away a crocodile that threatened the lives of local villagers.[16] Nguyễn Thuyên was considered the first person to write poems in Vietnamese. His poetry was modeled on the tonal and rhyming patterns of Chinese poetry and inspired many followers.[17]

The use of *chữ nôm* for creative purposes continued to expand, however, and left behind hundreds of literary examples.[18] It was used to record folk literature and came to be associated with Vietnamese cultural independence. In the 18th century, when *chữ nôm* writing reached its peak, many Vietnamese writers and poets used this script to compose their works.

Chữ nôm and *chữ nho* remained in use until the arrival of French missionaries and colonizers in the 19th century, when the promotion of a drastically different script came to dominate the writing of Vietnamese and eventually replaced the Chinese writing system to become the national script.

▮ *Quốc ngữ* 'national script'

Chữ quốc ngữ (孷國語 'script of national language'), or *quốc ngữ* (國語 'national script', *lit.* 'national language') refers to the script adapted from the Roman alphabet to writing Vietnamese. Aptly named, it has served as the official writing system for the Vietnamese language since the nation's independence in 1945. A distinctive feature of the script is the use of diacritics – often two on the same vowel letter – to mark tones and to indicate vowel quality. Primarily based on the Portuguese variation of the Roman alphabet, the script also incorporates elements from French, Italian, Spanish, Greek, and Latin spelling conventions.[19] This mingling of different ways of spelling has to do with the origin of the *quốc ngữ* script: it was designed by European missionaries in the first half of the 17th century who came to proselytize Catholicism in Vietnam. The missionaries recorded the Vietnamese speech in writing so as to be able to learn the language, but since their motive was primarily to use the script amongst themselves, they each followed their own languages' conventions of spelling and pronunciation.[20] Although their intention was not to teach the Vietnamese a new script and there was little concern as to whether the Vietnamese would be able to use the Roman alphabet at that time, a seed for *quốc ngữ* was planted.

THE STORY BEYOND

More about the origin of *quốc ngữ*

Romanized writing of Vietnamese was born out of the need of early Jesuit missionaries to learn to speak the language. It was essential for successful priests to deliver sermons in Vietnamese. Learning to write either the Chinese or the *chữ nôm* characters was perceived as very difficult. Like their colleagues in China and Japan, to whose earlier work on Romanized writing systems for Chinese and Japanese they most likely had been exposed,[21] Jesuit missionaries in Vietnam also made use of their native script to represent the speech sounds of the Vietnamese language. The year 1651 marked the publication of the first Romanized scheme of writing systematically designed for Vietnamese. It was presented in the French Jesuit missionary Alexandre de Rhodes's *Vietnamese, Portuguese and Latin Dictionary* (*Dictionarium Annamaticum, Lusitanum et Latinum*) and his compiled *Catechism* (*Cathechismus*). This system was eventually modified to become the established alphabetical script for Vietnamese.

The use of Romanized writing for Vietnamese was rather limited in the beginning. For about 200 years after its invention – that is, until the military conquest of Vietnam by France in the mid-19th century – it was restricted to the Catholic community. Even within this group, its use was very limited, possibly mainly as a tool for foreign missionaries to learn the language. Furthermore, the Catholic community occupied a marginal position in Vietnamese society. Its converts were commonly the most economically deprived and were viewed by the Confucian literati as "the quintessential social parvenus, outcast devotees of a foreign god, subversive and untrustworthy."[22] The Romanized writing system associated with the Catholic converts were possibly perceived with equally aversive disdain, and *chữ nho* continued to be the dominant form of writing as Confucian ideology remained the social mainstream.

So, how did the Roman alphabet eventually become the national script of Vietnam? It had to do with both the colonial policy of the French, who occupied Vietnam for nearly 100 years since the 1850s, and the nationalist movement of modern Vietnam that led to the nation's independence in 1945. In what follows, we will see how, within a period of less than 100 years, *quốc ngữ* transformed from a form of writing imposed by the French colonizers to a script that reflected cultural independence from France as well as from China. It will be good to keep in mind that the general linguistic landscape for most of this period consisted of four combinations of languages and writing systems: Chinese written in *chữ nho* characters, Vietnamese written in the Chinese-based *chữ nôm* script, Vietnamese written with the Roman alphabet, and French written in Roman letters.

THE STORY BEYOND

The French conquest

Over nearly a quarter century, from 1858 to 1883, Vietnam fell to the invasion of French military forces and became a colony of France. The conquest was first concentrated in the south and eventually spread to the north. French forces seized Saigon in 1859 and occupied three adjacent provinces in 1861. By 1867, France had gained power over more territories in the south and named the entire colony Cochinchina. It took another 16 years before the colonizers extended their control over the rest of the country. In 1883, a treaty was signed to make Tonkin (northern Vietnam) and Annam (central Vietnam) protectorates of France.

Under French colonial rules, the administration sought to eliminate *chữ nho* and *chữ nôm* to be rid of any Chinese influences. Replacing the Chinese writing system with the Roman alphabet was an important component of the French colonialist policy, because the colonizers recognized that the security of French dominance fundamentally rested on a shift in the cultural identity of the Vietnamese people from one that was "Chinese-inspired (or Chinese-reactive) towards a new colonial identity loyal to France."[23] The extant use of Chinese (*chữ nho*) or Chinese-like (*chữ nôm*) characters was perceived as an almost impenetrable obstacle to this endeavor. The Sinitic script was too complex and represented a culture that was too alien for the colonial administration to find ways to assimilate. Abandonment of the Chinese writing system was thus considered the only way to remove the barrier to bringing the Vietnamese closer under subjugation by the French.

THE STORY BEYOND

Colonial policy on Vietnamese language and writing

In a letter dated January 15, 1866, Paulin Vial, Directeur du Cabinet du Gouverneur de la Co-chinchine, articulated the view of the colonial administration on the current state of Vietnamese writing in the Chinese script.

> From the first days it was recognized that the Chinese language was a barrier between us and the natives; the education provided by means of the hieroglyphic characters was completely beyond us; this writing makes possible only with difficulty transmitting to the population the diverse ideas which are necessary for them at the level of their new political and commercial situation. Consequently we are obliged to follow the traditions of our own system of education; it is the only one which can bring close to us the Annamites of the colony by inculcating in them the principles of European civilization and isolating them from the hostile influence of our neighbors.[24]

The term "Annamites" referred to the Vietnamese people, and "our neighbors" referred to the Chinese.

In the beginning, Romanized Vietnamese promoted by the French was seen by the Vietnamese people as symbolic of French colonial control, while the traditional *chữ nho* and *chũ nôm* styles of writing represented resistance against French rule. French promotion of Romanization during this period was mostly in the colony in the south, where the occupation started. In northern Vietnam, Chinese writing maintained its prestige. In fact, *chữ nho* remained the high-status means of written communication overall and continued to be used for serious purposes during the late 19th century, including for anti-colonialism materials advocating for the Vietnamese national identity. The *nôm* script for vernacular Vietnamese, despite past endorsement by some of the ruling elites, largely continued to be seen as vulgar in the first half century of French rule.

The transition in the Vietnamese perception of *quốc ngữ* happened amidst the ambivalent attitude of the French colonizers towards the Romanized writing. On one hand, the colonizers made use of the Western script as a tool to dissociate the educated elites from traditional Confucian learning encoded in *chữ nho*. Elementary schools were set up in the major centers of the colony where indigenous students would learn to read and write Romanized Vietnamese. French language schools, often staffed by Catholic priests, were established in various locations of the colony. At the same time, as Romanized writing received broad promotion, the learning of the Chinese script was discouraged. In 1865, the termination of the Chinese-based examination system in the colony dealt "a final deathblow"[25] to Sinitic writing in the French colony. In 1910 *quốc ngữ* was made the script for all public documents.

On the other hand, the colonizers were wary of raising the literacy rate of the Vietnamese masses, for fear that they would become more difficult to subjugate. The very case of how the term *quốc ngữ* came to be used to refer to Romanized Vietnamese serves to illustrate the situation. According to John DeFrancis, the term *quốc ngữ* in the sense of "national language" rather than "national script" was initially used to refer to the Vietnamese language as opposed to Chinese long before the European missionaries arrived. It was later used by Vietnamese Catholic converts to refer to the Romanized writing of their own language. The French colonizers adopted this usage, possibly not entirely "conscious of its possible nationalistic implications relative to France"[26] at the time. When they became uneasy with the association of the "national language" with Vietnamese – a language other than French – it was already too late to do anything about the usage.

THE STORY BEYOND

When Romanized Vietnamese became *quốc ngữ*

The name *quốc ngữ* was not used to refer to the Romanization of Vietnamese until more than 200 years after Romanization had been practiced. It was first mentioned in 1867 in an article published in the newspaper *Gia Định Báo* (嘉定報), a government-sponsored publication all in Romanized Vietnamese. The article, written by a Vietnamese collaborator of the French colonizers, praised Romanized Vietnamese for being easy to learn in contrast with the complex and cumbersome Chinese script. Therefore, the name *quốc ngữ* was not created by the missionaries who first Romanized Vietnamese writing. Furthermore, it did not become widely used until the 20th century. Before that time Romanized Vietnamese had been called a variety of other names including "foreign characters," "European characters," "the European alphabet,"' "Latin characters," "Latin letters," "our characters," "our letters," and "the letters of our alphabet."[27]

The transformation in the Vietnamese perception of Romanized writing was marked by the establishment of the Tonkin Free School (*Đông Kinh Nghĩa Thục* 東京義塾) in 1907 in Hanoi.[28] Privately funded by the Vietnamese, the school advocated learning of modern science and new ideas from the West and Japan with the ultimate goal to modernize Vietnam. It strongly advocated using the Roman alphabet to write the Vietnamese vernacular and replacing character-based writing in Classical Chinese. Its graduates, predominantly young nationalists, naturally viewed *quốc ngữ* as the true representation of their Vietnamese identity. Although the school was shut down by the colonial regime in 1908, the shift in attitudes towards Romanized Vietnamese became irreversible.

Eventually, practical concerns secured the association of the alphabetical script with the concept of "national language." When Vietnam, a newly independent nation desperate for modernization, was faced with a high illiteracy rate, the Roman alphabet stood as a rational choice that would better serve the needs of the nation. *Chữ nho* and *chữ nôm* were completely abandoned, and *quốc ngữ* became the only officially recognized script for writing Vietnamese.

Notes

1 Taylor (2013, p. 5).
2 For example, DeFrancis (1977, pp. 26–27) and Nguyen (1984, p. 1).
3 DeFrancis (1977, p. 18).

4 Ibid., p. 21.

5 Nguyen (1984, p. 1).

6 Taylor (1983, p. 206); DeFrancis (1977, p. 23).

7 DeFrancis (1977, pp. 24–25).

8 This example comes from ibid., p. 24; also see Taylor (1983, p. 206).

9 See DeFrancis (1977, pp. 21–23).

10 See Rogers (2005, p. 76), Table 4.27 for a similar example, in which 美 and 母 form a composite character for mẹ 'mother.'

11 These two examples are both from ibid., Table 4.27.

12 See Nguyen (1984, pp. 10–11).

13 These three examples are all from Rogers (2005, p. 76), Table 4.27.

14 Ibid.

15 Le and O'Harrow (2007, p. 421).

16 DeFrancis (1997, p. 23).

17 Ibid.

18 Le and O'Harrow (2007, p. 421).

19 DeFrancis (1977, pp. 57–58).

20 Nguyen (1984, p. 6).

21 DeFrancis (1977, p. 51).

22 Le and O'Harrow (2007, p. 423).

23 Ibid.

24 Quoted by DeFrancis (1977) on p. 77 from a quote in Bouchot (1925, pp. 36–37).

25 DeFrancis (1977, pp. 79–81).

26 Ibid., p. 87.

27 Ibid., pp. 82–84.

28 Le and O'Harrow (2007, p. 425).

PART IV

Reforming the Chinese script

13 Phonetic writing before *pīnyīn*

THE CHINESE SCRIPT IS widely regarded as one of the most difficult in use. In China's recent history, embroiled in a national crisis of survival, the issue of writing became in itself a matter of life or death. The author Lǔ Xùn (鲁迅/魯迅, 1881–1936), a leading figure of the New Culture Movement (新文化运动/新文化運動 *Xīn Wénhuà Yùndòng* 1917–1921), cautioned with all sincerity: "Rid China of Chinese characters lest China dies!"[1] Lǔ Xùn was not the only one who saw Chinese characters as a serious impediment to learning and literacy, technological advancement, and overall modernization of the nation. A series of reform proposals were put forward from the late 19th to the mid-20th centuries, some more successful than others, arousing heated debates that have reverberated to this day. Meanwhile, rapid development in computer technology altered the competitive landscape of Chinese characters versus alphabetical writing once and again, posing new questions while offering new answers to the debates of writing reform. This chapter and the following few provide an overview of the script reform proposals and some of the changes that ensued during this time. The emphases are on phonetic writing (Chapter 13) – especially *pīnyīn* (Chapter 14) – character simplification (Chapter 15), and a few issues concerning the impact of computer technology on writing the Chinese language (Chapter 16).

As you probably already know, *pīnyīn* is currently the global standard for writing Chinese using the Roman alphabet and has been since 1982. *Pīnyīn* was an outcome of the script reform sponsored by the People's Republic of China (PRC) government in the 1950s–1980s. It was by no means, however, the first or only phonetic script that had been proposed or implemented for Chinese. To proselytize their religion among Chinese-speaking populations, Western missionaries devised Romanization systems for transcribing Mandarin in as early as the 16th century. About two and a half centuries later, with successive military and diplomatic conquests by foreign powers aimed to colonize China, the desire to write Chinese in a simpler script arose both in and outside of the country. Chinese intellectuals, eager to save the nation from foreign invasions, embraced the notion of phonetic writing by devising hundreds of phonographic scripts. Meanwhile, Western scholars designed Romanization systems that went on to serve as the standard in international communications for nearly a century. In this chapter, we will trace the major historical precedencies that led up to the eventual creation of *pīnyīn*. We will then take a closer look at *pīnyīn* in the next chapter.

Early attempts at Romanization (1580s–1620s)

The earliest attempts at writing Chinese with a phonetic script were by the Jesuit missionaries working in China in the late 16th century. Among them, Michele Ruggieri (罗明坚/羅明堅

Luó Míngjiān 1543–1607), Matteo Ricci (利玛窦/利瑪竇 *Lì Mǎdòu* 1552–1610), and Nicolas Trigault (金尼阁/金尼閣 *Jīn Nígé* 1577–1628) made especially significant contributions. Ruggieri and Ricci were pioneers in the endeavors to overcome the lingual-cultural hurdle the missionaries encountered in proselytizing Catholicism. They worked together in Macau (澳门/澳門 *Àomén*) and *Zhàoqìng* (肇庆/肇慶) and, during 1583–1588, compiled a Portuguese-Chinese dictionary to aid their work. A typical page in this dictionary consisted of a few columns: the first column was word entries in Portuguese arranged in the alphabetical order,[2] and the second column was Romanization of the Chinese words listed in the third column.[3] On the first few pages, there was also a fourth column with the word entries in Italian.

This dictionary adopted Ruggieri's Romanization system that used 16th-century Italian and Portuguese orthography to represent Mandarin syllables of the same era. Table 13.1 and Table 13.2 offer us a few examples.[4] Note that the sound system of 16th-century Mandarin was different from today's Mandarin,[5] so the specific speech sounds represented in the second and third columns may not always be the same.

Table 13.1 Romanization in the Portuguese-Chinese dictionary based on Italian orthography

Chinese character	Ruggieri's Romanization of 16th-century Mandarin based on Italian orthography	*Pīnyīn* Romanization of Modern Standard Chinese
战/戰	*cen*	*zhàn*
出	*cio*	*chū*
该/該	*cai*	*gāi*
看	*can*	*kàn*
花	*cua*	*huā*
水	*scioi*	*shuǐ*
子	*zi*	*zǐ*
菜	*zai*	*cài*

Table 13.2 Romanization in the Portuguese-Chinese dictionary based on Portuguese orthography

Chinese character	Ruggieri's Romanization of 16th-century Mandarin based on Portuguese orthography	*Pīnyīn* Romanization of Modern Standard Chinese
酒	*çiu*	*jiǔ*
草	*çau*	*cǎo*
日	*gi*	*rì*
当/當	*tam*	*dāng*
东/東	*tum* or *tu*	*dōng*
天	*tien* or *tiě*	*tiān*

Ten years later, in 1598, Ricci compiled a Chinese-Portuguese dictionary. What distinguished the Romanization system in this dictionary was that it marked Chinese tones and aspiration[6] with diacritics. According to Ricci, the tone and aspiration marks played an important role in offering clarity in written communication, so he ordered that all Jesuit missionaries use this system in their writing.[7] Unfortunately, the dictionary went missing and is yet to be found.[8] Towards the end of his career, in 1605, Ricci published in Beijing a work called *Xīzì Qíjì* (西字奇迹/西字奇蹟 *The Miracle of Western Letters*). It was a booklet of six pages containing three biblical stories he had written in Classical Chinese and handwritten in Chinese characters. The Chinese text was annotated using Ruggieri's Romanization system[9] to assist Western readers with pronunciation.

THE STORY BEYOND

Matteo Ricci in China

Ruggieri left China in 1588 and was never able to return. Ricci, however, stayed in China for another 22 years, during which time he visited many Chinese cities and established a number of Catholic churches.[10] In 1601, he made his way to the Forbidden City in *Běijīng* (北京), where, during the last years of his life, he served as an advisor to the *Wànlì* (万历/萬曆) emperor. Aside from his achievement in the study of Chinese linguistics, he translated the *Four Books* (四书/四書 *Sìshū*) of the Confucian classics – *Dàxué* (大学/大學 *Great Learning*), *Zhōngyōng* (中庸 *Doctrine of the Mean*), *Lúnyǔ* (论语/論語 *Analects*), and *Mèngzǐ* (孟子 *Mencius*) – into Latin and introduced Confucius' thoughts to Europe. He wrote and published on theology and science in Chinese. He was also known for introducing Western sciences to China and is considered the founder of Sinology (汉学/漢學 *Hànxué*), the study of China in the West.[11]

Twenty years after Ricci's *Xīzì Qíjì* was published, another missionary, Nicolas Trigault, produced a three-volume dictionary titled *Xī Rú Ěrmù Zī* (西儒耳目资/西儒耳目資 *Aid to the Eyes and Ears of Western Literati*), which was essentially a guide to the pronunciation of Chinese charactrs. The Romanization system Trigault used was based on Ricci's system in the *Chinese-Portuguese Dictionary*.

THE STORY BEYOND

Trigault's view of the Chinese writing system

Nicolas Trigault was quite proud of his accomplishment with *Xī Rú Ěrmù Zī*, which, like Ricci's *Xīzì Qíjì*, was likely to have earned admiration among his fellow scholars. His comment here betrays not only his satisfaction with the achievement, but also a perceived superiority of the Western alphabet over the Chinese writing system.

> At the invitation of Chinese academic friends, I have compiled a Chinese dictionary in three volumes. It brings together the vowels and consonants of Chinese in my own tongue, in such a way that a Chinese person could learn Western script in three or four days. The method I employed in making this dictionary has rather inspired the wonder of Chinese people. They have seen with their own eyes how a foreigner has put right the faults in their writing system which have long needed attention, which is a feat which naturally deserves commendation.[12]

Chinese intellectuals before Ricci's time were not completely uncritical of their difficult native script. As far back as in the *Sòng* dynasty, the historian Zhèng Qiáo (郑樵/鄭樵 1104–1162) already noted the simplicity of an alphabetical script while studying Sanskrit and made comments on the cumbersomeness of the Chinese writing in comparison.[13] Fāng Yǐzhì (方以智 1611–1671), a scholar-official in the late *Míng* to early *Qīng* dynasty also pointed out the advantages of Western alphabetical writing.[14] He observed that Western scripts represented words based on sounds, and the sounds, in turn, represented the meaning of the words. Thus, there existed a straightforward one-on-one relationship between words, sounds, and meaning. Chinese characters, on the other hand, were confusing because of "their interchangeability and borrowing."[15] That is, for semantic-phonetic compounds, the same sound element may indicate completely different pronunciations in different characters, and the semantic component only vaguely suggests the meaning of the character, if at all. Many characters take on multiple, unrelated meanings through phonological extension. Therefore, the relationship between sound, meaning, and the written graph is a lot more entangled and complex than alphabetical writing.

The missionaries' earliest attempts at phonetic scripts for Chinese were aimed primarily at helping Western scholars learn to read and pronounce Chinese characters and were not intended in any way to reform the Chinese script for the Chinese. Whatever impact they had on how the Chinese viewed their own writing system was probably momentary and minimal.[16] It would take at least another 200 years – and, perhaps more importantly, an imminent crisis of the nation's survival brought on by the attacks of Western powers – for the phoneticization of Chinese writing to become a major issue of debate.

Later proposals of phonetic scripts (1890s–1930s)

Propelled by an urgent desire to modernize China, progressive intellectuals launched what was later referred to as the National Language Movement (国语运动/國語運動 *Guóyǔ Yùndòng*). In a broad sense, the movement encompassed the development and standardization of phonographic writing, as well as the promotion of a national speech and the use of vernacular Chinese (instead of Classical Chinese) in writing. Starting from the late *Qīng* and lasting into the 1940s, the National Language Movement profoundly transformed how speech and writing were used in modern China.

Although the character-based writing system contributed to the emergence and development of Chinese nationalism in early history,[17] at the turn of the 20th century, it came to represent a part of the Chinese national identity considered necessary to be changed and renewed in the making of a new China. Faced with the crisis of a nation struggling to survive under the aggression of foreign powers, politically progressive intellectuals strived to find the fundamental cause of China's defeats and were eager to come up with proposals for solutions. Seeing that over 80% of their fellow citizens were unable to read or write,[18] they wrestled with the recognition that the difficult system of writing was a major obstacle and must be obliterated. Script reform thus became a remedy for not only the abysmally low rate of literacy but also the endangered survival of China.

Motivations for phonetic writing

The motivations for instituting phonetic writing in China had a lot to do with the socio-historical circumstances at the time. For the reformists, first and foremost was their desire to make it possible for every Chinese person to be able to read and write. The complicated traditional Chinese script, in their eyes, put the Chinese people at a great disadvantage compared to those in Europe, America, and Japan. Lú Zhuàngzhāng (卢戆章/盧戇章 1854–1928) observed that anyone above the age of ten in Europe and America, even those in remote and isolated areas, was able to read.[19] In stark contrast, as Cài Xīyǒng (蔡锡勇/蔡錫勇 1847–1897) lamented, in China, even those scholars who spent their entire lives reading books were not able to learn all the Chinese characters.[20] The extremely low literacy rate among the Chinese, in their mind, was caused at least in part by the fact that Chinese characters were too numerous and too complex. What was more, the Chinese writing system could also be confusing – the same sound was usually represented by multiple characters, and the same character often had multiple readings. The much more straightforward relationship between language and writing in alphabetical scripts was what the reformers wished to bring to the writing of Chinese.

Another dimension that made acquiring literacy in Chinese drastically more difficult was the stylistic difference between speech and writing. For the Chinese, being able to write did not simply mean being able to transcribe in characters or letters what one said; rather, one would have to write in the literary style, i.e. Classical Chinese (文言 wényán). As explained in Chapter 5, Classical Chinese was essentially a different language from Modern Standard Chinese. Thus, to become literate in China around the turn of the 20th century, one would not only have to master a complex and demanding script, but also have to learn an ancient language specifically reserved for writing.

THE STORY BEYOND

The speech-and-writing divide

Wáng Zhào (王照1859–1933), who designed "Mandarin Letters" modeling on Japanese *kana*, explained in the following passage how the disparity between speech and writing came to be and made it clear why it was a fundamental issue to address in script reform.

> Should one attempt to exhort the people [in China] to learn, to manage finances, to drill troops, and so forth, in contrast with other nations east and west, one becomes aware of the vast disparity between the difficulty for us and the ease for them. . . . When China's ancients created writing for the convenient use of the people . . . no separate literary language existed. . . . Later literati . . . put a premium on modeling themselves on the ancients. . . . Writing no longer followed the changes of spoken language, and the two became daily distant, with the result that there were no characters to serve as symbols for the language. . . . Now, in the various nations of the West, education prospers greatly, the arts of government flourish day by day, and even in Japan commands are unified and changes are rapid. Surely there are reasons for this in each case. The identity of speech and writing and the simplicity of their scripts are actually the most important factors.[21]

To save China meant to modernize China, and to modernize China required the development of science and technology. The reformers believed that writing Chinese in a phonetic script would not only greatly improve basic literacy of the Chinese population, but would also open up communicative channels for Chinese scientists to join international exchanges for the advancement of scientific learning and technological innovation. The traditional Chinese script, on the other hand, presented an enormous hurdle to this prospect. We will not go into details here on this topic, but we will return in Chapter 16 to look at the challenges presented by the Sinitic script to the development of modern information technology in China.

If the practical motivation for phoneticizing the Chinese script was to promote literacy and education and to develop science and technology, then the ideological motivation was to establish democracy in creating a modern China. For millennia, reading and writing Chinese characters had been the privilege of the educated few. The Chinese script, together with Classical Chinese, represented to the reform-minded scholars and politicians a non-democratic mode of written communication that had long deprived common Chinese of their basic rights to participate in society as citizens. It was considered outdated and incompatible with the modernization of China. By contrast, phonetic scripts, which were much easier to learn and to use, embodied the democratic ideal they were pursuing. Speaking of the phonetic scripts of other nations, Wáng Zhào (王照 1859–1933) expressly linked writing systems to the institution of political equality.

> [A]lthough the scripts of the other nations are shallow, each of the people throughout those nations are thoroughly conversant with them because language and script are consistent. Their letters are simple and convenient and, for even the dullest youths, the age they can speak is the age when they become conversant with writing. Therefore, it is the birth right of all to become specialists in the matters that are conveyed by their writing. Daily, they strive to refine themselves and make progress, no matter whether intelligent or stupid, noble or common, young or old, man or woman.[22]

Kāng Yǒuwéi (康有为/康有為 1858–1927) even went so far as to propose a common language and a shared script for the whole world. To be sure, this idealistic script would be nothing like the character-based system for writing Chinese, but a "simple and easy new script that would be extremely efficient."[23]

Companion Website

Exercise 13.1 Motivations for phonetic writing

The various proposals to phoneticize Chinese writing about a century ago may appear farfetched ideas from today's perspective. After all, to save China from its perils, what was required was much, much more than a simpler writing system. To build a strong nation with cultured citizens, the Chinese people must tremendously expand access to educational resources, an endeavor that would require profound changes of the Chinese society in both political and economic terms. It may be difficult to imagine that the reformers did not understand this; yet it is perhaps not difficult to understand that, in searching for solutions to China's problems, what stood out to the reformers were the fundamental distinctions between China and the West. To them, the difference between the complex Chinese writing system and the simpler Roman alphabet had come to symbolize the disparity in general national strength between China and the more industrialized foreign invaders. In comparison to those nations using phonetic scripts, China was seen as impoverished, weak, and illiterate as much as the

Chinese characters were seen as complicated, cumbersome, and impossible to learn. In this sense, the fact that many reform-minded intellectuals pinned their hopes of saving China on revolutionizing the writing system perhaps spoke louder about the cultural significance of the character-based Chinese script than any transformative power that reforming it had been presumed to possess.

Proposals by Chinese nationals

From 1892 to 1910, that is, during the last two decades of the *Qīng* dynasty, Chinese reformers came up with no less than 30 phonographic writing proposals,[24] drawing inspiration from an array of sources, both home and abroad. Lú Zhuàngzhāng (卢戆章/盧戇章 1854–1928), an educator of English and Chinese languages in Amoy,[25] made script reform his life-long pursuit. He devised a system called *Qièyīn Zìmǔ* (切音字母 'sound-spelling letters')[26] to write the local Chinese speech. It was based on the Roman alphabet, but Lú added new letterforms and increased the total number of symbols to 55. Published in his 1892 book *Yìmùliǎorán Chūjiē* (一目了然初阶/一目瞭然初階 *First Steps in Being Able to Understand at a Glance*), the script was the first alphabetical writing system designed by a Chinese for writing Chinese and marks the beginning of modern script reform in China.[27] What was distinctively innovative about this scheme was the use of word boundaries. Writing was no longer based on individual syllables but on words. That is, syllables of the same word were connected, yet neighboring words were separated with spaces, making the phonetic script much easier to read. Lú was also one of the first to adopt punctuations and horizontal text layout in writing Chinese.[28] All of these practices were maintained later on in *pīnyīn*.

A large number of the proposals, especially in the early stage, used either radicals or single strokes of Chinese characters to represent speech sounds. This type of scripts was inspired by Japanese *kana*. Sòng Shù (宋恕 1862–1910) was among the scholars who advocated strongly learning from Japan, a country that had quickly modernized through Western learning. Attributing Japan's success partly to its *kana* writing systems, Sòng declared, "now, we should emulate Japan . . . we need to devise many spelling systems for the area south of the Yangtze and Huai rivers to facilitate the studies of our children."[29] Wáng Zhào carried out Sòng's proposal. After having been in exile in Japan following the failure of the 1898 reforms in China (referred to as *Wùxū Biànfǎ* 戊戌变法 in Chinese; *Wùxū* was the name of the year and *biànfǎ* means "reform"), Wang returned in 1900 with a *kana*-style script. This syllabic script was called *Guānhuà Zìmǔ* (官话字母/官話字母 Mandarin Letters). Lú Zhuàngzhāng also borrowed ideas from *kana* and published in 1906 his second phonographic script using Chinese radicals to write Mandarin and a few dialects of *Mǐn* and Cantonese. In 1915, he published a third system of phonographic writing that made use of strokes of Chinese characters.

Rapid writing developed in the West also served as inspiration for Chinese phonetic scripts. In 1893, Mok Lai Chi from Hong Kong adapted Sir Issac Pitman's shorthand system to writing Cantonese. Mok's system was published in Pitman's *Phonetic Journal*, in which he wrote out the Chinese version of "the Lord's Prayer" using this script and stated that "from [this example] it will be seen that Phonography, even with half of its equipment and a slight alteration, can be safely used to represent the sounds of one of the most ancient and the most difficult languages in the world."[30] Three years later, Cài Xīyǒng also developed a phonetic script for the Chinese language based on shorthand, called *Chuányīn Kuàizì* (传音快字/傳音快字 'rapid graphs for transmitting sounds').

As the phoneticization movement went on, Romanization became the most popular choice among phonographic writing schemes. Scripts making use of character radicals or strokes maintained a degree of "Chineseness" in their appearance, but they lacked the international currency of the Roman alphabet, a script widely used in the Western world. Shorthand-style scripts did not gain much traction, having neither a Chinese appearance nor ready intelligibility for Western users. Eventually, the Latin alphabet became the winning script, and Romanization systems developed in this era paved the way for the design and adoption of *pīnyīn* half a century later. Besides Lú Zhuàngzhāng's *Qièyīn Zìmǔ*, two other well-known Latin scripts were Zhū Wénxióng's (朱文熊 1883–1961) *Jiāngsū Xīn Zìmǔ* (江苏新字母/江蘇新字母 'new alphabet for *Jiāngsū* speech') published in 1906 and Liú Mèngyáng's (刘孟扬/劉孟揚 1877–1943) *Zhōngguó Yīnbiāo Zìshū* (中国音标字书/中國音標字書 'Chinese sound-mark script') two years later. Zhū designed the script to write the Chinese speech of *Sūzhōu* (a city in *Jiāngsū*), his native language. However, he intended to one day modify the script to write Northern Mandarin.[31] This task was fulfilled by Liú's script, which was designed for *Běijīng* Mandarin. One improvement both of these scripts had over Lú Zhuàngzhāng's earlier system was that they did not create new letterforms and therefore used a significantly smaller set of symbols.[32]

THE STORY BEYOND

Progressive views on writing systems

Zhū Wénxióng and Liú Mèngyáng shared progressive views about the nature of writing systems. Zhū believed that, compared with creating a script new to the world, it is better to simply adopt an alphabet already widely in use.[33] Liú took it a step further and argued that written characters were nothing more than symbols. Choosing what writing systems to use was thus primarily a matter of suitability and usability, and there should not be such distinctions between "our scripts" vs. "their scripts."[34]

Phonetic scripts adopted before Pīnyīn

The majority of the phonetic scripts created before *pīnyīn* remained proposals on paper, but several of them were in fact adopted and went on to gain regional, national, or international currency. These included, in chronological order of their publication, (1) Wade-Giles, (2) Postal Romanization, (3) *Bopomofo*, (4) *Gwoyeu Romatzyh* (国语罗马字/國語羅馬字 *Guóyǔ Luómǎzì* 'national-language Romanization'), (5) *Latinxua Sin Wenz* (拉丁化新文字 *Lādīnghuà Xīn Wénzì* 'new Latinization'), and (6) Yale. The list was short, yet the history was complex because of the varied writing needs and social demands during a century of upheaval and change in China. A few of the phonetic scripts were designed by Chinese, and others by Westerners. Almost all of them used the Roman alphabet.

Wade-Giles, Postal, and Yale

The Wade-Giles system was one of the most widely used Romanization systems before *pīnyīn*. The name came from Thomas Francis Wade (威妥玛/威妥瑪 Wēi Tuǒmǎ 1818–1895), who designed the system in the 1860s to write *Běijīng* Mandarin, and Herbert Allen Giles (翟理

斯 Zhái Lǐsī 1845–1935), who later on perfected the system. The origin of the system was in *Mandarin Textbook* (官话课本/官話課本 *Guānhuà Kèběn*), the first Chinese language textbook in English, that Wade published in 1869 in his *Collection of Language for Self Teaching* (语言自迩集/語言自邇集 *Yǔyán Zìěr Jí*). Giles then revised and completed the system in his *Chinese-English Dictionary* of 1892. Both men were British diplomats in China, and a Romanization system of Mandarin Chinese based on the *Běijīng* dialect was necessary for their work. Because of Britain's global dominance, the system became widely used in English publications, including reference books and academic writing, and served as the de facto standard for transcribing Chinese for most of the 20th century. It was replaced by *pīnyīn* in 1979 in Mainland China but continued to be used in *Táiwān* for personal names, place names, and street names.

THE STORY BEYOND

Chinese words in English

In today's English writing, although *pīnyīn* has become the international standard for representing Chinese words, words that were borrowed into Chinese at earlier times may still be spelled in the Wade-Giles system. Below are a few examples. *Pīnyīn* (with tone marks omitted) is given in parentheses for comparison.

  kungfu (*gongfu*) 功夫
  Taichi (*Taiji*) 太极/太極
  I Ching (*Yi Jing*) 易经/易經 '*Book of Change*'
  Kungpao Chicken (*Gongbao* Chicken) 宫保鸡丁/宫保雞丁

Both Sinologists knowledgeable in Mandarin phonology, Thomas Wade and Herbert Giles designed the system primarily for the use of specialists like themselves. For non-specialists, therefore, the script was not always intuitive to learn or to use. A major inconvenience comes from its employment of the left apostrophe (') to represent aspiration. Table 13.3 lists examples in Wade-Giles and in *pīnyīn*. Note that tones in Wade-Giles are indicated with numbers 1 (first tone), 2 (second tone), 3 (third tone), and 4 (fourth tone) in superscript to the right of the syllable. If the apostrophe is omitted in writing, which non-specialists often do, then the distinction in aspiration disappears. The sounds /zh/, /ch/, /j/, and /q/ (represented here in *pīnyīn*), in particular, all become *ch* in writing, resulting in great ambiguity. *Pīnyīn* avoids this problem by using different letters. In total, Wade-Giles uses 20 letters of the Roman alphabet – *b, d, g, q, x,* and *v* are not used – while *pīnyīn* uses 25 (only *v* is not used).

Table 13.3 Differences between Wade-Giles and *pīnyīn* in marking aspiration

Wade-Giles	Pīnyīn	Character	Meaning
po¹	*bō*	播	'to spread'
p'o¹	*pō*	坡	'slope'
teng¹	*dēng*	灯/燈	'lamp'

Wade-Giles	*Pīnyīn*	Character	Meaning
t'eng²	*téng*	疼	'to ache'
kai¹	*gāi*	该/該	'should'
k'ai¹	*kāi*	开	'open'
tzu⁴	*zì*	自	'self'
tz'u⁴	*cì*	次	'number of time'
chu³	*zhǔ*	煮	'to boil'
ch'u³	*chǔ*	处/處	'to be located'
chü³	*jǔ*	举/舉	'to hold up'
ch'ü³	*qǔ*	曲	'melody'

The Postal Spelling System (邮政式拼音/郵政式拼音 *Yóuzhèng Shì* Pīnyīn) is a standardized Romanization system for Chinese place names. It was developed and adopted by the Imperial Postal and Telecommunication Services Joint Conference (帝国邮电联席会议/帝國郵電聯席會議 *Dìguó Yóudiàn Lián Xí Huìyì*) convened in Shanghai in 1906. Before China founded its own public postal and telecommunication system in 1881, foreign-run postal service had been using the Latin alphabet to transliterate Chinese place names. The spelling systems in use, however, were not uniform and could cause confusion. The Postal Spelling System passed at the conference decided to, for the most part, adopt the Wade-Giles system lest its apostrophes, diacritics, and dashes for ease of telegraphic transmission. However, spellings of place names already in common use, e.g. Foochow (福州 *Fúzhōu*), Canton (广州/廣州 *Guǎngzhōu*), and Amoy (厦门/廈門 *Xiàmén*), remained unchanged. In addition, some place names in *Guǎngdōng* (广东/廣東), *Guǎngxī* (广西/廣西), and *Fújiàn* (福建) were spelled according to the local speech rather than *Běijīng* or *Nánjīng* Mandarin. In a strict sense, therefore, Postal Romanization was not a coherent spelling system. Table 13.4 provides a few examples contrasting place names spelled in the Postal system, Wade-Giles, and *pīnyīn*. Postal Romanization was in common use until it was replaced by *pīnyīn* in the 1980s. The United Nations, in particular, adopted *pīnyīn* in 1977 as the standard spelling system for place names from Mainland China.

Table 13.4 Chinese city names in the Postal Spelling System, Wade-Giles, and *pīnyīn* without tone marks

Postal	Wade-Giles	*Pīnyīn*	Characters
Peking	*Pei-ching*	*Beijing*	北京
Nanking	*Nan-ching*	*Nanjing*	南京
Tientsin	*T'ien-chin*	*Tianjin*	天津
Chungking	*Chung-ch'ing*	*Chongqing*	重庆
Tsinan	*Chi-nan*	*Ji'nan*	济南
Tsingtao	*Ch'ing-tao*	*Qingdao*	青岛

Aside from the Wade-Giles system and the various other Romanization conventions represented in the Postal Spelling System, Yale Romanization (耶鲁方案/耶魯方案 *Yélǔ Fāng'àn*) was another system developed by Westerners to primarily serve the need of Westerners. In fact, the term "Yale Romanization" encompasses Romanization of four major East Asian languages: Mandarin, Cantonese, Japanese, and Korean, each developed by different authors. Yale Mandarin was designed by George A. Kennedy (1901–1960), a Sinologist at Yale University, in 1943 to teach Chinese to American troops to be deployed to China during World War II. At the time, of course, Wade-Giles was the international standard for Mandarin Romanization. The Yale system, however, was designed to be more intuitive as a language-learning tool, because its spelling was more closely based on the English pronunciation of Roman letter combinations. For example, the *pīnyīn* syllables *zhi, chi, shi,* and *ri* are spelled as *jr, chr, shr,* and *r* in Yale, much easier to pronounce for English speakers than the Wade-Giles *chih, ch'ih, shih,* and *jih.* Table 13.5 gives these and a few additional examples. In addition, Yale Mandarin dropped the left apostrophe (') used to represent aspiration in Wade-Giles; instead, it made use of *pīnyīn*-like pairs, distinguishing between *p-b, t-d,* and *k-g.* This also made it more user-friendly.

Table 13.5   Yale, Wade-Giles, and *pīnyīn* systems compared (tones not marked)

Yale	Wade-Giles	*Pīnyīn*	Characters
jr	*chih*	*zhi*	知
chr	*ch'ih*	*chi*	池
shr	*shih*	*shi*	是
r	*jih*	*ri*	日
ji	*chi*	*ji*	及
chi	*ch'i*	*qi*	七
xyi	*hsi*	*xi*	息

Bopomofo and Gwoyeu Romatzyh

Bopomofo (ㄅㄆㄇㄈ) and *Gwoyeu Romatzyh* (国语罗马字/國語羅馬字 *Guóyǔ Luómǎzì* 'national-language Romanization,' abbreviated *GR*), different from Wade-Giles, Postal, and Yale, were Chinese-designed phonographic writing systems. They were both sponsored by the Republic of China government[35] and were direct product of the National Language Movement that had been underway since the late *Qīng. Bopomofo,* a script based on archaic Chinese character forms, was adopted in 1918 as the official system to annotate pronunciation of the unified national language. Ten years later, the government published *GR,* a Romanization system, as it recognized the usefulness of using the Roman alphabet in communicating with Western countries. While the People's Republic of China government adopted *pīnyīn* as the standard Romanization script in Mainland China in 1958, both *Bopomofo* and *GR* continued to be used in *Táiwān* throughout the 20th century. They maintained their presence, together with a host of other phonographic systems, until this day, even after *Táiwān*'s adoption of *pīnyīn* as the official Romanization script in 2009. *Bopomofo,* in particular, is widely used in in educational settings. Students learn to use the script in elementary schools, and Chinese language instructors use it to teach their students.

Bopomofo was in fact the colloquial name of *Zhùyīn Fúhào* (注音符号/注音符號 'sound-annotating symbols,' abbreviated as *Zhùyīn*), which was originally named *Zhùyīn Zìmǔ* (注音字母 'sound-annotating letters'). The subtle switch from to *Zìmǔ* to *Fúhào* in 1930 was to emphasize the purpose of *Zhùyīn*: it was not to replace Chinese characters but to be used as an auxiliary script annotating Chinese characters in the pronunciation of the national language. The colloquial term came from the names of the first four symbols in the script: ㄅ (bō), ㄆ (pō), ㄇ (mō), and ㄈ (fō).

Ostensibly a *kana*-inspired script, *Bopomofo* is not a syllabary[36] (a syllabic writing system), nor is it an alphabet (a phonemic writing system); it is something in between. As shown in Table 13.6, a symbol may correspond to a single speech sound, as is the case for most consonants, or a sequence of sounds consisting of any of the following: a single vowel, a single semi-vowel, a vowel plus a semi-vowel, or a vowel plus a nasal. On what basis then, you may wonder, is the symbol-speech relation established in this script? It is based on traditional Chinese phonology, which analyzes a syllable into an initial consonant (which may be absent), a medial (which may be absent), and a rhyme. Intuitively to a Chinese speaker, each of these components assumes relatively equal status within a syllable and is thus represented by a separate symbol. Writing a syllable, therefore, usually requires two or three symbols.

Table 13.6 *Bopomofo* and *pīnyīn* comparison

Bopomofo	*Pīnyīn*	Structure	Status in traditional phonology
ㄅ	b	consonant	initial consonant
ㄊ	t	consonant	initial consonant
ㄏ	h	consonant	initial consonant
ㄚ	a	vowel	rhyme
ㄩ	ü	vowel	rhyme
ㄛ	o	vowel	rhyme
ㄧ	i/y	vowel/semi-vowel	rhyme/medial
ㄨ	u/w	vowel/semi-vowel	rhyme/medial
ㄞ	ai	vowel + semi-vowel	rhyme
ㄠ	ao	vowel + semi-vowel	rhyme
ㄣ	en	vowel + nasal	rhyme
ㄤ	ang	vowel + nasal	rhyme

THE STORY BEYOND

The origin of *Bopomofo* symbols

Bopomofo makes use of 37 symbols. Many of them are derived via phonetic borrowing from archaic forms of Chinese characters in the small seal script.[37] Below are a few examples.

ㄆ (p): archaic form of "扑 *pū*";
ㄎ (k): archaic form of "考 *kǎo*";
ㄒ (x): archaic form of "下 *xià*";
ㄙ (s): archaic form of "私 *sī*";
ㄠ (ao): archaic form of 麼, synonymous of 小 *xiǎo* 'little, small'.

Tones in *Bopomofo* are marked using diacritics similar to those in *pīnyīn*. First tone is not marked, but second (′), third (ˇ), fourth (`), and neutral (˙) tones are. The diacritics are placed to the upper right of the rhyme. For example, *Zhōngguó wénzì* (中国文字/中國文字 'Chinese script') in *Bopomofo* is written as:

ㄓㄨㄥ ㄍㄨㄛˊ ㄨㄣˊ ㄗˋ

In 1928, the Republic government published *GR*, a Romanization system designed by a group of linguists headed by Chao Yuen Ren (赵元任/趙元任 1892–1982). A prominent characteristic of this system was that tones were indicated in the spelling, circumventing the need to use diacritics, which had the tendency to be dropped in typing or handwriting. For example, the syllable *an* in four tones written in *GR* (*pīnyīn*) is *an* (ān), *arn* (án), *aan* (ǎn), and *ann* (àn). However, because the spelling rules were complicated, the system did not gain much public support and was not promoted for popular use.

THE STORY BEYOND

GR in *pīnyīn*

GR is in fact used along with *pīnyīn* in one particular case. The Chinese provincial names *Shānxī* (山西) and *Shǎnxī* (陕西/陝西) become indistinguishable in standard *pīnyīn* spelling when tone marks are omitted as they often are in Western text: both will be *Shanxi*. To solve this problem, *GR* spelling is adopted for this pair. The first tone *Shān* maintains the original spelling *Shan*, while the third tone *Shǎn* is written as *Shaan* with a double vowel.

Latinxua Sin Wenz

Latinxua Sin Wenz (拉丁化新文字 *Lādīnghuà Xīn Wénzì* 'new writing of Latinization,' aka *Zhongguo Latinxua Sin Wenz* or *Beifangxua Latinxua Sin Wenz*, abbreviated as *Latinxua* or *Bei-La*), published in 1929, was designed by Chinese scholars in exile in the Soviet Union in collaboration with Soviet linguists. Its immediate use was to raise the literacy rate of the large number of Chinese migrant workers living in the Soviet Union at the time. In this regard, it appeared quite effective: hundreds of thousands of copies of nearly 50 different types of books written in *Latinxua* were published in the Soviet Union, and Chinese workers were said to be able to read the newspapers and write letters using the script.[38]

Different from *Bopomofo*, *GR*, and the later implemented *pīnyīn*, *Latinxua* was proposed with full intention to achieve two ambitious goals: one, to completely replace Chinese characters, which the revolutionaries deemed incompatible with the modernizing China. Indeed, promoters of *Latinxua* were among the most radical in their view against the traditional writing system.[39] The second goal was to be able to write a variety of Chinese dialects (languages) in addition to the unified national language. As it spread to inside China in the early 1930s, *Latinxua* was met with antagonism from the Nationalist-controlled Republic government.[40] However, with support from the Communist leadership and a large number of left-wing intellectuals such as Lǔ Xùn (鲁迅/魯迅 1881–1936) and Cài Yuánpéi (蔡元培 1868–1940), a

Latinxua movement occurred on the national scale. Organizations appeared across China to promote and teach the script.[41] Within a few years, *Latinxua* systems for as many as 14 Chinese dialects (languages) were created.[42] In Northwestern China, an area under Communist control, the government adopted *Latinxua* as the official script.[43] By 1955, when the *Latinxua* movement finally ended, about 20,000 people had learned the script through more than 300 organizations,[44] and over 300 publications with half a million copies had been produced.[45] Although neither of the aforementioned goals was eventually realized, *Latinxua*, together with *Bopomofo* and *GR*, to say the least, served as the linguistic foundation for the development of a later Romanization system, *pīnyīn*.[46]

Notes

1 "汉字不灭，中国必亡！ / 漢字不滅，中國必亡！ (*Hànzì bú miè, Zhōngguó bì wáng!*)" Lǔ Xùn made this comment in his "Responses to rescue intelligence agents" (答救亡情报员/答救亡情報員) in October, 1936, not long before he passed away.

2 The Portuguese-Chinese dictionary was not the earliest foreign language dictionary in China, but it was probably the earliest to arrange entries in an alphabetical order.

3 Walle (2013, p. 183).

4 These examples are taken from the modern published version of the dictionary. See Yang (2001, pp. 112–113).

5 Ibid., pp. 208–209, quoted by Camus (2007, p. 4), suggested that the Mandarin of Ricci's time, that is, late *Míng* dynasty, "was not based on the Northern Beijing dialect, but, most probably was based on a commonly accepted Southern dialect variety of Mandarin, more specifically the dialect of Nanking and its nearby environs."

6 "Aspiration" is the linguistic term for the burst of air accompanying sounds like *p(ie)*, *t(ie)*, and *K(y)* in English. These sounds are considered aspirated. By contrast, sounds such as *b(ye)*, *d(ie)*, and *g(uy)* are unaspirated. Aspiration distinguishes the Chinese sounds *p(ai)*, *t(ai)*, and *k(ai)* from *b(ai)*, *d(ai)*, and *g(ai)*.

7 Yang (2001, p. 185).

8 Camus (2007, p. 4).

9 Yang (2001, p. 179).

10 Ibid., p. 171.

11 Ibid.

12 See Huang (1996).

13 Mair (2000, p. 302).

14 Ibid., pp. 105–106.

15 *Tōng Yǎ* (通雅, 1666 1.25b), quoted by Mair (2002, p. 106).

16 Ibid., p. 105.

17 DeFrancis (1950, p. 217).

18 There is no official record of China's illiteracy rate before 1949. However, the general view is it remained steady for the first half of the 20th century at 80%–85%. See Zhang (2005) for data after 1949.

19 Mair (2002, p. 110).

20 Ibid., p. 112.

21 Ibid., p. 121.

22 Ibid., p. 120.

23 Ibid., p. 111.

24 Tsu (2014, pp. 16–17).

25 An earlier Romanization of *Xiàmén* (厦门/廈門).

26 *Qiēyīn* is an earlier term used to mean *pīnyīn*, "spelling speech sounds." For this reason, early script reform is also referred to as "*qiēyīn* movement."

27 In his report published on January 13, 1958 in the *People's Daily* (人民日报/人民日報), "Current tasks in script reform (当前文字改革的任务/當前文字改革的任務)," Premier Zhōu Ēnlái (周恩来/周恩來) says: "Beginning from Lú Zhuàngzhāng's *qiēyīn xīn zì* (切音新字) in 1892, many patriots actively advocated script reform and created a variety of phonographic scripts (从一八九二年卢戆章的切音新字开始，当时我国的许多爱国人士也都积极提倡文字改革，并且创制各种拼音方案)."

28 Yán Fù (严复 1854–1921) was the first to use Western punctuation in writing Chinese. He adopted punctuation marks in his 1904 book translated from English *Yīngwén hàngū* (英文汉沽/英文漢沽 *English grammar explained in Chinese*). It was also the first book that used horizontal typesetting for Chinese text.

29 Mair (2002, pp. 107–108).

30 *The Phonetic Journal*, July 29, 1893, p. 470. Note that Mok confused "language" and "writing" by claiming that Chinese was "the most ancient" and "the most difficult in the world." Furthermore, the Chinese script was neither the most ancient nor, probably, the most difficult.

31 See Zhu (1956).

32 Zhū's script used variants of existing letters – the upside-down forms of five letters and the horizontal form of a sixth one – and Liú's script used only the 26 letters of the Roman alphabet.

33 See Zhu (1956). His original statement in Chinese is "与其造世界未有之新字，不如采用世界所通行之字母 / 與其造世界未有之新字，不如採用世界所通行之字母."

34 See Liu (1957). What Liú said in Chinese was "字也者，记号也，取其适用而已，无所谓人己之别 / 字也者，記號也，取其適用而已，無所謂人己之別".

35 The Republic of China was founded in 1911 after the last imperial dynasty, the *Qīng*, was overthrown.

36 As discussed in Chapter 3, Japanese *kana* scripts are strictly moraic rather than syllabic writing systems.

37 Chapter 21 offers an overview of the script styles.

38 Peng (2010, p. 14).

39 Chen (1999, pp. 168, 186).

40 Peng (2010, p. 14).

41 Ni (1987, p. 14).

42 Ibid., pp. 13–14.

43 Ibid., p. 26.

44 Ibid., p. 37.

45 Ni (1948) quoted by Chen (1999) on p. 186.

46 Wang (2002, p. 166).

14 *Pīnyīn*

AS WE LEARNED IN the previous chapter, Chinese reformers proposed and implement-ed a variety of phonographic scripts from the 1890s to the 1950s. Eager to promote lit-eracy in a mostly illiterate nation, they saw the phoneticization of Chinese writing as a doorway to broader access to education necessary for a stronger China. None of the proposals, however, was able to take hold in a country overwhelmed by foreign invasions, internal divisions, and a civil war. The founding of the People's Republic of China (PRC) in 1949 eventually made it possible to place writing reform once again on the national agenda. Sponsored by the PRC government, efforts began in the same year to study, plan, and carry out official changes to Chinese writing and continued well into the 1980s. This reform had two major aspects: popularization of *pīnyīn* (拼音) and simplification of Chinese characters. In this chapter, we will focus on *pīnyīn*, and we will discuss script simplification in the next chapter. If you took the brief tutorial on reading *pīnyīn* in Part I of this book, you will have already become familiar with the system and may also be able to rely on it to pronounce Chinese syllables and words. In this chapter, we will learn more about *pīnyīn*'s history, current uses, and spelling rules. First of all, however, let us consider what *pīnyīn* is and what it is designed to write.

What is *pīnyīn*?

Pīnyīn is a phonemic writing system that uses the Roman alphabet to represent Modern Standard Chinese (MSC), or *pǔtōnghuà* (普通话/普通話 'common speech'). *Pīn* (拼) means "to spell," and *yīn* (音) means "sounds," referring to "speech sounds," so *pīnyīn* literally means "spell (speech) sounds." The script makes use of 25 of the 26 Roman letters – *v* is not used – plus *ü*, and it marks tones with diacritics (e.g., *mā, má, mǎ* and *mà*).

The term *pīnyīn* may have slightly different meanings in English than in Chinese. In English, it is used as a proper name to refer specifically to the phonemic writing system designed for MSC under the PRC government. Used in this sense, it is an abbreviated form for *Hànyǔ pīnyīn fāng'àn* (汉语拼音方案/漢語拼音方案 'Chinese sound-spelling scheme') or *Hànyǔ pīnyīn*. In Chinese, however, *pīnyīn* can also be used in a general sense to mean "spelling (speech) sounds," or, in another term that is familiar to us, "phonographic." For example, *pīnyīn wénzì* (拼音文字; 文字 *wénzì* 'writing, script') can be understood as "phonographic scripts."

What does *pīnyīn* write? It is, in this regard, very different from *Latinxua*, the Romanization system we have previously discussed. As you may recall, *Latinxua* was intended not only to replace Chinese characters but also to write a range of Chinese languages. It was designed to enable autonomous Romanization of any variety of Chinese dialect and had hence underrepresented certain dialect-specific features. For instance, tones were not marked in *Latinxua* because dialectical variations, to a great extent, manifested in tonal differences. *Latinxua* provided the linguistic basis on which *pīnyīn* was created.[1] However, *pīnyīn* was designed for writing MSC only, and, at least for the foreseeable future, it is not used for writing regional dialects (languages).

Although the *pīnyīn* script, in linguistic terms, is a full-fledged writing system, its status is secondary to the character-based script: it has been primarily used as a pronunciation guide, for example, in printed Chinese text, on street signs, and in Chinese-language classrooms. It is also used to transcribe Mandarin speech or to represent Chinese in Western texts. According to the linguist *Zhōu Yǒuguāng* (周有光 1906–2017), who oversaw the development work of *pīnyīn*, the script was not meant to replace the character-based writing system, and "that was made clear when *pīnyīn* was promulgated."[2]

THE STORY BEYOND

Pīnyīn as an alternative script?

In a personal interview with John DeFrancis,[3] Zhōu Yôuguāng revealed that when *pīnyīn* was first created, the system was in fact "submitted for discussion" as a potential alternative script. Its original name also had the term "*wénzì* ('writing, script')" in it – *hànyǔ pīnyīn wénzì fāng'àn* ('Chinese phonographic writing plan'). The intention was to develop the *fāng'àn* ('plan') into a formal script over a period of ten years. When the National People's Congress approved *pīnyīn* in 1958, however, the term "*wénzì*" was dropped from its name, thus changing the nature of *pīnyīn* from a "writing plan" to an "annotation plan."[4] With the emergence of the Great Leap Forward (1958–1962), a campaign led by the Communist Party to rapidly industrialize China, the euphoric expectations of progress by uniquely Chinese means embraced the area of writing as well.[5] At around the same time, China fell into an economic crisis. As a result, work to reform Chinese writing became stalled[6] and did not resume until in the early 1970s.[7]

The status of *pīnyīn*, however, remained an issue of debate as the desire for a phonographic script rose and fell. In the early stages of research on natural language processing aided by computers, the vast and unsorted set of characters in the Chinese writing system presented enormous challenges to the digitization and processing of Chinese text. Frustrated developers saw *pīnyīn* as a solution, and this led them to propose having two full scripts for Chinese, *hànzì* (汉字/漢字 'Chinese characters') and *pīnyīn*, elevating the latter to a position on par with conventional characters. The idea or phenomena that a language is written in two distinctive scripts used for complementary purposes is referred to as **digraphia**.[8] Despite the advocacy by researchers as well as some linguists and language educators for *pīnyīn* to become a full script alongside Chinese characters, it never achieved this status in official terms. Further development in digital technology has also made it easier to process Chinese text on computers. On the other hand, *pīnyīn* has become indispensable in mediating the input of characters on computers, cell phones, and other modern electronic devices, leading some linguists to consider *hànzì* and *pīnyīn* already in a digraphic relationship.[9]

▉ History of *pīnyīn*

Motivations for creating *pīnyīn* came from, first of all, the PRC government's desire to establish a national and international standard for phonographic writing of Chinese. Under the Republic government (1912–1949), the official phonographic script was *Bopomofo*, a character-inspired system that continued to be used after the founding of the PRC and had been in use for almost four decades by the time the work on *pīnyīn* started. To establish a phonographic script for Chinese as an international standard, the PRC government came to recognize that *Bopomofo* needed to be replaced by a Romanization system because of the much greater international currency of the Roman alphabet. As we have learned in the last chapter, a variety of Romanization scripts was already in existence at the time to transcribe Chinese: most notably, Wade-Giles created by British scholars, *Gwoyeu Romatzyh* (*GR*) developed under the Nationalist government, and *Latinxua* sponsored by the Communist establishment. However, each of these systems had major shortcomings. For example, Wade-Giles employed diacritics that its users often mistakenly omitted, *GR* had complicated spelling rules, and *Latinxua* did not mark tones. The coexistence of these systems also caused much confusion. Adding to the chaos was the fact that personal names might be Romanized differently in different languages. For example, the name of Zhōu Ēnlái (周恩来/周恩來 1898–1976), the first premier of the PRC, was represented as "Chou Enlai" in English and "Tchou Enlai" in French.[10] Clearly, there needed to be a new, unified Romanization system to reduce confusion and aid communication across languages.

Another motivation for a new and improved Romanization system was to facilitate the PRC government's goal to promulgate Modern Standard Chinese or *pǔtōnghuà* as the standard speech for the nation. The new Romanized script was viewed as a necessary tool to help with the learning of *pǔtōnghuà* pronunciation, and thus, the script must be tailored to transcribing the sounds of *pǔtōnghuà*. *Pīnyīn* was designed with this in mind. Since its creation, it has been used as a pedagogical tool in teaching *pǔtōnghuà* to both native and foreign learners.

The work on a new phonographic script began as soon as the PRC government formed in 1949. Up until 1954, the effort was mainly on devising a script based on the strokes of Chinese characters. In 1955, the PRC government charged a team of about 20 specialists under the Committee of Chinese Writing Reform (中国文字改革委员会/中國文字改革委員會 *Zhōngguó Wénzì Gǎigé Wěiyuánhuì*) with the task of developing a Romanization system for Chinese. It was not until later that year, however, that the decision was made to adopt the Roman alphabet. Headed by Zhōu Yǒuguāng, the team of specialists began to develop what eventually came to be known as *pīnyīn*. The process took as long as three years – a "full-time job" in Zhōu's words.[11] Besides studying and comparing past Romanization systems, they considered hundreds of new proposals from the general public. About 1,700 phonographic writing schemes, some using the Roman alphabet, some not, were submitted to the committee.[12] In 1958, *pīnyīn* was published and became the official Romanization system in Mainland China.

THE STORY BEYOND

Adoption of the Roman alphabet

The decision to adopt the Roman alphabet instead of a native-based script to transcribe *pǔtōnghuà* did not come easily. At the early stage of *pīnyīn*'s development, Chairman Máo requested that the new system be based on Chinese characters. The committee charged with writing reform, after intensive deliberations, came up with six proposals, four based on Chinese characters, one on the Cyrillic script, and one on the Latin alphabet. A heated debate ensued. Máo eventually supported the adoption of the Roman alphabet. Premier Zhōu Ēnlái, in his speech in 1958, officially endorsed *pīnyīn* and concluded that "the adoption of the Latin alphabet will . . . not harm the patriotism of our people,"[13] ending the debate on script choice.

In the decades after *pīnyīn* was declared the official Romanization system of the PRC, it made strides in becoming the international standard. In 1979, the United Nations passed a resolution to adopt *pīnyīn* as the official system in transcribing Chinese personal and place names. Since that year, an increasing number of publishers in the West have switched to using *pīnyīn*.[14] In 1982, the International Organization for Standardization recognized *pīnyīn* as the standard Romanization for Chinese (ISO 7098). In *Táiwān*, a variety of Romanization systems, including Wade-Giles, *GR*, and the later-designed *Tongyong Pinyin* (通用拼音 *Tōngyòng pīnyīn*, 2002–2008), had been in concurrent use, before *pīnyīn* was adopted in 2009 as the official Romanization system.

Current uses of *pīnyīn*

Although rarely used as an independent writing system, *pīnyīn* has a range of important applications in modern education, communication, and information processing. *Pīnyīn*, first of all, has proved a highly useful pedagogical tool. Elementary-school students in Mainland China typically master *pīnyīn* in the first one or two months of their Chinese class before learning to read and write Chinese characters with the assistance of *pīnyīn*.[15] Vocabulary lists and Chinese texts at the elementary level are annotated using *pīnyīn* to help students pronounce characters new to them. Students may also read supplementary texts written completely in *pīnyīn*. *Pīnyīn* serves a similar function for foreign learners of Chinese as an Additional Language. Some college-level textbooks, for example, *Basic Spoken Chinese* and *Basic Written Chinese*,[16] use separate *pīnyīn* and character books, with the *pīnyīn* version dedicated to the training of students' speaking proficiency.

Pīnyīn is also used to organize textual information in Chinese. Modern print dictionaries use *pīnyīn* to order character and word entries and annotate their pronunciation. To look up a character, if one knows the pronunciation, one can simply locate it by its *pīnyīn* spelling according to the alphabetical order. Libraries also make use of *pīnyīn* in organizing their print catalogues.

Pīnyīn has a significant presence in the visual landscape of Chinese public spaces. Road signs and storefronts often carry *pīnyīn* underneath the characters. The annotation helps those not fully proficient in reading Chinese deduce the meaning of the characters and those who speak a non-Mandarin dialect learn the standard pronunciation that may be different from their own.[17]

Internationally, it is now standard practice to use *pīnyīn*, usually without tone marks, in publications in Western languages to represent Chinese words. For example, the current

Chinese president's name appears as *Xi Jinping* (习近平/習近平) in news media, and the capital city of China, as you know, is spelled *Beijing* (北京).

THE STORY BEYOND

Peking vs. *Beijing*

The name of the Chinese capital has been Romanized in at least two commonly seen forms: *Peking* and *Beijing*. Earlier we have learned that *Peking* is not based on the Wade-Giles system but rather on the less known Postal system. In Wade-Giles, the city name would be spelled as *Pei3-ching1* with tone marks indicated in numerals. There is more to the story.

In Chinese characters, this northern Chinese city is represented as 北京. 北 *běi* means "north," and 京 *jīng* means "capital." Thus, 北京 simply means "northern capital." *Beijing* is the *pīnyīn* representation of the city name in Modern Standard Chinese with the tone marks omitted. The other Romanized form, *Peking*, predates *Beijing* by many years, and registers the traditional pronunciation of 北京. European missionaries who came to China during the *Míng* dynasty (1368–1644) were the first ones to Romanize the city's name in writing. The *lingua franca* at the time was the *Nánjīng* speech, which pronounced the city name to something close to *pik-king*. Based on the prestigious *Nánjīng* Mandarin, Matteo Ricci (1552–1610) rendered it as *Pekin*. Due to a series of phonological changes in northern Mandarin around the mid-17th century, some scholars believe that the sounds represented in *Pekin(g)* came to change to the sounds represented by *Beijing*.[18] Thus, *Peking* and *Beijing* differ in the pronunciation they represent, and they are not alternative Romanizations of the same sounds.

Pīnyīn input methods are probably the most commonly used for entering Chinese characters on digital devices using a standard keyboard. Most educated speakers of Chinese today have learned *pīnyīn*, so using this kind of input methods requires minimal practice. After a *pīnyīn* syllable has been entered, the user is presented with a list of characters sharing the same pronunciation and makes a choice by selecting the desired character or entering a corresponding number on the keyboard. The process is not as straightforward as inputting pure *pīnyīn* text or English, but with continued improvements, such as the addition of context-based adaptive prompts, experienced users can input Chinese-character text with adequate efficiency for day-to-day communicative purposes.

Spelling rules

Can *pīnyīn* replace Chinese characters, after all? Sociocultural considerations aside, for *pīnyīn* to be used as a fully functioning script, it needs to overcome a number of linguistic challenges. Among these, word boundaries and homophony are the most significant. In 1988, Zhōu Yǒuguāng and his committee published an officially approved set of spelling rules for *pīnyīn*.[19] With these rules in place, some argued, *pīnyīn* was in a good position to tackle the challenges and become "a full-fledged script."[20]

Unlike reading and understanding text in Chinese characters, reading *pīnyīn* requires the marking of word boundaries for easier comprehension. Words are natural units of complete meaning in a language, so it helps readers understand the text when words are segmented. In Chinese character-based writing, word boundaries are typically not marked. Characters are placed right next to each other no matter how long the sentence may be. Readers must parse the text into words as they read based on their vocabulary knowledge and what they know about the context. This is workable because characters vary a great deal in shape and each character represents meaning in addition to sounds. For example, the short sentence 今天星期六 (*Jīntiān xīngqīliù*, 'Today is Saturday') may contain two words to most readers: 今天 (*jīntiān*, 'today') and 星期六 (*Xīngqīliù*, 'Saturday'). The five symbols all appear different from each other, and readers have the knowledge that 今天 (*jīntiān*, 'today') is a word and 星期六 (*xīngqīliù*, 'Saturday') is another word. They also know from experience that 天星 (*tiān xīng*) is not a word and neither is 期六 (*qī liù*). Thus, drawing the word boundaries as 今/天星/期六 (*jīn tiānxīng qīliù*) will not be correct. Marking word boundaries is imperative in *pīnyīn* writing, because Roman letters repeat each other much more frequently and individual letters do not represent meaning. For example, although reading and understanding "*jīntiānxīngqīliù*" is not impossible, it requires significantly more effort than "*jīntiān xīngqīliù*." Imagine reading a sentence much longer than this in English. Reading Chinese in *pīnyīn* without word boundaries would probably be just as difficult.

The primary role of the *pīnyīn* orthography rules is to standardize word boundaries in *pīnyīn* writing. They aim to ensure that, on one hand, syllables of separate words are separated, and on the other hand, syllables of the same words are written together. However, the spelling rules currently are neither taught at school nor strictly enforced, so many may be oblivious of their existence. For example, visitors in China may see signs such as in Figure 14.1, in which *pīnyīn* syllables are written completely separately with a space in between very two syllables. This practice likely mirrors the writing convention of syllable-based Chinese characters, but in this case it may obscure the distinction between proper names and general names and make the sign more difficult to understand. Based on *pīnyīn* orthography, the place name *Tong Hai* (通海) should be written as one word as *Tonghai*, because both syllables are part of a proper name, the name of a place. *Da Hui Cun* (大回村, *Dàhuí Cūn*, 'Dahui Village,' *lit.* 'Great Muslim Village') should be written as *Dahui Cun*, because *Dahui* is a proper name and *Cun* (村 *cūn* 'village') is a general noun.[21] Another reason why *pīnyīn* spelling rules are often not put into practice may be that word segmentation may not always be intuitive. In fact, scholars have found that being accustomed to the character-based system makes Chinese users lack a sense of "word."[22] The *pīnyīn* annotation for the smaller characters in the sign, for instance, may be segmented into *Chama Gudao (Majia Dayuan)* or *Chama Gu Dao (Majia Da Yuan)*, depending on whether we consider *Gudao* (古道 *gǔdào* 'ancient path') and *Dayuan* (大院 *dàyuàn* 'big yard') as one or two words each in themselves.

Another challenge that has been cited for *pīnyīn* in considering its potential as an independent writing system is the prevalence of homophony in the Chinese language. A great number of words in Chinese share the same pronunciation. Written in characters, they appear different; in *pīnyīn*, they are not distinct from each other. For example:

> *wēijī*: 危机/危機 'crisis'; 微机/微機 'micro computer'
> *yǒulì*: 有利 'beneficial'; 有力 'powerful'
> *yóushuì*: 游说/遊說 'to campaign'; 油税/油稅 'gas tax'
> *shíhuà* 实话/實話 'honest words'; 石化 (short form for 石油化工 *shíyóu huàgōng*) 'petroleum and chemical industry'

FIGURE 14.1 *Pīnyīn* on road sign

Some point out that homophony may not be as big a problem as many think.[23] In most cases, contextual information should provide sufficient help needed to disambiguate homophonous words. After all, if people have little difficulty understanding each other in speech, then there is no reason why they should have major problems differentiating homophones in reading. Occasionally when confusion arises, interlocutors in a face-to-face conversation could ask questions to clarify for each other; a reader of a book written in *pīnyīn*, however, would have little recourse. To solve this problem, some proposed adding a silent one-letter suffix to differentiate homophonous morphemes or words. The suffixes function somewhat like radicals in Chinese characters.[24] For example:

琵琶 *pípa-w* 'pipa (a Chinese musical instrument)'
枇杷 *pípa-m* 'loquat (a fruit)'

The "*w*" represented the *wáng* (王) radical, and the "*m*" represented the *mù* (木) radical, each present in the respective characters. Zhōu Yǒuguāng objected to this proposal on the ground that this would turn *pīnyīn* into an annotation system for Chinese characters rather than a writing system for the Chinese language, which would go against the basic principles of *pīnyīn*.[25]

Finally, the spelling rules also stipulate the use of punctuation in *pīnyīn*. Overall, the usage of punctuation marks in *pīnyīn* is similar to in English text. This means a few differences exist between punctuating *pīnyīn* writing and text in Chinese characters: *pīnyīn* uses a dot ('.') to represent a period, while character-based writing uses a circle ('。'). Character writing uses the symbol '、' to indicate a pause shorter than a comma, as in making a list; *pīnyīn* does not use this symbol and uses commas instead for such pauses. At the end of a line, a multisyllabic word may break and continue at the beginning of the next line. As in English, a hyphen is required to indicate that the word is not yet finished, and the hyphen must be placed between syllables.[26]

Companion Website

Exercise 14.1 Representing foreign place names and personal names in *pīnyīn*

As a final note: the official *pīnyīn* orthography rules adopt the principle of following the original. That is, the original Romanized forms are taken as the standard. This is also the principle used by the UN's Conference on Standardization of Place Names. By this principle, any foreign name will have only one written form: the Romanization used in its language of origin.

Notes

1 Taylor and Taylor (2014, p. 123).
2 Zhou (1958, p. 17), quoted by Sampson (1985, p. 159).
3 DeFrancis (1984, p. 275).
4 Zhao and Baldauf (2008, pp. 287–288).
5 DeFrancis (1984, p. 275).
6 Wang (2002, p. 83).
7 Ibid., pp. 97–105.
8 According to Tranter (2008, p. 133), "in practice scholars tend to use 'digraphia' to describe the relationship between the Roman alphabet and the native scripts (e.g., Unger, 2001), rather than the relationship between all the scripts." The "native script" in the case of Chinese refers to the character-based script.
9 Mair (1996, p. 205).
10 This example is from DeFrancis (1984, p. 256).
11 Father of pinyin. *China Daily*, March 26, 2009. Retrieved July 12, 2009. Reprinted in part as Simon, A. (January 21–27, 2011). Father of Pinyin. *China Daily Asia Weekly* (Hong Kong), Xinhua, p. 20.
12 See DeFrancis (1984, p. 262).
13 Cited by ibid., pp. 263–264.
14 Sampson (1985, p. 159).
15 In *Táiwān*, *pīnyīn* is used for Romanization alone rather than for educational and computer input purposes.
16 Kubler (2011).
17 Sampson (1985, p. 159).
18 Man (1990, p. 5).
19 For a reference book in English on the *pīnyīn* orthography rules, see Yin (1990).
20 Mair (1996, p. 205).
21 Refer to Zhou (2003). Note that if *Dahui Cun* is taken as a well-established place name as a whole, then it is preferably written as one word, *Dahuicun*. This is perhaps another example for how complex *pīnyīn* orthography rules can be in application.

22 Taylor and Taylor (2014, p. 26) cites a study by Hoosain (1991) that finds that Hong Kong middle-school students were not able to proficiently segment a Chinese text into words.
23 See Zhou (2003).
24 Ibid., p. 125.
25 Ibid., pp. 110, 125.
26 Ibid., p. 120.

15 Simplification of Chinese characters

A LONG WITH EFFORTS TO design and popularize a new Romanization system (*pīnyīn*) for Modern Standard Chinese, the PRC government implemented policies to simplify the character-based script. After work that spanned more than three decades (1953–1986), the result was what is commonly known in Chinese as *jiǎntǐ zì* (简体字/簡體字 'simple-style characters'). The simplified script is used today in Mainland China, Singapore, and Malaysia and is widely taught in the Chinese-language curricula in the West, while in *Táiwān*, Hong Kong, and Macau, the traditional (pre-simplification) script, referred to as *fántǐ zì* (繁体字/繁體字 'complex-style characters') in Chinese, remains the official style.

Script simplification under the PRC government incorporated work along two major dimensions: reducing the number of strokes within characters and downsizing and standardizing the overall inventory of characters. In this chapter, we will discuss both aspects with a focus on the process and outcome of the PRC's script reform. This reform was by no means, however, the first effort by the Chinese to systematically simplify the writing system in the modern era. In fact, earlier experimentation laid the groundwork for the implementation of this reform. We will begin by taking a look at some of these attempts.

▇ Early attempts at simplification (1900–1950s)

Although modern efforts to simplify the Chinese script did not come to fruition until the PRC's writing reform in the second half of the 20th century, they began about half a century before and had a significant impact on the reform. Lù Fèikuí (陆费逵/陸費逵 1886–1941) in 1909 published an article in the inaugural issue of *Jiàoyù Zázhì* (教育杂志/教育雜誌 *Education Journal*), calling for the use of folk characters in general education. He pointed out that folk characters had already been "used for every purpose but official documents and examinations."[1] If adopted for general education, they would aid learning and literacy and would have "nothing but benefits."[2] This was the first published proposal for simplifying characters and marked the beginning of the modern character-simplification movement.[3] In 1921, Lù Fèikuí proposed specific strategies for simplifying the writing system. These included limiting the number of frequently used characters, giving official status to the simplified characters already in wide use, and reducing the strokes of complex characters[4] – all principles followed by the PRC's script reform decades later.

During the New Culture Movement, progressive intellectuals such as Cài Yuánpéi (蔡元培 1868–1940), Hú Shì (胡适/胡適 1891–1962), Zhōu Zuòrén (周作人 1885–1967), and Lín Yǔtáng (林语堂/林語堂 1895–1976) were all supporters of script simplification. A major development took place in 1922, when the prominent scholar Qián Xuántóng (钱玄同/錢玄同

1887–1939) brought forward a bill to the Republic government calling for adopting simplified characters.[5] He pointed out that, for thousands of years, Chinese characters had constantly been reduced to simpler forms, and he advocated using such forms that were already in popular use as the accepted standard for writing Chinese.[6] Furthermore, he proposed to create new simplified characters: "existent simplified characters are not many, and we should . . . create many more simplified characters . . . so that the thousands of most frequently used characters, aside from those that have few strokes to start with, will all have simple forms."[7]

THE STORY BEYOND

Qián Xuántóng's arguments

In his "Bill to simplify and reduce the strokes of the currently used characters (减省现行汉字的笔画案/減省現行漢字的筆畫案 *Jiǎnshěng xiànxíng hànzì de bǐhuà àn*)" before the Preparatory Committee for Unifying the National Language (国语统一筹备委员会/國語統一籌備委員會 *Guóyǔ Tǒngyī Chóubèi Wěiyuánhuì*), Qián Xuántóng said,

> Script is originally a tool. Whether the tool is suitable for utilization should be based on the standard of its quality. Characters with many strokes are hard to write and are a waste of time, and thus are naturally unsuitable for use. Characters with fewer strokes are easier to write and save time, and thus are naturally suitable for use.

He pointed out that reducing the strokes in characters had been a constant trend since the earliest use of the Chinese writing system:

> From (the carved script of) oracle bones, to the bronze inscriptions, to the characters collected in *Explanations of Simple and Compound Graphs* (说文解字/說文解字 *Shuōwén Jiězì*, 100 CE), the number of strokes in characters were often reduced. Since the *Sòng* (960–1279) and *Yuán* (1206–1368) dynasties, people reduced the number of the strokes of the running script and created a simplified script (so-called 俗体/俗體 *sútǐ* 'popular script'). Over several thousand years, the strokes of characters have been reduced constantly.[8]

He also argued for the use of folk characters as the official standard:

> Since the *Míng* and *Qīng* dynasties, this kind of simplified characters, which circulates among the masses, was used in bookkeeping, pawn receipts, medical prescriptions, (vernacular) novels, and libretti for ballad singers (唱本 *chàngběn*); all the usages that are said to be not presentable (不登大雅之堂 *bù dēng dà yǎ zhī táng*). Now we should make every effort to promote these simplified characters and formally use them in education, literature, and art, as well as in scholarship and politics. We do not think that simplified characters are the unofficial style but instead they are the reformed style of the currently used characters. It is like our attitude toward vernacular literature: we do not think that vernacular literature is vulgar and shallower than Classical literature; it is a beautiful literature more advanced than the works written in Classical Chinese.[9]

With support from Chiang Kai-shek (蒋介石/蔣介石 1887–1975), president of the Republic of China (ROC), Qián in 1934 compiled a collection of about 2,400 simplified characters from a variety of sources: folk characters in popular use, folk characters used in Classical novels, characters simplified in cursive and running scripts, and variant characters in early dictionaries and stone inscriptions.[10] Based on Qián's work, in 1935, the Nationalist government in *Nánjīng*[11] put forth an official *First Set of Simplified Characters* (第一批简体字表/第一批檢體字表 *Dìyī Pī Jiǎntǐ Zì Biǎo*), which contained 324 folk characters. Due to strong objection from some conservative members of the government,[12] however, this list was abolished the next year. Nonetheless, research on character simplification received significant attention among the educational circles,[13] and reference materials on a simplified script were published, including a *Simplified Character Dictionary* (简体字典/簡體字典 *Jiǎntǐ Zìdiǎn*) containing 4,445 characters, a *Collection of Commonly Used Simplified Characters* (常用简字表/常用簡字表 *Chángyòng Jiǎnzì Biǎo*) with 3,150 characters,[14] and, in 1937, a collection called *Simplified Characters: the First List* (简体字表第一表/簡體字表第一表 *Jiǎntǐzì Biǎo: Dì Yī Biǎo*) with 1,700 characters.[15] Later that year, the Second Sino-Japanese War[16] (1937–1945) broke out.

THE STORY BEYOND

Liberated characters

During the Second Sino-Japanese War, efforts to simplify the Chinese script continued in areas controlled by the Communist Party, the so-called liberated areas (解放区/解放區 *jiěfàng qū*). A large number of simplified characters were used in books, newspapers, and other printed materials circulated within the *jiěfàng qū* Below are a few examples (traditional characters in parentheses):[17]

拥 (擁 *yōng*), 护 (護 *hù*), 卫 (衛 *wèi*), 胜 (勝 *shèng*), 运 (運 *yùn*)

动 (動 *dòng*), 艺 (藝 *yì*), 习 (習 *xí*), 团 (團 *tuán*)

These characters all have their origin in calligraphy works by the *Táng* dynasty master Yán Zhēnqīng (颜真卿 709–785). As the war ended, the use of the *jiěfàng qū* characters spread to the rest of the country and gained the nickname *jiěfàng zì* (解放字), "liberated characters."[18]

After the founding of the PRC in 1949, the ROC government in *Táiwān* eventually decided to maintain the traditional script that continued to be used till this day. This decision, however, appeared to have been based more on political than linguistic concerns. In fact, in 1952, Chiang Kai-shek reopened the subject of character simplification and a committee was set up to conduct research on this topic. The initiative had significant support from the public,[19] but the idea again met with strong objection from some conservative members of the legislature.[20] By the time when the PRC government on the Mainland had successfully implemented their script reform, the issue of character simplification quickly became politicized for Táiwān. The Republic government decided to maintain the traditional script, taking a position clearly opposing that of the Mainland government.

THE STORY BEYOND

Táiwān's shift in attitude toward script simplification

The PRC government pushed forward their writing reform and published an official list of simplified characters in 1956. This caused script simplification, an issue originally supported by both the Nationalists and the Communists, to become highly politicized. Chiang Kai-shek and his government changed their attitude, as the Taiwanese scholar Lin An-wu (林安梧 1957–) explained:

> Because our political opponent promoted the simplified style, we [had no choice but to] advocate the traditional script. In philosophical terms, we were on the opposing side of the enemy, the "passive" side. We were the slaves of the powerful "active" side and were forced to take the opposing position.

Chiang Kai-shek stopped advocating for character simplification. In fact, anyone who dared to do so would have been labeled a "red hat" and considered a collaborator of the Communists.[21]

Script simplification by the PRC (1950s–1980s)

Character simplification

Over the long history of changes that happened to the Chinese character inventory, although the number of symbols grew as new characters were created and added to the pool, the number of strokes within characters decreased overall. This was because, as the amount of writing activities increased, simplicity and ease of writing became more and more important. Consequently, characters containing fewer strokes were usually preferred in major script reforms and style changes. When the First Emperor, Qínshǐhuáng (秦始皇 259–210 BCE), took measures to standardize the script to be used across the newly unified China, among the existent styles, character forms with fewer strokes were generally adopted to form the so-called small seal script (小篆 xiǎozhuàn),[22] the official script of the Qín (秦) dynasty. For example, Figure 15.1 shows four variant forms of the character for "cart," the modern 车/車 (chē) character, in oracle bone and bronze inscriptions. The simplest form (i.e., the character on the far left) was eventually adopted with revision as the standard form in the small seal script.[23] Characters of the small seal script were further simplified when the clerical script (隶书/隸書 lìshū) was created as an unofficial style to meet the increased demand in administrative record keeping. The clerical style was much faster to write and eventually became the official script of the Hàn (汉/漢) dynasty, the dynasty following the Qín. From the clerical script came the cursive script (草书/草書 cǎoshū), the standard script (楷书/楷書 kǎishū), and the running script (行书/行書 xíngshū). The cursive and running styles continued the trend to simplify character forms by connecting or omitting certain strokes while writing in a more fluid manner.

FIGURE 15.1 Four variants of the character 车 in oracle bone and bronze inscriptions
Source: Adapted from Seybolt and Chiang (1979, p. 8)

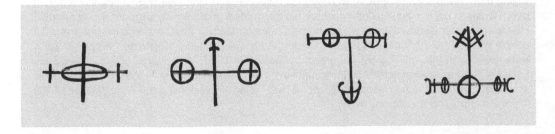

Initiatives to reform the Chinese script in the modern era continued the historical trend to simplify the character forms. As you may recall from the previous chapter, the PRC government began its work on writing reform as soon as it was officially formed. In October 1949, with Máo Zédōng's support, the Chinese Writing Reform Association (中国文字改革协会/中國文字改革協會 *Zhōngguó Wénzì Gǎigé Xiéhuì*) was established. Its initial focus was to devise a phonographic script for Chinese. However, script simplification soon became one of the key components of the overall writing reform, and new committees were set up within the government to head the relevant research and development efforts. Eventually, in 1954, the Committee for Chinese Writing Reform (中国文字改革委员会/中國文字改革委員會 *Zhōngguó Wénzì Gǎigé Wěiyuánhuì*) was created under direct supervision of the State Council (国务院/國務院 *Guówùyuàn*) as an organ to oversee the various aspects of script simplification. In 1985, it was renamed to State Language and Writing Work Committee (*Guójiā Yǔyán Wénzì Gōngzuò Wěiyuánhuì* 国家语言文字工作委员会/國家語言文字工作委員會). The change of name signaled the end of major reform work, though the Committee remained directly under the State Council. Finally, in 1994, it became part of the Ministry of Education.

Although the central government of the PRC was the chief promoter and architect of the writing reform, simplification of the Chinese characters, at least in its early stage, was not entirely a top-down endeavor. The Committee actively sought and considered input from the general public, who also took it seriously to participate in the process. In 1955, the Committee issued its *Plan for Simplifying Chinese Characters (Draft)* (汉字简化方案草案/漢字簡化方案草案 *Hànzì Jiǎnhuà Fāng'àn Cǎoàn*) and invited feedback from various groups and agencies. Within half a year, it received more than 5,000 letters or written opinions, and about 200,000 people of varied educational levels took part in the discussion.[24] In 1956, the State Council published the revised *Plan for Simplifying Chinese Characters* (汉字简化方案/漢字簡化方案 *Hànzì Jiǎnhuà Fāng'àn*).

THE STORY BEYOND

Political debate

The reform efforts started off among heated debate and intense controversy characterized by the political sensitivity of that time. One prominent scholar and critic of the reform, Chén Mèngjiā (陈梦家/陳夢家 1911–1966), commented, "[People] have opposing views but do not dare express them." Verbal exchanges between those involved were deeply emotional. Because of his criticism, Chén Mèngjiā was charged with "portraying the new China as a cold, dense forest that is dark and without the light of day" and accused of "appealing only to emotions in attacking people, of fearing disorder and hating Marxism." Another critic, Guān Xī (关西/關西), expressed his concern by saying that "[even Chairman Mao] who was not a specialist in language and writing studies [had been deceived by] the vigorous propaganda that the masses unanimously support writing reform." His view was criticized as a "rude accusation of Chairman Mao. . . [that] exceeds the limits of what people will endure."[25] Some critics of the script reform were labeled "Rightists," and their views were silenced in the Anti-Rightist Campaign by the end of 1957. In January 1958, Premier Zhōu Ēnlái (周恩来) gave a speech, "The immediate tasks in writing reform (当前文字改革的任务/當前文字改革的任務 *Dāngqián wénzì gǎigé de rènwù*)," officially endorsing the simplification of the Chinese script. The debate was over.

To what extent are the simplified characters simplified? The 1956 *Plan* consisted of 515 simplified characters and 54 simplified **radicals**.[26] Before simplification, the 515 characters averaged 16.8 strokes per character; after simplification, they averaged 8.16 strokes per character, a 49% reduction.[27] Of course, this effect will be less pronounced when measured in a regular text that contains not all simplified characters. In an article of 2,258 characters, for example, it was found that simplified characters reduced the total number of strokes by 22.6%.[28] This percentage may also change depending on the type of the text measured. An alternative measure that can be informative is to look at the 2,000 most frequently used characters. For these characters, simplification reduced the average number of strokes per character from 11.2 to 9.8 by 12.5%.[29]

How different is the "simplified script" from the "traditional script"? This question may not be easy to answer. The 1956 *Plan* contained 54 simplified radicals that would generate a great number of characters simplified by analogy, but it was not clear which characters specifically should be simplified in that manner. For example, the radical 廣 (*guǎng*) was simplified as 广, and by analogy, the characters 礦, 曠, and 鄺 (all pronounced *kuàng*) would be simplified as 矿, 旷, and 邝. Were there other characters containing 廣, such as 爌 (*huǎng*) and 橫 (*huǎng*), that should also be simplified? Questions like this did not have clear answers, because the work to further spell out the simplified character forms was not done until about a decade later. In 1964, the Committee published a *General Table of Simplified Characters* (简化字总表/簡化字總表 *Jiǎnhuàzì Zǒngbiǎo*) on the basis of the 1956 *Plan*, and "the simplification of Chinese characters became an accomplished fact."[30] The *General Table* was reissued with slight revisions in 1986 and contained a total of 2,235 simplified characters (two less than the 1964 publication) divided into three categories. Table 15.1 provides a few examples (traditional characters in parentheses) for each of them.

Table 15.1 Examples from the 1986 General Table of Simplified Characters

Chart	Examples
Chart 1: 350 independent simplified characters that cannot be used as combinatory elements to form other characters	办 (辦), 标 (標), 才 (纔), 奋 (奮), 护 (護), 烂 (爛), 灭 (滅), 台 (台, 臺, 檯, 颱)
Chart 2: 132 independent characters and 14 radicals that can also be used as elements to form other simplified characters	爱 (愛), 尔 (爾), 丰 (豐), 几 (幾), 门 (門), 亲 (親), 义 (義), 与 (與) 讠 (言), 饣 (食), 纟 (糸), 钅 (金)
Chart 3: 1,753 characters simplified by analogy based on the second chart	迩 (邇), 弥 (彌), 祢 (禰), 玺 (璽), 猕 (獼) 讥 (譏), 叽 (嘰), 饥 (饑), 机 (機), 玑 (璣)

Do the 2,000-plus simplified characters in the 1964/1986 *General Table* represent the difference between the simplified and the traditional scripts? The answer may be yes and no. The *General Table*, though much more elaborate than the 1956 *Plan*, was still not an exhaustive list of all simplified characters. In particular, Chart 3 provided characters in simplified forms only within the coverage of the *Xīnhuá Zìdiǎn* (新华字典/新華字典 *New China Dictionary*), 1962 edition, which contained about 8,000 characters. Given that the total number of Chinese characters might be in the range of 80,000 to 100,000, there was little doubt that more simplified characters existed beyond those in the *General Table* if we were to apply the simplification mechanisms consistently to the entire inventory of Chinese characters. On the other hand, the 8,000 or so characters in the *Xīnhuá Zìdiǎn* were sufficient for most reading and writing purposes in Modern Standard Chinese. Beyond that, a great portion of characters was variant or archaic forms found mostly in works of Classical Chinese. Simplification of these characters might not serve great practical purpose. For instance, in the aforementioned example, 爌 (*huǎng*) and 橫 (*huǎng*) were archaic variants of modern-day characters 晃 (*huǎng* 'bright') and 幌 (*huǎng* 'curtain'). Their simplified forms, based on the *Plan* or the *General Table*, should contain the 广 instead of the 廣 component. However, such forms did not seem to exist.[31] For written communication in Modern Standard Chinese, the 2,235 simplified characters in the *General Table* might be all that were necessary and might well represent the difference between the simplified and the traditional script. If we take the 8,000 as the base, then this distinction is at about 27%.

After the 1956 *Plan* and between the 1964 *General Table* and its 1986 reissuance, the Committee issued a *Second Plan for Chinese Character Simplification (Draft)* (第二次汉字简化方案草案/第二次漢字簡化方案草案 *Dìèrcì Hànzì Jiǎnhuà Fāngàn Cǎoàn*) in 1977. The draft contained a total of 853 characters organized in the same categories of the 1964 *General Table*. This plan did not receive popular support, however. The general opinion was that the characters had been oversimplified so as to lose visual connections with their traditional counterparts and to appear difficult to distinguish from each other in reading. The *Second Plan* was eventually abolished in 1986, soon after which the 1964 *General Table* was reissued to reaffirm its status as the standard set of simplified characters.

One major criticism against character simplification, from the time when script reform was proposed until this day, was the potential loss of the "cultural history" encoded in the characters. An example critics often cite is the character 愛 (*ài*) for "love." Its simplified counterpart 爱 (*ài*), as they point out, no longer contains the component 心 (*xīn*) that represents "heart." "Heartless love" thus becomes one of the representative cases for the "lack of logic" in script simplification. Supporters of the reform point to the fact that the character 爱 is not a modern invention; rather, it is a folk character that has been in use for thousands of years before the script reform, and the reform simply gives it an official status. In fact, most of the simplified characters either have or are related to a character that has historical roots. Among the 2,235 simplified characters of the *General Table*, 521 are basic simplified characters, and the rest is simplified by analogy from the 521 basic forms. About 79% of the 521 basic characters are historical forms, and only about 21% are created after the founding of the PRC (Table 15.2).

Table 15.2 Historical roots of the 521 basic simplified characters[32]

Number (percentage) of characters	Period	Examples (traditional characters in parentheses)
67 characters (13%)	Pre-*Qín* (before 221 BCE)	布 (佈), 才 (纔)
92 characters (18%)	*Qín* and *Hàn* dynasties (221 BCE - 220 CE)	碍 (礙), 办 (辦)
32 characters (6%)	Three Kingdoms, *Jìn*, and Northern and Southern dynasties (220–589 CE)	爱 (愛), 笔 (筆)
29 characters (6%)	*Suí*, *Táng* and Five Dynasties (581–960 CE)	参 (參), 蚕 (蠶)
80 characters (15%)	*Sòng*, *Liáo*, *Jīn* and *Yuán* dynasties (960–1368 CE)	边 (邊), 标 (標)

Table 15.2 Continued

Number (percentage) of characters	Period	Examples (traditional characters in parentheses)
53 characters (10%)	*Míng* and *Qīng* dynasties (1368–1911 CE)	罢 (罷), 表 (錶)
57 characters (11%)	Republic of China (1911–1949)	袄 (襖), 坝 (壩)
111 characters (21%)	People's Republic of China (1949–1956 when the *Plan for Simplifying Chinese Characters* was published)	肮脏 (骯髒), 拥护 (擁護)

Important sources of simplified characters also include folk characters and characters written in the cursive style. See Tables 15.3 and 15.4 for a few examples.

Table 15.3 Examples of folk characters

Traditional character	Simplified/folk character	*Pīnyīn*	Meaning
萬	万	wàn	'ten thousand'
塵	尘	chén	'dust'
體	体	tǐ	'body'
竈	灶	zào	'stove'
寶	宝	bǎo	'treasure'
膚	肤	fū	'skin'
蠶	蚕	cán	'silkworm'

Table 15.4 Characters simplified based on the cursive script

Traditional character	Simplified character	*Pīnyīn*	Meaning
門	门	mén	'door'
為	为	wéi	'to do'
車	车	chē	'vehicle'
東	东	dōng	'east'
發	发	fà	'hair'
會	会	huì	'to meet'
盡	尽	jìn	'to exhaust'

Character set reduction

This aspect of script simplification might be less known because its impact on the day-to-day use of characters was less conspicuous. Learning about the related issues, however, may help us better understand the nature of the Chinese writing system at the macro level.

How many Chinese characters are there? If you recall, we considered this question in Chapter 7. Adding to the earlier discussion, a look at the number of characters recorded in Chinese dictionaries (Table 15.5) reveals that the size of the character set has expanded dramatically through history. The largest dictionary contains more than 100,000 characters – a mind-boggling number if we consider that alphabetical writing systems typically contain 20 to 50 symbols or even the fact that only 3,000 to 4,000 characters are needed for basic literacy.

Table 15.5 Number of characters in major dictionaries[33]

Dictionary	Number of characters	Period	Date
Cāngjiépiān, Yuánlìpiān, Bóxuépiān	3,300	*Qín*	221–206 BCE
Shuōwén Jiězì	9,535	Eastern *Hàn*	100 CE
Yùpiān	16,917	*Liáng*	543
Guǎngyùn	26,149	Northern *Sòng*	1011
Hóngwǔ Zhèngyùn	32,200	*Míng*	1375
Kāngxī Zìdiǎn	47,043	*Qīng*	1716
Zhōnghuá Dà Zìdiǎn	48,000	ROC	1916
Xiàndài Hànyǔ Dà Zìdiǎn	56,000	PRC	1986–1990
Zhōnghuá Zìhǎi	85,568	PRC	1994
Yìtǐzì Zìdiǎn	106, 333	ROC	2000

This excessiveness may lie in a few factors. First of all, the nature of the writing system determines that the character set is an open one. Chinese characters represent morphemes. Because the number of morphemes is infinite, the number of characters, in theory, is also limitless. When new ideas or concepts occurred, new characters were often created in order to represent them. Another reason was the lack of standardization. It was not uncommon for a character used in different geographical areas or in different time periods to have somewhat different forms. These graphic variants of the same character, called *yìtǐ zì* (异体字/異體字 'variant style character'), make up for a significant portion of the character inventory, and some characters may have multiple *yìtǐ zì*. In *Shuōwén Jiězì* (100 CE), for example, about 89% were distinctive characters, and the remaining 11% were variant forms. Forty percent of the characters in the *Kāngxī Dictionary* (1716) were *yìtǐ zì*.[34] In the modern dictionary *Cíhǎi* (1979 edition), the percentage of variant forms recorded was 27%.[35] *Yìtǐ Zì Zìdiǎn*, the dictionary that has the greatest number of characters in Table 15.5, is in fact a dictionary specialized in documenting variant forms. Seventy percent of characters collected in its sixth edition are *yìtǐ zì*.

The large number of characters in active use today may also be a result of the variation in **register** employed in speech and in writing. Although we say that the Chinese writing system represents the speech of Modern Standard Chinese, in writing, the delineation between Modern Standard Chinese and Classical Chinese can be rather fuzzy. Expressions from Classical Chinese are often mixed in modern text to make it sound more formal. As a result, words that are particular to Classical Chinese are also part of today's Chinese lexicon and written symbols used to represent such words, as well, are part of the character inventory.

It is often desirable and, in some cases, necessary to put a limit on the number of characters. First of all, there are psychological constraints as to how many characters human users may realistically store for active recall from memory. This number has been suggested to be somewhere between 7,000 to 8,000.[36] Limiting the number of characters used is also feasible, since not all characters are used with equal frequency (Table 15.6). In fact, in non-specialized publications, the 1,000 most frequently used characters constitute about 90% of all the characters used. Adding the next 1,400 most frequently used characters would increase this coverage rate to 99%. This means that if the reader only knows the 2,400 high-frequency characters, she would encounter one new character in about every hundred on average in non-technical reading. Consistent with these numbers, criterion for achieving literacy in Chinese is set at about 2,000 characters, and elementary school graduates are expected to know about 2,500 characters.[37]

Table 15.6 Coverage rate of most frequently used characters in writing Modern Standard Chinese[38]

Number of characters	Coverage rate
500	80%
1,000	91%
2,400	99%
3,800	99.9%
5,200	99.99%
6,600	99.999%

Computer processing of Chinese text also makes it necessary to limit the number of characters used. The list of characters provided to computers must be a finite one. The *Basic Collection of Character Coding Graphs in Exchange of Information* (信息交换汉字标码字符集基本集/信息交換漢字標碼字符集基本集 *Xìnxī Jiāohuàn Hànzì Biāomǎ Zìfú Jí Jīběn Jí*, GB 2312–80) published in Mainland China in 1981 contained 6,763 characters, and the *Standardized Character Exchange Code for General Use* (通用汉字标准交换码/通用漢字標準交換碼 *Tōngyòng Hànzì Biāozhǔn Jiāohuàn Mǎ*) published in *Táiwān* two years later included 13,051 characters. These numbers have been increasing, however. Unicode 10.0, the current computing industry standard for handling text, defines a total of 87,882 "CJK unified characters" (characters shared in representing Chinese, Japanese, and Korean).[39]

Official efforts were made to limit the number of characters in use. As part of the script reform, such efforts mainly consisted of eliminating variant characters. After the National Conference on Script Reform in 1955 (全国文字改革会议/全國文字改革會議 *Quánguó Wénzì Gǎigé Huìyì*), the government published a list of 810 characters with variants and proclaimed that the variants, 1,053 in total, be eliminated. For instance, the character 并 (*bìng*) was chosen to be the standard form, and its variants 並, 竝, and 併 were abolished. The character 杯 (*bēi*) replaced its variant forms 盃 and 桮. The character 酬 (*chóu*) was chosen as the standard to replace its variants 酧, 詶, and 醻.[40] Elimination of the variant forms was the first major step of the script reform and a step taken before the character forms were simplified.

After the script reform, more recent efforts were to standardize the most frequently used portion of the character set. In 1988, the Mainland promulgated the *List of Generally Used Characters of Modern Chinese* (现代汉语通用字表/現代漢語通用字表 *Xiàndài Hànyǔ Tōngyòng Zìbiǎo*), which contained 7,000 characters, the most frequent 3,500 of which constituted the *List of Frequently Used Characters of Modern Chinese* (现代汉语常用字表/現代漢

語常用字表 *Xiàndài Hànyǔ Chángyòng Zìbiǎo*).[41] In 2013, the PRC government, on the basis of previous work, published a new *List of Standardized Characters for General Use* (规范汉字表/規範漢字表 *Guīfàn Hànzì Biǎo*). This list contains 8,105 characters, including 3,500 most frequently used ones for elementary and literacy education, 3,000 frequently used characters for publishing, lexicography, and information processing, and 1,605 less frequent characters for personal names, place names, science and technological terminology, and study of Classical Chinese at elementary and secondary schools.[42]

THE STORY BEYOND

Limit of character use in Japan and South Korea

In Japan, elementary school students are expected to learn 996 *kanji* by the time they graduate, and in South Korea, high school students learn up to 1,800 *hanja*.[43] Limitations as such are workable partly because *kana*, the Japanese moraic script, and *hangeul*, the Korean alphabet, are fully able to write Japanese or Korean without the use of Chinese characters. *Kanji* or *hanja*, however, may be used to disambiguate homophones.

▮ International impact

Since the 1970s, the simplified script has gained increasing prominence in Chinese-speaking regions outside of China and in other areas of the world. In 1971, the People's Republic of China replaced the Republic of China (*Táiwān*) as the official representative of China at the United Nations (UN). The simplified script has since then served as the UN's official writing system for Chinese. Singapore implemented script simplification of its own in 1969, but in 1974, the country officially adopted the PRC's version of simplified script (which was different from the original Singaporean version). Similarly, Malaysia also adopted the simplified characters of the PRC in the early 1980s. Today, the traditional script is still used as the only official Chinese script in *Táiwān*, Hong Kong, and Macau. Schools in these regions use traditional characters exclusively. Schools in Singapore and Malaysia use the simplified characters exclusively though the use of traditional characters is not officially discouraged. Literacy rates of regions using the Chinese script, traditional or simplified, are consistently high: as of the late 2010s, adult (15+ years) literacy rates in Mainland China, Hong Kong, Macau, and *Táiwān* are 96%–99%, and youth (15–24 years) literacy rates are all above 99%.[44] Chinese as an Additional Language curricula in the United States has gone through a transition from the traditional to the simplified script, and almost all of them now teach the simplified script with some offering the traditional script as an option to students.[45]

The language and script reform in the PRC from the 1950s to the 1980s reshaped the linguistic reality in Mainland China. Today, most educated Chinese speak *pǔtōnghuà* (i.e., Mandarin or Modern Standard Chinese) in addition to their local dialects,[46] read and write simplified Chinese characters (and many are also proficient in reading the traditional script), and use *pīnyīn* in their day-to-day life. Mandarin, the simplified script, and *pīnyīn* are also taught to and used by an increasing number of Chinese learners outside of China. Although there was much debate on the Romanization and simplification of the Chinese script earlier in the 20th century, as we have learned in the previous chapters, that debate appears to have been largely settled.

Notes

1 Zhou (1961, p. 321).
2 Ibid., p. 321.
3 Ibid.
4 Ibid.
5 Zhou (2003, p. 60).
6 Ibid., pp. 60–61.
7 Zhou (1961, pp. 322–323).
8 Zhou (2003, pp. 60–61).
9 Ibid., p. 61.
10 Qian (1999, pp. 471–472); cited by Yang (2015).
11 The *Nánjīng* government escaped to *Táiwān* after the defeat by the Communist Party in the late 1940s, and the Republic of China continued to exist in *Táiwān* until this day.
12 See Renmin chuban she (1956, p. 36) and Zhang, Wang, Li, and An (1997, p. 10). The senior Nationalist Party official Dài Jìtáo (戴季陶, 1891–1949) is often cited as the leading conservative against script simplification.
13 Zhou (2003, p. 61).
14 Yang (2015).
15 Zhou (1961, p. 326).
16 Commonly referred to in China as "Anti-Japanese War" (*Kàngrì Zhànzhēng* 抗日战争/抗日戰爭)
17 Zhang et al. (1997, pp. 100–110).
18 Zhou (1961, p. 326).
19 A poll conducted by the *United Daily News* in 1954 found that 60% (7,315) of those participated (12,122) were supportive of simplifying the writing system. See Yang (2015).
20 Zhang et al. (1997, p. 18); cited by Yang (2015). Also see Renmin chuban she (1956, p. 36).
21 Translated from He and Jiao (2014, p. 118).
22 See Chapter 7 for a brief discussion of the script styles in Chinese writing.
23 This example is from Seybolt and Chiang (1979, p. 8).
24 Wang (2009). Also see Seybolt and Chiang (1979, p. 2).
25 All quotes in this "Story Beyond" are from Seybolt and Chiang (1979, p. 4).
26 Radicals, or "section headers" (部首 *bùshǒu*) in the character index of a Chinese dictionary, are seen as graphic roots for generating characters.
27 Zhou (1961, p. 341).
28 Ibid., p. 341.
29 Ibid., p. 341.
30 Seybolt and Chiang (1979, p. 11).
31 A search for the simplified forms yielded no results from the Chinese character set in macOS Sierra 10.12.6.
32 These examples are from Zhou (2003, pp. 66–67).
33 Adapted from Chen (1999, p. 135), with new entries added.
34 Ibid., p. 148.
35 Zhou (2003, p. 75).
36 Ibid., pp. 76–77.

37 Chen (1999, p. 136).

38 Adapted from ibid., p. 137, Table 8.2.

39 https://en.wikipedia.org/wiki/CJK_Unified_Ideographs.

40 Zhou (2003, p. 62).

41 Ibid., p. 79.

42 The State Council (2013).

43 1,600 according to Zhou (2003, p. 80)

44 See Central Intelligence Agency. (n.d.), Hong Kong Council of Social Service. (n.d.), UNESCO Institute for Statistics. (n.d.), and Ministry of Foreign Affairs, Republic of China (*Táiwān*) (2011, February 21).

45 Xing (2006, p. 105): "For programs in teaching and learning Chinese as FL outside China, the simplified version has gradually gained ground and become the first choice because of student demand."

46 The majority of Chinese speak a local dialect that is different from *pǔtōnghuà*.

The script reformers in early 20th century, for instance, felt a desperate need in a Chinese dictionary. You may recall that we have in an earlier chapter discussed some of the efforts that mounted into the Chinese writing system. Here we examine the relationship in the past [...]

16 Writing and technology in modern China

I N RECENT HISTORY, THE Chinese writing system was perceived as a major impediment to the modernization of the nation when most of the Chinese citizens were unable to read and write. In an earlier chapter, we reviewed a few of the multitude of proposals put forth during the late 19th to the mid-20th centuries for writing Chinese using alternative, phonographic scripts. These proposals signified a crisis of the Chinese script against the backdrop of a nation struggling to remake herself in an increasingly globalized world. The low literacy rate, however, was not the only concern the script reformers had during that time. Another major challenge was the difficulty the character-based writing system created in developing and using modern technology to acquire, organize, process, transmit, retrieve, and translate through machines or electronic devices information coded in the Chinese script. In this chapter, we will, without getting into the technological details, discuss two of these challenges and the debates around them: ordering information and inputting Chinese text on computers.

Ordering information

Have you ever thought about how textual information in the English language can be ordered? A good example to consider is the conventional dictionary. To English users, looking up a word in a physical dictionary is a fairly straightforward process. Word entries are typically arranged in the alphabetical order *a–z*: words with the first letter *a* come before words with the first letter *b*; among words with the initial letter *a*, those with the second letter *a* come before those with the second letter *b*; and so on. To find a word, one simply follows this logic to locate the string of letters that corresponds to the first letter, and then the second, the third, until one finds the whole word. The knowledge of the alphabetical order, for native readers, is usually learned in childhood – perhaps with the aid of a little song – and is generally a painless and insignificant process. When applied to sorting words, the alphabetical order ensures that the sequencing in the outcome is strict and consistent. That is, any two words are reliably sorted in the same order under the alphabetical rule regardless of who is doing the sorting or for what purpose.

Companion Website

Exercise 16.1 Alphabetical ordering of English words: an artificial example

---

The same cannot always be said, however, for looking up for a character in a Chinese dictionary. You may recall that we have already talked about this in Chapter 7, when we first introduced you to the Chinese writing system. Here we will elaborate a little more on this topic.

First of all, it is important to note again that most modern Chinese dictionaries list characters in the alphabetical order based on the *pīnyīn* notation of the characters' pronunciation. If you know how a character is pronounced, then looking it up is almost as straightforward as consulting an English dictionary. However, there may be a couple of complications: one, the same syllable may occur in various tones. Characters sharing the same *pīnyīn* spelling are usually arranged in the order of neutral (e.g., *ma*), first (*mā*), second (*má*), third (*mǎ*), and fourth (*mà*) tones. So, if you know which tone the target character has, it will be easier to locate it. Another complication is that the same syllable bearing the same tone may be represented by more than one (and as many as 167![1]) characters. These characters cannot be differentiated by their sounds and therefore must be arranged based on their forms. In particular, it is the number of strokes in the characters that counts: characters with fewer strokes come before those with more strokes. For example, 马 玛 码 蚂 are all pronounced *mǎ*. They are likely arranged in this order in relation to each other because 马 (3) has the fewest strokes, 玛 (7) has more, 码 (8) even more, and 蚂 (9) the greatest number of them all. If you know what the character looks like, counting the strokes will help you get to it faster. Otherwise, you will need to patiently go through the list of homophones until you find the character that matches the one you are looking for.

The process gets much more complicated when you only know what a character looks like and wish to find out its pronunciation and meaning by looking it up in a dictionary. In this scenario, all we have to rely on is the graphic form of the character. As we discussed in Chapter 7, we must understand how characters are categorized in a dictionary based on section headers (部首 *bùshǒu*) or radicals, that is, recurring elements in characters that are often (but not always) indicative of the characters' rough semantic category. Table 16.1 shows a few more examples.

Table 16.1   Examples of a few radicals

Radicals	Sample characters		
氵 'water'	河 *hé* 'river'	淹 *yān* 'to submerge'	渴 *kě* 'thirsty'
扌 'hand'	指 *zhǐ* 'finger'	打 *dǎ* 'to hit'	折 *zhé* 'to fold'
辶 'walk'	边/邊 *biān* 'edge'	达/達 *dá* 'to arrive'	远/遠 *yuǎn* 'far'

Let us review the process of locating a character based on its graphic form in a conventional dictionary. Suppose we want to find out the pronunciation of the first character in Table 16.1, 河. We will need to first locate its section header in the radical index. The **radical index** is a list of section headers arranged based on their number of strokes. Radicals with fewer strokes come before radicals that have more strokes. In this case, the radical for the character 河 is 氵, which has three strokes. We can find this radical in the three-stroke section of the radical index. The radical index leads us to a page number that points to the 氵 section of the character index. The **character index** is a list of characters arranged by radical. Here we see a list of all characters that have the 氵 radical. These characters are arranged by the number of strokes of the whole character lest the number of strokes of the radical. In our case, if we take 氵 out of 河, the remaining part 可 has five strokes. Thus, we look for the five-stroke subsection within the 氵 section of the character index. Here, we most likely see more than one character: 沫, 泄, 沽 . . . until we find 河, with a page number attached to it. We turn to that page of the dictionary and will be able to locate the entry 河 *hé* 'river.'

As you see, the radical indexing method is much more cumbersome than alphabetical indexing. What's more, it is not guaranteed that any given character can be located this way. There are characters that do not contain a radical that is easy to identify or is among the list of the 200 or so section headers. For these characters, the dictionary may have a supplemental list in which the characters are arranged solely by the number of strokes. For example, the *Contemporary Chinese Dictionary*, 5th edition,[2] has such a list with 491 characters in it, including both single-component characters (e.g., 丁 *dīng*, 正 *zhèng*, and 或 *huò*) and compound characters (e.g., 就 *jiù*, 靠 *kào*, and 赢 *yíng*).

THE STORY BEYOND

O friend, where art thou?

The complexity in ordering information pertains not only to Chinese lexicography, but also to other large databases that require information to be sorted in order to facilitate its retrieval. Some examples are store inventories, library catalogues, and hotel registrations. The Sinologist Victor Mair related an anecdote that might be particularly revealing in this respect.[3] In likely the late 1980s, before the cell phone era or even the wide availability of landlines in China, Mair went to visit friends who lived in an apartment complex of about 10,000 residents – typical of the Chinese "living districts" (生活小区/生活小區 *shēnghuó xiǎoqū* 'apartment complexes') of that time. The workers at the housing office had great difficulties locating his friends' names. "The files were not arranged in any logical fashion that is intended to facilitate finding one out of 10,000."[4] Eventually, he had to give up seeing his friends.

It has been argued that the challenge in ordering information that the Chinese writing system poses may hold the answer to the well-known "Needham Question."[5] The British Sinologist Joseph Needham (李约瑟/李約瑟 1900–1995), after carefully studying and documenting the history of Chinese science and technology and its influence on the West, asks: "Why, then, did modern science, as opposed to ancient and medieval science, develop only in the Western world?"[6] He deems it a puzzle that modern science did not develop in China despite the country's sustained lead over the Western world in most of the major areas of science and technology from ancient times up to the recent two or three centuries.[7] Scholars' responses to this question, for the most part, have come from considerations of social, political, and economic factors.[8] However, a few scholars have also specifically argued for the impact of the Chinese writing system.[9] The logic in their arguments seems to, at least in part, hinge on the observation that the Chinese script has made it difficult to order information and has therefore inhibited the development of taxonomy or scientific classification.[10] For example, "to understand which of the two types of script, alphabetic or ideographic, is best suited to classification, one needs only compare Western and Chinese dictionaries."[11] In traditional Chinese encyclopedias as well, because of the lack of an organizing mechanism such as alphabetization, information is often grouped into complex categories from celestial phenomena to terrestrial matters that do not aid well swift and accurate retrieval of information.[12] Arguments have also been made for the concreteness of Chinese characters[13] and the shallowness in their representation of speech.[14] All in all, the Chinese script is thought to be less conducive to abstract theoretical thinking than the alphabetical writing system. Whether such arguments can be substantiated with sufficient empirical evidence may remain a question. Nonetheless, the difficulties Chinese characters presented in the early stage of information technology were no doubt significant.

Companion Website

Exercise 16.2 Chinese characters and scientific creativity

Computer input methods

In the early age of personal computers, inputting Chinese text on a PC was one of the most challenging problems and was often referred to as "the bottleneck"[15] of Chinese information processing.[16] In fact, the challenge was so great that, by the early 1990s, despite decades of research in this area, computing in China, Japan, and Korea was still mostly done in English.[17] *Hànzì* (Chinese), *kanji* (Japanese), and *hanja* (Korean) can be collectively referred to as "*Han* characters" or "CJK unified ideographs"[18] in computer encoding. To be able to input CJK characters on a computer, the characters will first have to be encoded into bits (usually represented with the value "0" or "1"), the only form recognizable by a computer. This was, of course, also true for any other symbols used to write any other languages, but what made encoding Chinese characters much more challenging was the sheer size of the inventory. For example, the first national standard for simplified script encoding published by the PRC in 1980, also known as "GB 2312,"[19] included 6,763 characters in its Basic Set intended for ordinary use and another 14,276 in the Supplementary Set for specialized users.[20] In fact, CJK characters, since they were encoded, have constituted the majority of symbols one can possibly process on a computer. In the current version of Unicode (Version 10.0, June 2017), 87,882 out of the 136,755 symbols – that is, about 64% used in a total of 139 scripts – are CJK characters.

Once the characters had been encoded, there was still the challenge of inputting them using the keyboard. How to effectively link the tens of thousands of characters to the dozens of keys on a regular keyboard? Once it was clear that the QWERTY keyboard was becoming the industry standard, much collective and individual effort was expended in solving this particular problem in the 1970s and 1980s. By the early 1990s, more than 700 inputting schemes had been developed, "with new ones being proposed at the rate of about one per fortnight."[21]

The large number of input methods can be divided into two camps: shape-based and sound-based. The great majority of the 700-plus input schemes were of the first kind. The shape-based approach generally decomposes Chinese characters into recurring components of various sizes, from meaning-bearing radicals down to single strokes, which are then assigned letters or numerals to be keyed in on a standard keyboard. The *Wŭbĭ* (五笔/五筆, short for五笔字型/五筆字型 *Wŭbĭ Zìxíng* 'five strokes') method developed on the Mainland and *Cāngjié* (仓颉/倉頡 '(name of the mythical figure credited for the invention of the Chinese script') used in *Táiwān* and Hong Kong were among the most popular examples of this type. This approach relied solely on the graphic information of the characters, and it is particularly useful when the typist did not know how a character was pronounced. In the 1990s, when personal computers were not yet readily accessible in Mainland China, authors often took their manuscripts to professional typists and paid a fee at a per-thousand-character rate to get them processed. Invented in 1983, *Wŭbĭ* was one of the most commonly used methods by typists for inputting simplified characters. It was a configurative scheme that delegated characters to five zones on the QWERTY keyboard based on the type of their initial strokes: horizontal (一), vertical (|), down-left slant (丿), down-right slant (乀), and bent (乛). Each character was input by hitting a series of one to four keys. Professional typists favored this method because, compared to the phonetic input methods at the time, it had very low code redundancy – that is, a given string of keys almost always corresponded to a unique character – and allowed them to type at a high speed. The downside, however, was that it required significant training to develop high-level proficiency.

The most popular type of input methods today uses the sound-based approach. The *pīnyīn* method in Mainland China and the *zhùyīn* (注音, i.e., *Bopomofo*) method in *Táiwān* are both of this kind. These days, most everyone who writes in Chinese on a computer uses this kind of approach. On the Mainland, for example, students usually learn *pīnyīn* in elementary school, so most computer users can start inputting *pīnyīn* without learning any additional code. *Pīnyīn*-based input software is also the most readily available – these days they come preinstalled on Windows or Mac operating systems. In fact, *pīnyīn* became the PRC's standard for Romanized writing of Chinese around the same time as experimentation started with computer inputting of Chinese characters, and it has been the basis of the phonetic approach from the get-go.

Over the years, the accuracy and speed of *pīnyīn* input methods have improved as the technology becomes more sophisticated. First of all, replacing the syllable-based conversion mechanism with a word-based system solved the homophone problem. As previously mentioned, one major drawback of *pīnyīn*-based input methods is their relatively high code redundancy. This is because homophones abound in the Chinese language. For example, inputting the *pīnyīn* syllable *ma*[22] on a Macintosh computer using its native *pīnyīn* input method for simplified Chinese characters[23] brings out 18 characters that share the same pronunciation (tones not considered). The user will then need to pick the intended character out of this list. As one may imagine, inputting Chinese text syllable by syllable could be a rather inefficient process. In a word-based system, instead of inputting a single *pīnyīn* syllable to get a single character, users input whole words that contextualize and disambiguate homophonic characters. As a result, accuracy and speed both significantly improve. This can be accomplished because only a small minority of words in modern Chinese is monosyllabic – about 2,500 in a list of 60,000 word entries, based on one study.[24] By the early 1990s, most *pīnyīn*-character conversion systems have made use of the word-based mechanism.[25] This could be considered a new stage in the development of computer input methods for Chinese.

THE STORY BEYOND

The monosyllabic myth and its impact on character input mechanism

With the popularization of *pīnyīn* and the continuous improvement in *pīnyīn*-based character-conversion applications, the phonetic method for inputting Chinese characters has come a long way. The path it has taken, interestingly, illustrates the influence of the "monosyllabic myth," that is, the idea that Chinese words consist of single syllables. The development of the *pīnyīn*-character conversion system largely went through three stages – syllable-based, word-based, and sentence-based stages – each resulting in improved accuracy and efficiency. The fact that inputting *pīnyīn* syllable by syllable was the first solution that came to mind might indicate an implicit yet inaccurate understanding of Chinese as a monosyllabic language, the notion referred to as the "monosyllabic myth." It was a misconception perpetuated by the morphosyllabic Chinese writing system: because writing was done on a syllable-by-syllable basis and word boundaries were not marked, although the majority of words in Modern Standard Chinese contained more than one syllable, Chinese users tended to conceptualize the basic structure of the Chinese language in terms of syllables rather than words.

Since then, *pīnyīn* input methods have significantly evolved. Today, the most popular input applications among average users support sentence-length *pīnyīn* parsing. The previous generation of word-based conversion was effective in distinguishing homophonic syllables situated within polysyllabic words, but it was still helpless when the words consisted of single syllables. This problem is solved when contextual information at the sentence level is taken into account. As an example, let us look at how the standard *pīnyīn* input method on a Macintosh computer[26] handles the three *de* – 的, 地, and 得 – in Chinese (Table 16.2). Pronounced exactly the same, these three particles are represented with different characters in writing because they have different grammatical functions: roughly speaking, 的 connects a noun and its preceding modifier, 地 is used between a verb and its modifier, while 得 connects a verb (or an adjective functioning as a verb) and the complement[27] following it, all within the same phrase.

Table 16.2 The three *de* particles in Chinese

Structure			Example
Modifier	的	Noun	高兴的孩子/高興的孩子 *gāoxìng de háizi* 'happy children'
Modifier	地	Verb	高兴地跳舞/高興地跳舞 *gāoxìng de tiàowǔ* 'happily dance'
Verb/adjective	得	Complement	高兴得笑个不停/高興得笑個不停 *gāoxìng de xiào ge bùtíng* '(so) happy (as to) not stop laughing'

When we type one of the above phrases, the computer defaults to the first *de* (的) until more information is given from the word following 高兴/高興 (*gāoxìng* 'happy, happily'). At that point, the computer application adjusts accordingly to provide the correct character form. The writer can monitor the result during typing and may still need to revise a few characters here and there – "such an intermediate stage of checking and revising will always exist."[28] However, the overall accuracy has reached above 97%.[29]

In terms of efficiency, some have pointed out that typing Chinese on a computer using *pīnyīn* has become faster than English thanks to the development of increasingly sophisticated input software.[30] One particularly helpful feature of such software allows users to key in a sentence by only typing the first letter of each *pīnyīn* syllable. The letter combination usually is sufficient information for the application to "figure out" the entire sentence. For example, to type 我们明天一起吃饭好吗/我們明天一起吃飯好嗎 (*wǒmen míngtiān yìqǐ chīfàn hǎoma* 'how about we have dinner together tomorrow'), one may simply type *wmmtyqcfhm*. That is, seven letters instead of 29. And the software is intelligent enough to put together the correct sentence. This kind of "predictive text," however, is not currently an option for typing English on a QWERTY keyboard. The "what you type is what you get" approach for the English alphabet since the beginning of computers has remained unchanged, and the typing speed of English text has accordingly remained unchanged. On the other hand, many will probably agree that Chinese input methods have developed in such a way that the initial hurdles posed by the Chinese writing system have been largely overcome.

Notes

1 One hundred sixty-seven different characters are pronounced *yi* based on the *Contemporary Chinese Dictionary* (*Xiàndài hànyǔ cídiǎn* 现代汉语词典/現代漢語詞典), 5th edition, published in 2007 by the Commercial Press in Beijing.
2 Chinese Academy of Social Sciences (2007).
3 Mair (1991).
4 Ibid., p. 1.
5 For example, Logan (1986); Bodde (1991).
6 Needham (1956, p. 214).
7 Lin (1995, p. 270).
8 For example, Needham (2013) and Lin (1995).
9 Logan (1986, pp. 47–48, 54).
10 Bodde (1991), cited by Hannas (2003, p. 257).
11 Logan (1986, p. 57). Note that the Chinese writing system is referred to as "ideographic," but we know that this is not an accurate characterization. See Chapter 8.
12 Mair (1991, p. 1).
13 Logan (1986, p. 55).
14 Hannas (2003, pp. 244–262).
15 Liu (1991).
16 The term "information processing," when applied to computer science, refers to the use of algorithms to transform data on computers.
17 Mair (1991, p. 1).
18 Sometimes Vietnamese is also included in this set, thus "CJKV Unified Ideographs." The set incorporates traditional and simplified characters for writing Chinese, *kanji* for Japanese, *hanjia* for Korean, *chữ nôm* for Vietnamese, as well as phonographic scripts for these languages.
19 GB stands for 国标/國標 *guóbiāo*, a short form for 国家标准/國家標準 *guójiā biāozhǔn* 'national standard.'
20 Liu (1991, p. 10).
21 Mair (1991, p. 5).
22 Tones are usually not marked when inputting Chinese characters via *pīnyīn*.
23 The computer runs the Mac OS High Sierra operating system, version 10.13.2.

24 Zhou (1991, p. 20).

25 Yin (1991, p. 27).

26 The operating system is the same as above.

27 In Chinese grammar, a "complement" to a verb is a word or phrase that provides information about the action that the verb represents. In the example "高兴得笑个不停 (*gāoxìng de xiào ge bù tíng* 'so happy that (one) cannot stop laughing')," "笑个不停 (*xiào ge bù tíng* 'cannot stop laughing')" describes the main verb (in this case, an adjective functioning as a verb) "高兴 (*gāoxìng* 'happy')."

28 See Hannas (2003, pp. 244–262).

29 Yin (1991).

30 For example, Tom Mullaney. See Zhang (2016).

PART V

Identity and gender in writing Chinese

17 Handwriting and personhood

TO UNDERSTAND THE ROLE of handwriting in the construction of the Chinese personhood, it is useful to evoke a metaphor Yen (2005) suggests: the writing of Chinese characters, to the Chinese people, is like "a secondary face."[1] This concept can be illustrated by a Chinese saying, *rén rú qí zì, zì rú qí rén. Rén* (人) means "person, human, personhood," *rú* (如) "to resemble," *qí* (其) "his, her, its," and *zì* (字) "handwriting." Thus, "one's personhood resembles one's handwriting, and one's handwriting resembles one's personhood." That is to say, Chinese people tend to expect the inner traits of a person to align with the qualities seen in her handwriting, and vice versa. "It takes no more than one written character to reveal one's heart,"[2] said the *Táng* dynasty calligrapher Zhāng Huáiguàn (张怀瓘/張懷瓘).

人如其字，字如其人
rén rú qí zì, zì rú qí rén

Furthermore, handwriting as a secondary face is "the layer of oneself that comes directly into contact with the world."[3] In other words, one's handwriting is the part of the person that is the most easily seen or often the only part visible to others. For this reason, for instance, candidates of the civil service exams placed a premium on beautiful and elegant calligraphy, hoping to create a favorable impression on exam viewers. This tradition has carried over to today's college entrance tests and still propels student candidates to strive for graceful and mature, or at least neat, handwriting on their test papers. During the author's high school years in the 1990s, her teacher constantly urged the class to practice writing characters in their spare time, because she believed that good handwriting was crucial to creating a positive impression and that a positive impression on the test markers could sometimes make the difference between a first-tier and a second-tier university in admissions decisions. Even though the students understood those to be extreme cases, they did not dare to take the teacher's advice lightly. They practiced when they could, critiqued each other's styles, and took great care to write well on their test papers.

Handwriting and moral character

In imperial times, one's calligraphy was tied to the moral character or quality of the calligrapher.[4] The Chinese term for this concept is *rénpǐn* (人品 'character, moral standing'), in which *pǐn* (品) means "grade, class, quality."[5]

If one's *pǐn* is high, then every dot and stroke he writes is teemed with an air of purity (清 *qīng*), unbending will (刚/剛 *gāng*), elegance (雅 *yǎ*) and uprightness (正 *zhèng*).

If one's *pǐn* is low, even if his work looks impressive with deceptive vigor and strength, his untamed and flamboyant violence can nevertheless be detected.[6]

Being a moral person was the prerequisite for being a recognized calligrapher. As the late *Míng* and early *Qīng* calligrapher Fù Shān (傅山 1607–1684) said, *zuòzì xiān zuòrén*, "to write good calligraphy, one must first be a good person."

作　字　先　做　人
zuò　zì　xiān　zuò　rén

For this reason, good calligraphy did not necessarily mean beautiful calligraphy. Fù Shān famously stated that "rather than clever, beautiful, deft, and affected, I prefer being awkward, ugly, disconnected, and straightforward."[7] This preference for honest, inner beauty above pretentious, superficial beauty is deeply rooted in traditional Chinese culture.

The concept of *pǐn* describes not only the moral quality of a person, but also the quality of calligraphy works. In calligraphy *pǐn* is not necessarily beautiful execution of the lines and dots or skillful arrangement of the characters on the writing surface. Rather, it is a general quality similar to those that define a moral person – purity, elegance, and uprightness. Not surprisingly, such a quality is often believed to derive from the calligrapher. If the calligrapher is a noble person, then his work most likely possesses this quality in the perception of the viewers. If the calligrapher lacks moral character or strength, then the calligraphy she produces will not be recognized as superior works. A telling example is the infamous high-ranking official of the Northern *Sòng* dynasty, Cài Jīng (蔡京 1047–1126 CE). A highly skilled calligrapher, Cài Jīng was at one time regarded one of the four great calligraphy masters of his time, collectively known as *Sū Huáng Mǐ Cài* (苏轼/蘇軾 Sū Shì, 黄庭坚/黄庭堅 Huáng Tíngjiān, 米芾 Mǐ Fú, and at first 蔡京 Cài Jīng). He proved, however, a treacherous official whose corrupt deeds contributed to the downfall of the Northern *Sòng*. For this reason, his name was later replaced by that of Cài Xiāng (蔡襄 1012–1067 CE), a scholar-official known for his uprightness and integrity. Since then, when people speak of *Sū Huáng Mǐ Cài*, the family name Cài has changed its association to Cài Xiāng.[8]

Appreciating works of calligraphy inherently requires identifying oneself with the moral values of the calligrapher and therefore says much about one's own moral preferences. This is also why students of calligraphy are carefully selective about which calligrapher's models to emulate. They invariably select calligraphers with high moral standing, especially those with unwavering loyalty to their nation.[9] One such example is the famed *Táng* dynasty calligrapher Yán Zhēnqīng (颜真卿 709–785), who served the Xuánzōng emperor (玄宗 685–762) and his successors. As a loyal governor, he fought the revolting forces during the Ān Shǐ rebellion (安史之乱/安史之亂 *Ān Shǐ Zhī Luàn*). As minister of law, he was outspoken against corrupt high-ranking officials, resulting in him being repeatedly demoted. His uprightness was hailed by commoners, and his standard-script calligraphy of what is widely known as the "Yán style" (颜体/顏體 *Yántǐ*) is said to possess the same quality of unbending honesty. To this day, Yán Zhēnqīng's calligraphy works in the regular script are some of the most popular options calligraphy students choose to use as models.

Copying the characters on paper is believed to be inseparable from absorbing the moral vigor of the calligrapher. Thus, no matter how accomplished a calligrapher is in his art, if his *pǐn*, or moral character, is questionable, his works will not receive the same respect and will be shunned by most calligraphy students. The infamous chancellor of the *Sòng* dynasty, Qín Huì (秦桧/秦檜 1090–1155), for example, was perhaps as good a calligrapher in terms of skills as the most respected masters. Because of his role in the political execution of the loyal military general Yuè Fēi (岳飞/岳飛 1103–1142), however, he is regarded a traitor against the *Hàn* Chinese people. As a result of his poor moral reputation, few students imitate his calligraphic style. The calligraphy of Yuè Fēi, on the other hand, is highly respected until this day, even though its artistic accomplishment is considered secondary to that of Qín Huì.[10]

Handwriting and personality traits

In modern China, aside from academic achievement, excellent handwriting can also be associated with a range of other inner and outer qualities. Some believe that those who write beautifully are physically more attractive and admit to behaving differently around those with elegant handwriting.[11] Others consider graceful handwriting a reliable indicator that the writer is patient, composed, and dependable. Those who write large characters in cursive style are thought of as more free-spirited and outgoing, while those who use small, standard-script characters in neatly arranged rows give the impression of being disciplined, reserved, and detail oriented. Most people bestow respect and admiration on those who have beautiful handwriting, because it is perceived as the combined result of talent, aesthetic sensitivity, and persistence, all qualities of a refined person.

The idea that handwriting reveals the writer's personality traits is hardly a modern notion. The *Táng* dynasty calligrapher Sūn Guòtíng (孙过庭/孫過庭 648–703 CE) analyzed personality characteristics exhibited in brush strokes and came up with nine distinctive patterns. According to him, each personality had weaknesses discernible in calligraphic styles. For example, an upright person tended to produce strokes that were straight and unadorned but lacking in charm. A careful and reserved person was often too restrained in brush maneuvers. The brush strokes of a mild-tempered person might fall short in vigor and strength, and a vane person's calligraphy was too often affected by the prevalent fashion.[12]

However, it is important to understand that, much as handwriting is considered revelatory of the writer's personal traits and character, it is also understood as potentially deceptive.[13] On one hand, handsome handwriting is still taken by the Chinese as an indicator of positive character traits and abilities; on the other hand, however, it is no longer a definitive mark of distinction in personhood, if it ever has been. After all, in this digital age, handwriting has become less of a required skill in daily life, and the willingness to devote a large amount of time and energy to honing this skill is in general declining. It is understood, therefore, that sloppy handwriting may mislead the viewer into underestimating the inner qualities of the writer, and that pretty handwriting cannot always be trusted to reveal the writer's appearance, character traits, or morality.

Companion Website

Exercise 17.1 Social impetuses for improving handwriting

Parallels between calligraphy techniques and moral preferences

The connection between handwriting and personhood, as Yen (2005) argues, finds evidence in a series of parallels between the moral inclinations of Confucianism and the preferred calligraphic techniques of the classical tradition. A *jūnzǐ* (君子), or a cultivated person, is emotionally and intellectually profound and is, therefore, humble and reserved. Thus, a person who constantly brags about his accomplishments is hardly considered a cultivated person. Likewise, in the execution of a calligraphic stroke, preference is often given to a hidden tip (藏锋/藏鋒 *cángfēng*) over an exposed tip (露锋/露鋒 *lùfēng*). To achieve the hidden tip, the brush starts off going in the opposite of the intended direction and then wraps back around, covering the pointy mark made by the tip of the brush. The result is a stroke with a rounded rather than a sharp end (Figure 17.1). Roundedness in one's disposition – for instance, the ability to communicate without being abrasive – is also a desired quality in the cultivation of a proper, noble person in the Confucian ideal.

FIGURE 17.1   Hidden tip vs. exposed tip

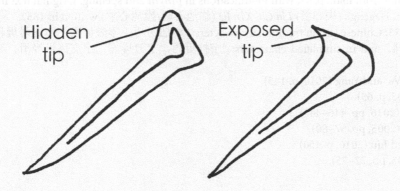

Similarly, being highly controlled is another desired characteristic in both brush techniques and a noble person's temperament. The calligraphy brush is light in weight, but maneuvering of the brush should preferably make it appear a very heavy instrument. Brush movement should be slow and sluggish rather than swift or light. Fast and careless brush movements may result in strokes that are blatant, excessive, or showy, which are all disfavored qualities of a refined person.

Table 17.1   Parallels of desired qualities in Chinese calligraphy and personhood

Calligraphy	Personhood
Roundedness	Cooperativeness with one another
Steady force	Strength
Fullness	Profundity
Being controlled	Composure
Clumsiness	Sincerity
Hidden tip	Modesty

Being humble, reserved, and controlled are not the only desired qualities shared by traditional Chinese calligraphy techniques and the concept of the noble person from the Confucian perspective. Table 17.1 summarizes a list of such qualities in matching pairs. These parallels illustrate further the close connection between handwriting and personhood in the Chinese tradition. Keep this in mind when you practice calligraphy, as it is understanding as such that gives the act of brush writing its cultural significance – when you understand the ideal person calligraphers aim to cultivate, you can more fully appreciate the meaning of calligraphy as you pick up a brush to participate in this time-honored tradition.

Notes

1 Yen (2005, p. 70).
2 书则一字已见其心/書則一字已見其心, from Zhāng Huáiguàn's *On Writing* (文字论/文字論)
3 Yen (2005, p. 64).
4 Ibid., p. 64.
5 Ibid., p. 66.
6 Translation from ibid., p. 67, with modifications in *pīnyīn* and spelling. Original text in Chinese is from Zhū Hégēng's (朱和羹) *Lín Chí Xīn Jiě* (临池心解/臨池心解) written in 1852.
7 Ibid., p. 73. Chinese text in traditional characters: "寧拙勿巧，寧醜毋媚，寧支離毋輕滑，寧直率毋安排," and in simplified characters: "宁拙毋巧，宁丑毋媚，宁支离毋轻滑，宁直率毋安排"
8 Xiang, Wu, and Yang (2016, p. 145).
9 Yen (2005, p. 65).
10 Zhuang (2016, pp. 446–447).
11 See Yen (2005, pp. 57–80).
12 Wang and Liu (2016, p. 150).
13 Yen (2005, pp. 72–75).

18 Sexism in the Chinese writing system

I T MIGHT BE SOMEWHAT odd to consider that a system of writing could in some way register gender relations. We've defined **writing** as the graphic representation of language (speech) in a specific and systematic manner. If a writing system encodes sexism, then at what linguistic level does this encoding take place? In other words, what linguistic unit of the writing system is *inherently* sexist? Only when we can demonstrate the inherence of sexism in a script can we claim that it is, in any degree, sexist. This is because we may otherwise fall into the trap of confusing writing with language and inaccurately attribute the gender bias in speech to the writing system. Indeed, we need to clearly distinguish between language (speech) and writing in this case. Sexist words, phrases, and statements belong to the realm of speech rather than writing, even though they may be represented in graphic marks when we encounter them. For example, in reading printed text we may come across the highly offensive word "bitch" used to refer to a female person. This may trigger in our mind a connection between the combination of the letters <b-i-t-c-h> and the highly sexist and offensive notion in this term. However, the true bearer of the sexist idea is the English word (think speech) [bɪtʃ],[1] and the letter combination <b-i-t-c-h> just happens to be the way this word is represented visually in writing. There is little that is inherent about the letters, or their combination, that makes them sexist. For this reason, it would be illogical to say that the Roman alphabet is sexist.

So, what does it mean to say that a writing system is sexist? It means that the script itself has built-in gender biases. Such biases can be shown to exist without evoking sexist expressions in the language that the script is customarily used to write; instead, evidence comes from intrinsic elements of the script. In the case of the Chinese script, we can look at individual characters to determine whether there is gender-based bias in the derivation or construction of their forms.[2] We will do that in the latter part of this chapter. First, let us take a brief look at gender bias against women in China.

The status of women in China

In China, as in many societies of the world, sexism against women is unfortunately deep-seated and has characterized both pre-modern and modern times.

Women in pre-modern China

The marginalization and oppression of women in imperial China (221 BCE–1911 CE) is believed to have its roots in Confucianism, the predominant doctrine or ideology that, for millennia, governed how Chinese people thought and behaved. The Confucian social structure, in particular its patriarchal family hierarchy and the corresponding marginalization of women in the public sphere, has long been criticized as a major source of sexism in the Chinese society.[3] Some often-quoted examples come from the Confucian Classics[4], the prerequisite, foundational literature for men to enter the ruling class in imperial China. Although writings in the Classics do not uniformly depict women as inferior, unworthy, or evil, scholars point to passages in these books that apparently do.[5] For example, in the *Book of Odes* (诗经/詩經 *Shījīng*), one reads:

> When a baby boy was born he was laid on the bed and given jade to play with, and when a baby girl was born she was laid on the floor and given a tile to play with.[6]

Again in the *Book of Odes*:

> A clever man builds a city wall/A clever woman overthrows it/Beautiful is the clever woman, but she is an owl, a hooting owl/A woman with a long tongue, she is a promoter of evil/Disorder is not sent down from Heaven, it is produced by women/Those who cannot be instructed or taught are women and eunuchs. . . . And therefore the women have no public service. They have to abide by their silkworm work and their weaving.[7]

In the *Book of Documents* (尚书/尚書 *Shàngshū*), the term *pìnjī sīchén* (牝鸡司晨/牝雞司晨), meaning "the hen (instead of the rooster) announcing dawn," is used to caution against women playing any role in the public sphere. This is because, as one scholar expounds, the belief was that "if women are [were] entrusted with tasks involving contact with the outside, they will [would] cause disorder and confusion in the Empire, harm and bring shame on the Imperial Court, and sully sun and moon."[8]

The patriarchy of imperial China allowed little space for women in the public domain. From low-ranking officials to the emperor high above, it was almost exclusively men who controlled and directly participated in governing and operating the state. Women were not only considered unfit for such responsibilities, but were also largely deprived of the education that would have prepared them for formal roles outside the domestic realm. This system kept women out of social positions that would put them on par with men and perpetuated the oppression and marginalization of women.

In pre-modern China, women's "proper" place was in the family: "They have to abide by their silkworm work and their weaving."[9] However, this did not mean that women enjoyed higher status than men in the household. On the contrary, Confucian teaching required women to abide by "three obediences and four virtues" (三从四德/三從四德 *sāncóng sìdé*).[10] A good woman was to obey her father before she was married (*wèijià cóngfù* 未嫁从父/未嫁從父), her husband after getting married (*jìjià cóngfū* 既嫁从夫/既嫁從夫), and her sons after her husband died (*fūsǐ cóngzǐ* 夫死从子/夫死從子). A virtuous woman must also possess feminine morality (*fùdé* 妇德/婦德), display proper speech (*fùyán* 妇言/婦言), maintain a modest manner and appearance (*fùróng* 妇容/婦容), and work diligently (*fùgōng* 妇功/婦功).[11] These moral standards relegated women to a status inferior to the men around them in the domestic realm.

Women in modern China

The Chinese Communist Party (CCP) government, during the Máo era (1949–1976), carried out a series of legal reforms and social campaigns designed to promote gender equality. The Marriage Law in 1950 abolished arranged marriages and concubinage, granting women the freedom to marry and to divorce according to their own will. The Electoral Law in 1953 gave women equal rights to vote and be elected. Successive campaigns to eradicate illiteracy (1952, 1956, 1958) improved millions of women's ability to read and write. The first Constitution of the People's Republic of China (1954) made a clear statement that women and men should have equal rights. Needless to say, the women's liberation movement that began in the 1920s in China achieved important successes during the Socialist reforms. Post-reform women in general enjoyed much more personal and professional freedom and higher social standing, and the effect has been profound and far-reaching. For example, according to a 2012 study of women's leadership, China has not only the highest percentage of female business executives in Asia, but also a higher percentage than many Western countries.[12] Máo Zédōng (毛泽东/ 毛澤東 1893–1976) was famously quoted as saying "women hold up half the sky" (妇女能顶 半边天/婦女能頂半邊天 *fùnǚ néng dǐng bàn biān tiān*).[13] A CCP slogan at the time, this statement has become a common saying for asserting women's equal status in China and remains popular to this day.

In the post-Máo era (1977-present), however, gender equality has deteriorated under the impact of market-economy reform in both the public and domestic spheres. According to researchers, women's status saw a gradual downturn in employment and education. Census figures in 2010 showed that only 60.8% of urban working-age women were employed, a 16.6 percentage point drop from 1990 and 20.3 percentage points lower than that of men.[14] The wage gap between women and men had also grown steadily, with urban women earning 69% the amount of men.[15] Men continued to be favored over women in admission to university programs and in hiring into the public as well as the private sectors.[16] In 2011, an amendment was made to the Marriage Law that made it more difficult for divorced women to own proper-ty,[17] putting women at a great disadvantage in home ownership. Increasing unemployment in the early stage of reform spurred a movement calling on women to quit their jobs and return to the home.[18] Staying home as a caregiver is not only becoming more acceptable, but is also glorified once again as a path to fulfillment for women.[19] Keeping a second "wife" (包二奶 *bāo èrnǎi*) is becoming more common among wealthy men, reminiscent of traditional marriages between one husband and multiple wives.

THE STORY BEYOND

Sobbing in a BMW

Increased commodification in the Chinese culture has also had a negative impact on how Chinese women are perceived as well as on how they perceive themselves.[20] For example, young women increasingly place more emphasis on material wealth when choosing potential marriage partners. One infamous incidence that occurred in the popular dating show *If You Are the One* (非诚勿扰/非 誠勿擾 *Fēi Chéng Wù Rǎo*) in 2010 illustrates this point well. One of the female participants, when asked by an unemployed male guest if she might enjoy bike riding with him, responded that she "would rather be sobbing inside a BMW than smiling on the back of a bicycle."[21] The video went viral on the Internet, and the episode has become an infamous example for the rise of materialism and shift in the values of Chinese women coming of age in recent decades.

Sexism in Chinese characters

As we have seen in previous chapters, the development of the Chinese writing system has been influenced at almost every turn by evolving power relations and social systems. Has the status of woman influenced the writing system as well? In particular, is sexism encoded in the Chinese writing system?

A focal point in investigating sexist bias in the Chinese script has been the character 女 (nǚ), meaning "female" or "woman." Commonly regarded as a pictograph, this character is thought to represent the image of a woman. In the oracle-bone script, the character suggests a woman kneeling – or seated on her heels, as Chinese people typically did in ancient times – with two hands crossed in front of her (Figure 18.1). Some scholars consider this a posture of submission,[22] as if the woman is sitting quietly listening to instructions from her husband. Others point out that in the oracle-bone script and the bronze script, characters that represent female persons – 女 (nǚ 'female, woman'), 母 (mǔ 'mother'), and 妻 (qī 'wife') – all have a curved bottom stroke, indicating a kneeling or sitting posture. By contrast, characters such as 人 (rén 'person') and 大 (dà 'big (derived from the image of a person stretching his arms out)') – have straight strokes suggesting a standing posture.[23] It seems that there is a general association of a female person with a more yielding, passive, or obedient posture in Chinese characters.

FIGURE 18.1   The character 女 (nǚ 'female, woman') in oracle-bone script

Sexism against the female also manifests in compound characters that have 女 as the radical (the semantic element). As some scholars point out,[24] among the hundreds of characters of this kind, a large number denote negative attributes that often have to do with a person's moral character or inner quality. For instance:

姦 jiān 'wicked, treacherous, evil'
妖 yāo 'seductive and evil'

妄 *wàng* 'preposterous and arrogant'
嬬 *ruò* 'weak, timid, and lazy'
婪 *lán* 'ambitious and avaricious'

When such characters express positive meanings, they are usually complimentary of women's physical appearance. For example:

婉 *wǎn* 'beautiful, graceful'
婷 *tíng* 'elegant'
妍 *yán* 'beautiful'
姣 *jiǎo* 'pretty'
媛 *yuán* 'beautiful woman'

Furthermore, some of the compounds may demonstrate expectations or practices of a patri-archal society in which women have an inferior role. For example, a woman holding a broom is one that fulfills the role of a wife. Peace and contentment are achieved when a woman is under her husband's roof.

婦 *fù* "wife, woman" = 女 + 帚 *zhou* "broom"
安 *ān* "peaceful, content"[25]

Companion Website

Exercise 18.1 Diagnosing compound characters

Do these compound characters encoding gender bias serve to confirm and reinforce gender inequality in the Chinese society? Does the use of these characters cause a writer or reader to be more prone to sexist beliefs or practices? With perhaps the exception of discussions among scholars, the issue of sexist characters does not seem to have sparked a lot of attention among users of the Chinese writing system, and there has not been much talk of a formal script reform based on this issue. From a linguistic perspective, however, this lack of attention may be understandable. Users of Chinese characters do not need to consciously analyze the sexist connotation within the characters in order to appropriately use them – and indeed they do not seem to. This is because a writing system, in its essence, is a set of symbols (graphemes) used to represent speech, and the same graphemes can be used to write and convey messages that are either sexist or not. The meaning of the messages derives primarily from the speech being written rather than the internal structure of the graphemes used to record that speech. Sexist characters may be used to fight for the protection of women's rights just as well as they may be used to demean and devalue women. Although some of the Chinese characters are evidently sexist in construction, the continued existence of gender inequality in China, however, may have little to do with that reality.

Notes

1 [bɪtʃ] is the IPA representation of the English word *bitch*.
2 Fan (1996) is one example study that has done so.
3 Goldin (2000) references a list of works in his article (p. 133 and note 1).
4 The Confucian Classics are referred to in Chinese as *Sìshū Wǔjīng* (四书五经/四書五經 'Four Books and Five Classics'). The five classics refer to *Shījīng* (诗经/詩經 *Book of Odes*), *Shàngshū* (尚书/尚書 *Book of Documents*), *Lǐjì* (礼记/禮記 *Book of Rites*), *Yìjīng* (易经/易經 *Book of Changes*), and *Chūnqiū* (春秋 *Spring and Autumn Annals*. The four books are *Dàxué* (大学/大學 *Great Learning*), *Zhōngyōng* (中庸, *Doctrine of the Mean*), *Lúnyǔ* (论语/論語 *Analects*), and *Mèngzǐ* (孟子 *Mencius*).
5 For example: Fan (1996); Li (2000); Yuan (2005); and Foust (2016).
6 Translated by *Lín Yǔtáng* (林语堂/林語堂). (1977). *My Country and My People*. Heinenmann: Asia, p. 131, as quoted by Fan (1996) on p. 98.
7 From the poem "I see on high (瞻仰 *Zhānyǎng*)," translation quoted from Fan (1996, p. 98).
8 Quoted by ibid., p. 98, from Van Gulik. (1974). *Sexual Life in Ancient China*. Leiden: E. J. Brill, pp. 86–87.
9 Ibid.
10 The "three obediences" first appeared in *Yí Lǐ* (仪礼/儀禮 *Book of Etiquette and Ceremonial*) *and* the "four virtues" in *Zhōu Lǐ* (周礼/周禮 *Rites of Zhou*).
11 Lee (2000, p. 470).
12 Tuminez (2012).
13 Although this well-known slogan has been commonly attributed to *Máo Zéngdōng*, there is no clear source of this attribution. See Zhong (2009).
14 Attané (2012). Data come from "Surveys on the social status of Chinese women (*Zhōngguó fùnǚ shèhuì dìwèi chōuyàng diàochá*)" carried out jointly by the Federation of Chinese Women and the National Office of Statistics in 1990, 2000, and 2010.
15 Otis (2015).
16 Fincher (2013).
17 Brannigan (2015). The "judicial guidance" stated that, on divorce, property should no longer be split between the couple but be awarded to the person whose name is on the deeds. The norm in China has been to put the man's name on the deeds even though the woman also contributes to the purchase.
18 Fincher (2013).
19 Fan (1996, p. 105).
20 Ibid., p. 96.
21 Bergman (2010).
22 Fan (1996, p. 96).
23 For example, Su (1999).
24 Fan (1996) is one example.
25 Examples of compound characters are taken from ibid.

19

Nǚshū

Women's script

Ǔ SHŪ (女书/女書), LITERALLY "WOMEN'S SCRIPT," is a writing system invented and used by unschooled, rural women in southern *Húnán* (湖南) province to write the local Chinese dialect.[1] It is unknown when exactly the script was invented, but many believe that it had been in use for at least hundreds of years until sometime in the 20th century.[2] Girls and women in the area nowadays receive education in the standard Chinese script, so *nǚshū* is no longer employed for regular writing purposes. Nonetheless, the story of *nǚshū* is an illuminating case of ingenuity, endurance, and mutual support among women. For many generations since *nǚshū*'s invention, the women educated themselves in the script and used it to compose letters and poems, record songs and stories, write autobiographies, and so on. Much of the *nǚshū* writing was shared among female friends on various social occasions. In this manner, *nǚshū* served as the vehicle of life-sustaining literary activities among peasant women in a male-dominant culture. It continues to capture the fascination of researchers and students in linguistics, anthropology, and other related disciplines. As an introduction to the *nǚshū* script, this chapter aims to answer a few of the basic questions regarding this remarkable legacy.

Who, where, and when?

There is much mystery about the origin of the *nǚshū* script. It is generally believed to have been invented by women living in the *Shàngjiāngxū* (上江圩) region of *Jiāngyǒng* (江永) county located on the southern edge of *Húnán* province (Figure 19.1). Women in this area, like those in the rest of China, historically had little opportunity to receive formal education. They were largely illiterate in the standard *hànzì* (汉字/漢字 'Chinese characters') writing system, the character-based script that they referred to as *nánshū* (男书/男書 'men's script'). Some proposed that *nǚshū* developed from the oracle-bone script,[3] essentially claiming on its behalf a history as long as that of *hànzì*. Some speculated that it had been around for more than 1,000 years.[4] However, most scholars believe that *nǚshū* likely has a much briefer history compared with *hànzì*. In one of the more conservative cases, scholars suspect that the script did not come into existence until in the 18th century and began to fall out of use in the 20th century.[5]

The difficulty in delineating the timeline for the development and use of *nǚshū* was, first of all, due to the script's limited scale in use. It appears that *nǚshū* was only used by women in a small cluster of villages in the *Shàngjiāngxū* region. There was little evidence for its spread outside of that area. In addition, there was almost never systematic teaching or learning of the script. Rather, it was passed down from one generation of women to the next through informal interactions. Another reason was that *nǚshū* had been ignored by almost everyone outside the community of female writers, including the men living amongst them. Besides

FIGURE 19.1 Location of *Jiāngyǒng* (江永) county. The map on the left shows the *Yangtze* River (长江/長江 *Chángjiāng*) in China and the location of *Húnán* province to the south of the river. The Yangtze River is usually regarded as the demarcation between northern and southern China. The map on the right shows the location of *Jiāngyǒng* (江永) county in *Húnán* province.

perhaps a handful of researchers, most of the men seemed to have dismissed writing in *nǔshū* as merely "something that women did" and therefore unworthy of their serious attention.[6] Such contemptuous attitudes could be seen from the names some men gave to the script – for example, "ant graphs" or "mosquito crawls," hinting at the long and slender strokes commonly used in the script – and the fact that many did not know what to call the script at all.[7] Scholars who noticed the *nǔshū* script either thought of it as an inferior variant of *hànzì* or found it difficult to bring to the attention of a wider research community. For instance, in 1954, Zhōu Shuòyí (周硕沂/周碩沂), a local researcher at the *Jiāngyǒng* County Office of Cultural Affairs, reported the script to the National Science Academy in Beijing but received little response.[8]

Nǔshū did not survive unscathed the social movements accompanied by radical ideological changes in mid- to late 20th-century China. In the 1950s, the script was suspected of being a secret code used for subversive purposes, and its use was prohibited.[9] During the Cultural Revolution (1966–1976), the script was regarded as part of the "four olds (四旧/四舊 *Sì Jiù*)" – old culture, old ideas, old habits, and old customs – and was banned along with the cultural conventions and practices that had provided the foundation for its application. Most of the texts were destroyed, and those who knew the script stopped using it or teaching it to others. By the 1980s, there were no more than a few elderly women who were still able to read and write *nǔshū*. The last proficient user of the script passed away in 2004.

Although *nǔshū* was in obscurity to the broader world for most of its history, it is by no means "a secret script," as it was incorrectly accused to be in the 1950s, or as popular media sometimes romantically portray it to be much later.[10] Most of the texts written in *nǔshū* were lyrics for ballads to be performed in public, for instance, at weddings and festivals, where the display of letters or other documents written in *nǔshū* was sometimes a matter of pride.[11] Men were not excluded from these occasions. The fact that the script was little known was perhaps more indicative of the lowly status of the women writers than any intention to keep the women's communication private.

Companion Website

Exercise 19.1 *Nǚshū* in contemporary media

◼ What does *nǚshū* look like?

Figure 19.2 shows the first few lines of a poem written in *nǚshū* glossed with *hànzì* characters. The page layout is the same as *hànzì* writing in the traditional style, so the poem is intended to be read in columns from right to left. To those literate in *hànzì*, it may not be difficult to detect formal similarities between some of the *nǚshū* symbols and their *hànzì* counterparts in this poem. Table 19.1 shows a few examples of corresponding symbols in the two scripts.[12] Indeed, standard Chinese characters are considered an important source for *nǚshū* graphs. In one study of *nǚshū* documents, among the 719 graphs identified, 439, or approximately 61%, are believed to have been derived from *hànzì*.[13] This still leaves a significant percentage, however, that does not appear related to standard Chinese characters.

Table 19.1 Corresponding symbols in *nǚshū* and *hànzì*. The same *nǚshū* symbol may correspond to multiple *hànzì* characters.

Nǚshū graph	*Hànzì* in the traditional script	Pronunciation and meaning in Modern Standard Chinese
	包	*bāo* 'to wrap, bag'
	苞	*bāo* '(flower) bud'
	胞	*bāo* 'womb'
	白	*bái* 'white'
	柏	*bǎi* 'cypress'

As you can see from these examples, if we assume that the *nǚshū* graphs have been derived from *hànzì* in form, then we can see that they tend to tilt the *hànzì* characters clockwise by about 45 degrees, resulting in diamond-shaped symbols. The highest point of the symbols is on the upper right, and the lowest point, the lower left. A single graph may contain 1 to 20 strokes. Unlike *hànzì* characters, *nǚshū* graphs consist of few horizontal or vertical

FIGURE 19.2 Part of a poem in *nǚshū* glossed with *hànzì* characters. *Hànzì* symbols are supplied to the left of the corresponding *nǚshū* graphs.

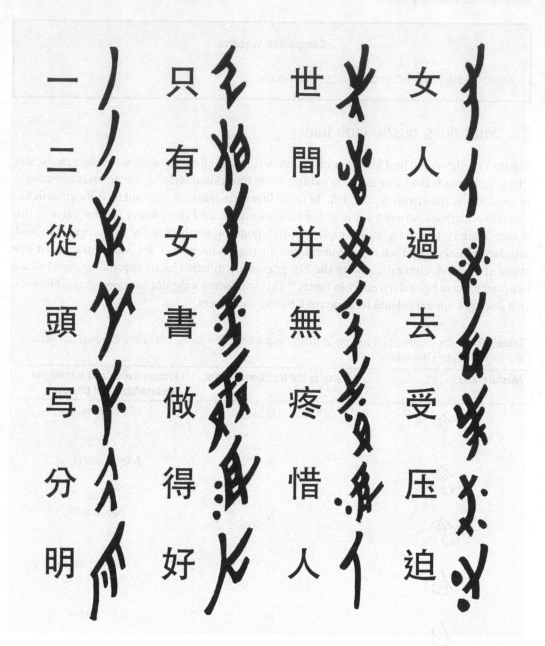

strokes, and most strokes are "slants," stretching either from the upper right to the lower left or from the upper left to the lower right. Other basic strokes of *nǚshū* include circles, round dots, and curves, all of which are less commonly used in *hànzì*. In writing *nǚshū*, small, thin, and uniform strokes are considered a beautiful hand.[14] Although almost all the extant *nǚshū* documents are written in ink with a brush, the strokes are linear and fine with little variation in width, which may indicate that the script did not originate in brush writing.[15] It has been suggested that *nǚshū* stroke forms are derived from embroidery.[16] Indeed, embroidery featured significantly in the lives of the *nǚshū* writers, and the women often incorporated *nǚshū* characters into the design of their embroidery work.

What kind of writing system is *nǚshū?*

Nǚshū appears to share a number of features with *hànzì*. Like in *hànzì*, the individual graphs in *nǚshū* are discretely arranged on the writing surface, each occupying about the same amount of space. Word boundaries are not marked. *Nǚshū* symbols are arranged on a page in the same way as *hànzì* characters. Also, as previously discussed, a large number of *nǚshū* graphs appear to have visual counterparts in *hànzì* and have probably been derived from *hànzì*. Of course, in addition to visual similarities, the two scripts are used to write varieties of the same language, Chinese. *Nǚshū* was used to write *Xiāngnán tǔhuà* (湘南土话/湘南土話 'local speech of southern *Xiāng*'), a sub-variety of the *Xiāng* (湘) dialect (language). This was the speech used by the women who wrote in *nǚshū* on daily occasions among family members, relatives, friends, and acquaintances from the local area, and it was also their mother tongue. Many in the *nǚshū* region, including the *nǚshū* users, typically only spoke *Xiāngnán tǔhuà*. Some might also speak the *Xiāng* dialect used in a broader region. As we have learned earlier in this book, *Xiāng* (including *Xiāngnán tǔhuà*) is not mutually intelligible with Mandarin. Nonetheless, *Xiāngnán tǔhuà* (or *Xiāng* in general) is similar in syntax and morphology and shares lexical cognates and regular sound correspondences with Mandarin.[17] Also like Mandarin, its morphemes usually consist of single syllables.

Given the much commonality, is *nǚshū* the same kind of writing system as *hànzì*? In other words, does it represent *Xiāngnán tǔhuà* in the same linguistic manner as *hànzì* represents Modern Standard Chinese? There is one key difference between them: unlike *hànzì* characters, each *nǚshū* symbol does not correspond to a morpheme or a meaningful syllable – instead, it represents a meaningless syllable – and the same symbol is used to write a number of morphemes sharing the same pronunciation. This is why, without context, it is possible for a *nǚshū* graph to mean a range of different things. *Nǚshū* is a script in which a grapheme by and large represents the sounds of a syllable without referencing meaning. It is a syllabic writing system or a **syllabary**.

Does *nǚshū* have as many graphs as *hànzì*? We know that a syllabic system of writing works the best when the number of distinctive syllables in the language is limited. MSC has about 1,840 possible syllable shapes, and 1,359 are actually used,[18] making it a less ideal fit for a syllabic writing system. *Xiāngnán tǔhuà* is very much like MSC. It has 23 consonants, eight vowels, and seven tones. With tonal variations included, a total of 1,316 distinctive syllable shapes are actually used in speech.[19] It is important to note here that the actual number of *nǚshū* characters, excluding graphic variants, that have been found in extant documents is significantly smaller – 719 to be exact, according to one researcher.[20] The main reason for the difference is that *nǚshū* writing is limited in its topics and style, and stock phrases are often used. Still, it may be somewhat surprising that *nǚshū* is a syllabic script rather than a morphosyllabic one like *hànzì*. Some consider it likely that the *nǚshū* script started out like *hànzì* with each symbol representing a morpheme but gradually evolved to a simpler sound-script relationship, so that most of its graphemes only represented syllables and were no longer tied to specific meanings.[21]

Learning to read *nǚshū* may not be a straightforward process. Although the relationship between sound and script is predominantly one graph for one syllable, there is a significant amount of overlap: the same graph can represent several similar, yet sometimes unrelated, syllables, and the same syllable may occur in a number of variant graphic forms. Interpretation of *nǚshū* texts, therefore, relies to a great extent on contextual knowledge and familiarity with their themes and vocabulary. What does help is that almost all the *nǚshū* texts are written in verse with fixed sentence lengths: mostly seven syllables, and some five. In fact, many of them are meant to be chanted in a certain melody following the oral tradition of the local culture, as it often happened at routine gatherings where female friends did their spinning, weaving, or embroidery together. The singing perhaps relieved some of the boredom in the repetitive tasks,[22] but there is more to it. What were some of the themes of the ballads written in *nǚshū*? What were the social functions that they served? We will discuss these questions in the next section.

What is *nǚshū* used to write and why?

In this section, we are shifting the focus from how writing was done to what was being written and why. The verse format of *nǚshū* writing is clearly indicative of its social function and literary value beyond routine communicative purposes. Indeed, *nǚshū* was not just a tool that enabled women to keep in touch with each other through writing, it also made it possible to provide and receive peer support in a predominantly patriarchal culture.

The low social status of women in the *Shàngjiāngxū* villages was reflected in the local customs of naming and genealogy. Boys were given "book names" besides "milk names" before their first birthdays. Book names were used for formal occasions and were recorded in the family lineage. Girls, however, only received milk names or nicknames, and they were excluded from the genealogy of their natal families.[23] Upon marriage, they officially became wives or daughters of their husbands' households. It was perhaps no wonder that parents were less inclined to invest in the education of their daughters.[24] Boys went to school and learned to read and write *hànzì* characters, or *nánshū* ('men's script'). Girls were usually not considered worthy enough to learn *hànzì*, and had to rely on haphazard peer tutoring if they wanted to master *nǚshū*. Many writers had a few years' schooling at the most and were far from having acquired functional literacy in *hànzì*. *Nǚshū* was a necessary and effective vehicle for its women writers to actualize self-expression and forge group solidarity. In what follows, we will examine the sociocultural impetuses for the various kinds of writing in two drastically different stages of these women's lives: first before marriage and then during or after marriage.

THE STORY BEYOND

Geo-economic reasons for the low status of women

The small region of southern *Húnán* province where *nǚshū* was used, like most other areas in China, sustained a culture that was predominantly male centered. Besides ideological reasons rooted in Confucianism, there were geo-economic reasons for women's low status. For example, as Endo (1999) explained, this area was blessed with mild climate, ample rain, and fertile soil, and it was thus ideally conditioned for agricultural productivity. Generally, men alone were able to handle the labor required to produce sufficient crops for the whole family. Women's participation in farm work was not required. Instead, they were expected to perfect such womanly crafts as weaving, sewing, and embroidery as well as to do other domestic chores. Men were the livelihood earners, and women took care of the men. Such division of labor served as the economic basis for discrimination between genders.

Before marriage

Women in the *Jiāngyǒng* region conducted their lives according to a variety of local customs and rituals. One such important custom was for unrelated young girls to become "sworn sisters," that is, close female friends who were mutually supportive and whose relationship was expected to last for life. Sworn-sisterhood was sometimes prearranged by the families of the girls but often grew out of frequent companionship among friends in day-to-day activities. Girls in the area began to take on a significant share of housework when they reached age ten or so. Many kinds of household chores were done together with village girls of about the same age.[25] A group of young female friends would also spend time together doing embroidery and singing songs almost on a daily basis. In this group, regular companions of the same age – and sometimes one or two years apart – might decide to become sworn sisters.[26] A girl could have more than one sworn sister. Before they each got married, sworn sisters would spend a lot of time together, visiting the local temple to attend festivals, sleeping over at each other's houses, etc. This period of devoted friendship before marriage was generally regarded the happiest time in a girl's life.[27]

Nǚshū writing was indispensable to the development of sworn-sisterhood. At the outset of the relationship, the girls would exchange letters written in *nǚshū* on folded fans (Figure 19.3) or silk handkerchiefs to acknowledge the sisterhood. As the relationship continued, more letters could be written and exchanged inviting each other to visit, responding to the invitation, or deciding on a time to meet and go to festivals to the local temple. At the temple, they would deposit their prayers, recorded in *nǚshū* characters, to the goddesses. Besides fans and handkerchiefs, letters could also be written on rectangular sheets of red paper. Such letters were meant to be read by the addressees only and were preferably delivered by female carriers.[28] On almost every day, sworn sisters and their friends would sing songs together while doing needlework. The lyrics of the songs were written down in *nǚshū*. Along with reading lyrics and singing songs, the girls would practice together writing in *nǚshū*, helping each other learn. Such teaching and learning were informal and most likely unsystematic but were also motivated and earnest – it has been proposed that the impetus for women to create *nǚshū* was so that sworn sisters would be able to communicate after they had married and moved away from each other.[29]

Getting married and after marriage

To most women of the *nǚshū* era, unfortunately, marriage meant the end of a happy adolescence and the beginning of a life filled with hardship and suffering. Marriages were usually

FIGURE 19.3 *Nǚshū* fan, *Qīng* dynasty
Source: Photograph by Wú Yáoqí, collection of Hunan Museum, China

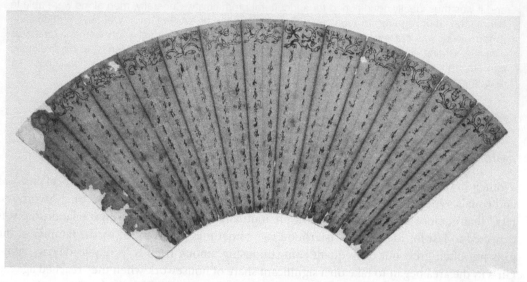

arranged by parents and matchmakers, which could mean that the young women had never met their husbands before the wedding. Getting married could also mean moving away from their home villages, making it very difficult to spend time again with their sworn sisters and other friends. Due to women's low status in the married household as daughters-in-law or wives, it was common that they were treated as not much more than free labor to do chores around the house or even abused by their husbands. In the event that their husbands died or abandoned them, if they had grown sons to support them, they would be very lucky; otherwise, life would become even harder.

Such harsh realities of the married life make lamenting women's misfortune a predominant theme of texts written in the *nǚshū* script. In fact, plaintiveness set the basic tone of the local marriage custom on the bride side. About a month before the wedding was to take place, sworn sisters and other female friends would gather at the house of the bride-to-be and sing songs for about three days. These songs, recorded in *nǚshū*, were lyrical accounts of women's grievance over the doom and gloom of marriages. Singing was often accompanied by tears and served as a channel for women to openly lament and vent against their parents for marrying them off and against the miseries they would have to suffer after getting married.[30] At the end of the singing and crying, the bride would be escorted to the groom's house where the wedding ceremony would take place.

One important type of writing in *nǚshū* is related to the local wedding custom. On the third day of the marriage, a member of the bride's family would be sent to bring the bride back to her home village. She would be presented by female friends or relatives an important ritual text called the "third-day book" (三朝书/三朝書 *sānzhāo shū*).[31] It was a cloth-bound book with songs or letters written in *nǚshū* in the first few pages followed by blank pages that the bride could fill in later on. The book was usually prepared by the bride's sworn sister or mother. The content of the writing had a few recurring themes: friends would lament the painful separation forced upon them, relatives would urge the bride to be an obedient and pleasing daughter-in-law, and everyone would advise her to accept the new circumstances as there were no alternatives and wish her happiness in the marriage.[32] The book was meticulously made, often adorned with embroidery on the cover or colorful paint on an inside page.

Through the ups and downs of their marital and social life, women wrote letters, recorded stories, and composed autobiographies using the *nǚshū* script. When the times got difficult, they would write letters to their female friends to seek support and sometimes visit and briefly stay with their sworn sisters for comfort and consolation. When traveling storytellers came to the village, they were enthusiastic audience and would write down in *nǚshū* the tales they heard from the performances.[33] Autobiographic writing of the women was almost exclusively focused on the tragic experiences of the authors. The writing was possibly presented to the goddesses at the local temple, registering the authors' wish to alleviate their pain and suffering.

Despite the rich variety and significant volume of writing that has been done in *nǚshū*, what remain for us to see today are a small number of samples. This had to do with the local custom as well. At the time of a woman's death, it was customary to burn her *nǚshū* documents so that she would be able to read them in her afterlife. This practice resulted in an almost complete loss of *nǚshū* writing and made it difficult to locate original documents created before the early modern period.[34] The materials did survive, however, revealed to us extraordinary creativity and forbearance of the women writers of *nǚshū*.

Notes

1 It has been proposed that men, instead of women, were the creators of *nǚshū* before *hànzì* was in use, and that women preserved the script when men adopted *hànzì* (see Chiang, 1995, p. 49). However, the idea remains a theory so far.
2 For example: ibid., p. 49; (Idema, 2009, p. 4).
3 This idea is mentioned in Idema and Grant (2004, p. 543).
4 Lee (2002) wrote: "[T]his group creates its own oral and written language that is transmitted over a thousand years from one generation to another" and "scholars asserted that *Nushu* was widely practiced in Shangjiangxu Township, Jiangyong County, southern Hunan Province of China, for more than one thousand years" (p. 101), but no sources were cited for these claims. Lee also wrote: "allegedly, the development of *Nushu* language was most likely to be initiated 1,000 years ago, and just who were the creators of *Nushu* has been disputed and remained unknown" (p. 106). However, in this second case, the sources Lee cited for the origin of *Nushu* were local legends (p. 115, Note 9). There did not seem to be any archeological or historical evidence that could confirm the claim.
5 Idema and Grant (2004, pp. 543–544).
6 See Lee (2002, p. 106) for references cited regarding men's attitude toward *nǚshū*.
7 Chiang (1995, p. 47).
8 Ibid., p. xvi. According to Zhōu Shuòyì's *Bǎidù Bǎikē* (the Chinese equivalent of Wikipedia) page (https://baike.baidu.com/item/周硕沂, accessed August 3, 2017), he reported the script to the Central Academy of Social Sciences two years later, in 1956, and received responses from Zhōu Yǒuguāng (周有光), who was in charge of the writing reform at the time.
9 Idema and Grant (2004, p. 544).
10 For example, Lisa See's 2014 novel *Snow Flower and the Secret Fan*, which was made into a film of the same name in 2011.
11 Idema (2009, p. 4).

12 Corresponding in a visual sense, but not in a strict sense between the two scripts, because the two scripts are different in nature.

13 Chiang (1995, p. 55).

14 Endo (1999).

15 Chiang (1995, p. 68).

16 Ibid., p. 49; Endo (1999).

17 Ibid., p. 20.

18 Rogers (2005) mentions "the 1359 occurring syllable shapes in modern Chinese" on p. 29.

19 Chiang (1995, p. 22).

20 This number is based on 24 *nǚshū* texts that have a total of 1,535 graphs with variants. Ibid., p. 50.

21 Idema and Grant (2004, p. 543).

22 Idema (2009, p. 5).

23 Chiang (1995, p. 24).

24 Ibid., p. 16.

25 Ibid., p. 32.

26 The term in Chinese for sworn sisters was *lǎotóng* (老同 *lit.* 'old same') or *tóngnián* (同年 *lit.* 'same year') if the girls were born in the same year or *jiébài zǐmèi* (结拜姊妹/結拜姊妹 'sworn sisters') if they were not born in the same year.

27 Idema and Grant (2004, p. 547).

28 See Chiang (1995, p. 64).

29 Endo (1999).

30 Chiang (1995, p. 18).

31 Another version of description for *sānzhāoshū* maintains that it was delivered to the bride's marital home – instead of her natal home – on the third day of her marriage. (Lee, 2002, p. 105).

32 Idema and Grant (2004, p. 548).

33 Chiang (1995, p. 34); Idema and Grant (2004, p. 542).

34 See Chiang (1995).

20 Script choice in writing Japanese

T HE WRITING OF JAPANESE in the modern, public context is probably more complex than that of most languages today. Japanese writing employs a mixture of four scripts: the morphographic *kanji*, the two moraic *kana* systems, *hiragana* and *katakana*, and the Latin alphabet referred to in Japanese as *rōmaji*. Theoretically, three of the four scripts – with *kanji* being the exception – would be able to fully represent the Japanese language each on their own. In other words, if the writer so wished, she would be able to write only and entirely in any one of those three scripts without major hindrance. However, a mixed script is generally preferred. It is therefore important for an average writer to understand when to use which script. Indeed, a writer of Japanese must be able to do so correctly in order to be considered genuinely proficient. In this chapter, we take the inquiry a step further to examine and understand both the linguistic constraints and the socio-cultural expectations associated with script choice by native Japanese speakers. We will see that these choices, consciously or unconsciously, are often associated with the writers' social identities and may be used to manipulate or construct such identities.

Linguistic constraints

Japanese script variation manifests predominantly at the lexical level (or, strictly speaking, the morphemic level). That is, choices of which script to use are often made word by word. Words of Sinitic origin that have long been part of the Japanese lexicon are usually represented in *kanji*, and so are many native Japanese words. Almost all *kanji* have both an *on* reading modeled on the original Chinese morpheme and a *kun* reading coming from the indigenous Japanese morpheme. For example, the character 木 representing 'tree' may be used to write either the Chinese loanword *moku* (*mù* in Modern Standard Chinese) or the Japanese word *ki*, both meaning 'tree.' If the words in question are verbs, then the stems are often (partially) written in *kanji* and the inflections are represented in *hiragana*. For instance, 食べた (*tabeta*) consists of the *kanji* and *hiragana* 食べ(る) 'to eat' and the inflectional ending た that indicates the completion of the action. In addition to grammatical particles and inflectional endings, *hiragana* is also used for native Japanese lexical items, such as もう (*mou* 'already'). Recent loanwords, especially those from the West, are of course not associated with *kanji*. They are usually written in *katakana*, for example, ビジネス (*bijinesu* 'business') and ミルク (*miruku* 'milk'). *Katakana* is also used for onomatopoeia, as in ドキドキ (*dokidoki* 'thump thump') describing a throbbing heart, or for indicating emphasis. In some cases, loanwords, especially acronyms from languages written with the Roman alphabet, including English, French, German, and Portuguese, can be represented directly in Roman letters or *rōmaji*.[1] One example is the acronym OL, used in Japanese to mean "office lady," referring in the Japanese context to female office workers who perform secretarial tasks. A few more examples are: NG for "not good," CM for "commercial," PV for "promotional video," and JR for "Japanese Railway." In speech, they are pronounced as individual letters in Japanese-style pronunciation. OL will be pronounced as *ōeru*, for example.

As you can imagine, one Japanese sentence is often written in a mixture of scripts. The example below is a sentence with all four scripts represented.

私は東京のJETプログラムで英語を勉強しました。
Watashi-wa Tōkyō-no JET *puroguramu-de Eigo-o benkyōshi-mashita.*
'I studied English at the JET Program in Tokyo.'

The pronoun 私 (*watashi* 'I'), the nouns 東京 ('Tokyo') and 英語 (*eigo* 'English'), and part of the verb stem 勉強 (し) (*benkyō* 'study') are represented in *kanji*. *Hiragana* is used to write the particles attached to the pronoun and nouns indicating topic (は *-wa*), possession (の *-no*), location (で *-de*), and direct object (を *-o*). It is also used for the verbal inflection (ました *-mashita*) attached to the verb stem. The word プログラム (*puroguramu* 'program'), an English loanword, is written in *katakana*. The English acronym JET for the Japan Exchange and Teaching Programme[2] is in *rōmaji*.

Furthermore, there is not always a consistent one-on-one relation between a word and its usual script. Although in most cases, a given word is conventionally written in one of the scripts regardless of context – and it thus often makes sense to say "this is a *kanji* word" or "that is a *hiragana* word" – a large number of lexical items can be written in two or more scripts. For example, Table 20.1 are some of the words found to occur in *kanji*, *hiragana*, or *katakana* with almost equal probability.[3] For our convenience, we will refer to these as triple-script words.

Table 20.1   Japanese triple-script words: examples

Kanji	Hiragana	Katakana	Romanization	English meaning
朝顔	あさがお	アサガオ	*asagao*	'morning glory'
梅	うめ	ウメ	*ume*	'plum'
桜	さくら	サクラ	*sakura*	'cherry'
鉛筆	えんぴつ	エンピツ	*enpitsu*	'pencil'
切符	きっぷ	キップ	*kippu*	'ticket'
虎	とら	トラ	*tora*	'tiger'
鳥	とり	トリ	*tori*	'bird'
蛍	ほたる	ホタル	*hotaru*	'firefly'
麦	むぎ	ムギ	*mugi*	'wheat'
人参	にんじん	ニンジン	*ninjin*	'carrot'

What, then, determines for the writer which form to use? As we will see in the next section, script choices cannot be explained solely on the basis of grammatical or lexical constraints. They are motivated by extra-linguistic factors as well.

Extra-linguistic factors

As a matter of fact, *kanji*, *hiragana*, and *katakana* have distinctive socio-cultural associations in Japan. In one study, when asked to provide key words that describe the qualities they associate with each of the scripts, Japanese native writers came up with adjectives that clearly separate the three scripts from each other, as shown in Table 20.2:[4]

Table 20.2 Descriptors by Japanese native writers for qualities associated with script choice based on Iwahara et al. (2003)

Script choice	Qualities associated with script
Kanji	hard, difficult, intellectual, vigorous, old, male, formal
Hiragana	soft, round, tender, simple, lovely, feminine, childish
Katakana	hard, angular, foreign, cold, new, sharp, inorganic

These socio-cultural associations matter a great deal in the writing of triple-script words and have been found to predispose native writers to choosing one script over another based on the qualities most congruent with the given context. For example, in an interesting experiment, Japanese university students were asked to come up with lists of Japanese celebrities they regarded as most compatible with qualities associated with *kanji*, *hiragana*, and *katakana* respectively. They had little difficulty coming to an agreement regarding such lists: the ex-Prime Minister Hashimoto Ryūtarō (橋本龍太郎) and the *enka*[5] singer Kitajima Saburō (北島三郎) were perceived as *kanji*-compatible celebrities. The television comedian Tamori (タモリ) and baseball star Ichirō (イチロー) were considered most compatible with *katakana*. The actress and fashion designer 篠原ともえ (Shinohara Tomoe) and TV comedian and actor Akashiya Sanma (明石家 さんま) were thought to be most closely associated with *hiragana*. Note that such associations between the celebrities and the script have nothing to do with the script in which the persons' names are written; it is about the prominent personal characteristics that the celebrities exhibit as perceived by the students and how well these characteristics match up with the distinctive qualities the various scripts are perceived to possess.

Then, the students were given a made-up scenario in which the celebrities opened up shops that needed to be named. They were asked to choose among the triple-script words names for the shops and to write them down in any script they considered appropriate. No surprise – they most frequently used the type of script most strongly associated with the personal characteristics of the celebrities. For instance, for "Mr. Hashimoto Ryutarō opened a shop named _____," a significantly higher percentage of students wrote the name in *kanji* than in the other two scripts.

The choice of script is one of the most important factors in marketing Japanese consumer commodities, and much thought goes into how brand names are written. The Japanese automaker Toyota and motorcycle manufacturer Suzuki both use *katakana* even though the brand names were originally family names, and family names are usually represented in *kanji* or *hiragana*. The choice of *katakana* creates an impression of being modern, high-tech, and international. In fact, most of the tech companies in Japan preferred *katakana* over *kanji* branding. Toyota and Mazda switched to *katakana* years ago (though Nissan still uses *kanji* along with Roman letters). Toyota's logo design, in particular, went through several changes in script.[6]

Table 20.3   Names of Japanese automakers in *katakana* and *kanji*

Romanization	*Katakana*	*Kanji*
Honda	ホンダ	本田
Toyota	トヨタ	豊田
Suzuki	スズキ	鈴木
Mazda	マツダ	松田

By contrast, Japanese companies that have a distinguishingly long history often choose to stay with their original *kanji* names to emphasize their time-honored heritage. Mitsui (三井) and Sumitomo (住友), both multi-industry international corporations, trace their roots to merchants in the Edo period (1603–1867) and have maintained their branding in *kanji* in honor of their founders.[7]

Another example to illustrate the point here is from Japan's alcoholic beverage industry. As you may have noticed, brand names for *sōchū* or *sake*, which are traditional Japanese beverages, tend to have *kanji* brands. Beer and whisky, which are later Western imports, usually have their brands represented in *katakana*.

Table 20.4   Brand names of Japanese beverages

白鶴	Hakutsuru (sake)
菊正宗	Kikumasamune (sake)
キリン	Kirin (beer)
アサヒ	Asahi (beer)
サッポロ	Sapporo (beer)

Violation of script choice conventions could achieve emphatic effects, much like using bold or italics in writing English, and it is a tactic sometimes used in advertisement.[8] For example, a catchphrase in Japanese is used to market the plush toys of the brand *Tarepanda*, and it is written entirely in *rōmaji* to achieve this eye-catching effect: *sawaruto yawarakaku igaito sittori siteiru*,[9] meaning "when you touch it, (you'll find) it soft and unexpectedly but comfortably moist." In conventional orthography it would have been written as 触ると柔らかく意外としっとりしている in a mixture of *kanji* and *hiragana*.

Extra-linguistic factors that influence script choice may also include the gender or age of the author or the target audience as well as the stylistic features of the writing. In general, the use of *kanji* is perceived by the Japanese as indicative of erudition on the part of the author or the readership, who tends to be expected to be male or of middle age or above. Since the cursive-stroked *hiragana* is usually associated with softness or femininity, the author or the audience is more often expected to be young or female. It also conveys a sense of tradition as compared with *katakana*. *Katakana*, with its straight or angular strokes, is often associated with modernity and pop culture, a perception that may have to do with the fact that new, Western loanwords are usually written in *katakana*. This script is generally perceived as suggesting a young and masculine identity. The use of *rōmaji* is more dominantly related to commerciality or consumerism and is often associated with young, female authors or readers.[10]

Companion Website

Exercise 20.1 Japanese authors' script choices

These script stereotypes are reflective of the social stereotypes rooted in cultural-historical context. For instance, *hiragana* is perceived as suggesting femininity and familiarity not just because of its soft curved shape in contrast to the sharp angular lines of *katakana* or because of its relatively simple form compared to *kanji*. It is also because historically *hiragana* was the script used by women to communicate their private thoughts and to create literary works, when *kanji*, the official script at the time, was almost exclusively used by men or for official correspondence. Because of this, *hiragana* was referred to as *onnade* (女手 'woman's hand') while *kanji* was also called *otokode* (男手 'man's hand'). *Kanji* has also been the script associated with formal education and thus intellectual cultivation and erudition from its early use to this day.

THE STORY BEYOND

Kanji aptitude testing

Proficiency in *kanji* in modern Japan is still an important skill, and official agencies play the role of measuring and recording individual performance through testing. For instance, the Japan *Kanji Aptitude Testing Public Interest Foundation* (日本漢字能力検定協会 *Nihon Kanji Nōryoku Kentei Kyōkai*) administers a 12-level *kanji* aptitude test. It assesses the ability to read and write *kanji*, to know the *on* readings and *kun* readings, to know the stroke order, and to use *kanji* in sentences. Level 1 is the highest. Levels 10 through 5 correspond to what elementary-school students learn. Level 2 is roughly what high school graduates are expected to be able to do. Most Japanese do not go beyond Level 2. College students who pass Level 2, however, may have an advantage in applying for jobs. Level 1 is very difficult, and typically fewer than 15% of those who take it are able to pass.[11]

Similarly, the association of *katakana* with modernity and pop culture and that of *rōmaji* with commerciality are rooted in the more modern reality of the Japanese society. *Katakana* is the script used to write Western loanwords, which occur more predominantly in the context of urban pop culture than elsewhere. In particular, *katakana* has come to convey the modern, metropolitan, and often international feel of popular youth culture. *Rōmaji*, the use of which is a legacy of the Occupation period (1945–1952), is frequently used in advertising or public signage to catch consumers' attention for products and services. It signifies non-indigenousness and conveys a cosmopolitan appeal. Often the meaning of the words or expressions matters less than its decorative value, and the Roman letters were used to generate a visual impact.[12]

Companion Website

Exercise 20.2 Script choice in popular literature[13]

Although correlations between aspects of socio-cultural identity and choices of script may be strong, they should not be interpreted as indicators of rigid categories dichotomizing writers of Japanese into various opposing social groups such as male vs. female, old vs. young, or, as will be discussed in the following example, heterosexual vs. homosexual. It is found that in texts tailored to lesbian readers published in periodicals, the proportion of characters written in *katakana* was significantly higher than in texts of the same nature targeting heterosexual Japanese housewives.[14] Furthermore, the use of *katakana* in lesbian literature is also found to be more innovative.[15] A morpheme that is conventionally written in *hiragana* (e.g., けど 'but, however'), for instance, may be represented in *katakana* (i.e., ケド) instead. The preferential use of *katakana*, however, does not necessarily suggest a tendency towards a lesbian identity and could possibly be explained by other factors such as modernity. Because historically lesbian identity in Japan came out of the Women's Liberation movement in the 1970s, it is closely associated with notions of the modern, which may be indexed by the use of *katakana*. In other words, lesbian identity and modernity are "co-indexed" in a similar script choice. As another example, it is also found that young gay men more often prefer to use *hiragana* to *kanji* in representing their own names in online posts than their heterosexual counterparts.[16] The choice of *hiragana*, however, might not necessarily represent an affinity to femininity. Rather, it could simply suggest a more playful and informal presentation of one's self.

THE STORY BEYOND

Script choice in periodical titles

One of the studies discussed above looks at periodicals published with lesbian women and housewives as their respective target audience. Distinctive script choice is apparent in the titles of these periodicals. The two publications tailored to housewives, 婦人之友 (*Fujin no Tomo* 'Women's Friend') and すてきな奥さん (*Suteki na Okusan* 'Lovely Wife') have titles written in *kanji* or a combination of *kanji* and *hiragana*. The ones for lesbians, *TypeMx* and *Labrys Dash*, were in *rōmaji*, each containing an English word. According to the researcher, these titles are not merely a stylistic choice but are revealing of housewives and lesbians "occupy[ing] different spheres in Japanese society."[17] In this sense, the use of English words and *rōmaji* for journal titles could simply be an expression of in-group identity and may not have much to do with the group members' being lesbian.

Notes

1 Smith and Schmidt (1996); Frank (2001, p. 210).
2 The word "programme" uses British spelling (with "-me" at the end) in the original name of the organization.
3 Iwahara, Hatta, and Maehara (2003, pp. 379, 395).
4 Ibid., p. 385.
5 *Enka* (演歌) is a popular music genre that stylistically resembles traditional Japanese music.
6 If you would like to know more, here is an interesting article to read: http://japantravelcafe.com/japanese-language-nihongo/learning-japanese-from-car-names-toyota-katagana.

 7 Noguchi (2009).
 8 Iwahara et al. (2003, p. 379).
 9 Tranter (2008, p. 142).
10 Based on Table 1 from Smith and Schmidt (1996, p. 50); also see Frank (2001, p. 209).
11 Koichi (2011).
12 Tranter (2008, p. 149).
13 Based on study conducted by Smith and Schmidt (1996).
14 Frank (2001).
15 Ibid., p. 222.
16 O'Mochain (2012).
17 Frank (2001, p. 217).

PART VI

Chinese characters in art and literature

21 Chinese calligraphy

▇ The Chinese script as foundation for calligraphy

In East Asia, calligraphy (Chinese 書法 *shūfǎ*, Japanese 書道 *shodō*, Korean 書藝 *seoye*) is a form of art that enjoys high social, cultural, and historical prestige. A time-honored tradition, East Asian calligraphy traces its origin to at least the oracle-bone script in China 3,000–3,500 years ago.[1] Calligraphy in the Chinese tradition has also had a long history in Korea and Japan, where the art form was introduced no later than the 6th century CE. In pre-modern China, the educated elite considered calligraphy the most prestigious form of art – and the most important of the "three perfections (三绝/三絕 *sān jué*)" that cultured scholars strove to accomplish:[2] calligraphy, painting, and poetry. In today's China, brush calligraphy remains the most widely practiced form of visual art. Calligraphy classes are part of the standard curriculum for elementary school students. Extracurricular training such as weekend or summer courses is also readily available. It is not rare for children and adults alike to practice calligraphy at home, and it has become increasingly common for older retirees to write water calligraphy[3] in public parks as morning exercises (Figure 21.1). In China and Japan, students of calligraphy can take national tests and be certified on a full scale of technical and artistic accomplishment.

FIGURE 21.1 Water calligraphy in a public park
Source: Photograph by Laura Vermeeren; used with permission

What makes calligraphy a thriving art form in East Asia? It has to do with, among other factors, the characteristics of the Chinese writing system. First of all, as a morphographic script, the Chinese writing system requires a large number of symbols. Recall that basic literacy in Chinese usually means being able to read and write 2,000 to 3,000 characters. Calligraphers may master significantly more, and this large number of symbols provides them with a rich visual repertoire for creating their works. Furthermore, Chinese characters are composed of a variety of strokes. Calligraphers have considerable freedom to vary the shapes and thickness of the individual strokes as well as how they relate to each other in the overall compositions of the characters. Such are the expressive resources at the disposal of the calligraphers when they create new styles.

Chinese calligraphy matured as an art form along with traditional Chinese painting. In pre-modern China, the painter-calligrapher, who was also usually a scholar, created calligraphy and painting in the same studios using the same tools and materials. For this reason, it is perhaps no wonder that traditional Chinese calligraphy and painting share the same aesthetic principles: vitality (气韵生动/氣韻生動 *qìyùn shēngdòng* 'life-like energy'), balance, and individuality are among the fundamental criteria in evaluating the merit of either painting or calligraphy.

You may wonder whether, to appreciate and enjoy Chinese calligraphy, one needs to be able to read the Chinese script and understand what is written. After all, calligraphy works usually contain meaningful texts, whether they are thousands of characters or single characters. To answer this question, it is important to understand that Chinese calligraphy is primarily an abstract art. It is much less about what is written than the rhythm, vitality, and balance of the marks created by the successive spontaneous movements of the brush. Indeed, Chinese calligraphy is valued "purely for the sake of the satisfactory nature of its lines and groups of lines."[4] In this sense, it speaks a universal artistic language that transcends the linguistic information encoded in Chinese characters.

Calligraphic evolution of the Chinese script

The Chinese script has no doubt changed significantly over its long history, and these changes are calligraphic in nature. That is, they are changes in the appearance of the script. The modern character 馬 (traditional) or 马 (simplified) for "horse," for example, looks very different from the character in the oracle-bone inscription, as shown in Table 21.1. We learned in an earlier chapter[5] that, besides the ancient oracle-bone script and the standard script presented in this table, there have been a few other major script styles. These include, in a roughly chronological order, bronze script, seal script, clerical script, running script, and cursive script. In that chapter, we noted – and it may be worthwhile to remind ourselves here – that, although we conventionally use the term "script" to refer to these styles, they are in fact different stylistic variations of the same script, the morphographic Chinese script. The fact that we give them different names indicates substantial differences between the styles, but their distinctions are merely in the visual forms of the characters, and they do not change the nature of the writing system per se. The Chinese script remains consistently morphographic whether it is in the oracle-bone script, the standard script, or any other script style in between.

Table 21.1 Changes in appearance of the Chinese character *mǎ* 'horse'

Oracle-bone script	Modern script (traditional)	Modern script (simplified)	*Pīnyīn*	Meaning
𤕟	馬	马	*mǎ*	'horse'

To calligraphers, the historical variations in the form of Chinese characters offer rich artistic resources. An accomplished calligrapher usually masters more than one style and is capable of drawing inspiration from multiple varieties to create her or his own personal style. Students of calligraphy typically start with one style – most commonly the standard script – tracing, copying, and emulating masterpieces produced by renowned calligraphers in the ancient past, and they then move on to similar practice with other styles. In what follows, we will take a look at each of the major script styles, in particular their historical background, visual characteristics, and the stories behind their creation.

Oracle-bone script

The earliest recognized archeological evidence we have to date of Chinese writing is characters inscribed on so-called oracle bones during the late *Shāng* (商) dynasty (1200–1050 BCE). The writing was done on ox shoulder blades (牛骨 *niú gǔ*) or turtle undershells (龟甲/龜甲 *guī jiǎ*) for divination purposes, hence the name *jiǎgǔwén* (甲骨文: 甲 *jiǎ* 'shell,' 骨 *gǔ* 'bone,' 文 *wén* 'writing') in Chinese and "oracle-bone script" in English. Ancient kings and their diviners used oracle bones to predict the future: A piece of bone or shell would first be inscribed with a question or an inquiry. It would then be subject to heat until it cracked. A diviner would look at the cracks and come up with an answer to the inquiry by interpreting the patterns the cracks had formed. The prediction made by the diviner would then be carved on the same piece of bone or shell. Sometimes, what actually transpired would also be recorded following the actual event. In this fascinating manner, a piece of oracle bone constitutes a historical record of events that took place several thousand years ago. The oracle bones discovered to date contain 4,000–4,500 different characters, only about 1,200 of which have been deciphered.[6] It is likely that many of the characters dropped out of use, and only about 20% still exist in a transformed form in today's script.

THE STORY BEYOND

Chinese characters representing oracle-bone cracks

A number of Chinese characters originally may have been pictographs representing cracks on oracle bones:[7]

卜 *bǔ* 'to predict, to divine'

兆 *zhào* 'divination cracks'

占 *zhān* 'to prognosticate'

吉 *jí* 'auspicious'

What does the oracle-bone script look like? Figure 21.2 offers one example. As seen in the image, the characters contain almost entirely straight lines: horizontals, verticals, or slants. There are few curves, circles, or dots, stroke types that are more commonly used in later scripts. The lines are thin and vary little in width. These characteristics probably have to do with the hard surface and the sharp writing tools used in the inscription of the characters. We may also observe that the size of the characters are not entirely uniform, some distinctively larger than others. The characters are arranged in columns but are not yet aligned horizontally.

FIGURE 21.2   Oracle bone from the reign of King Wu Ding (late *Shāng* dynasty, ca. 1200 BCE) National Museum of China

Source: CC BY-SA 3.0 (https://creativecommons.org/licenses/by-sa/3.0)

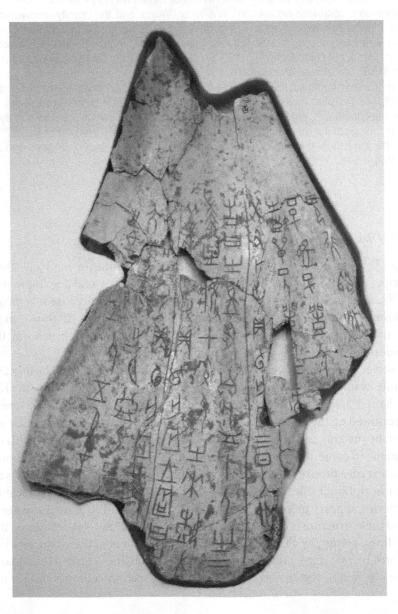

THE STORY BEYOND

Discovery of the oracle bones

The oracle bones are said to have been discovered by a scholar-official named Wáng Yíróng (王懿荣/王懿榮, 1845–1900), then the director of the Qīng imperial college in 1899. Wang fell ill to malaria that year and was prescribed traditional Chinese medicine to treat the disease. One of the ingredients he received was the so-called dragon bones (龙骨/龍骨 lóng gǔ). Upon close examination of the small pieces of bones in the package, Wáng was surprised to notice that they bore character-like carvings. Convinced that this could be evidence for early Chinese writing, he sent his subordinates to trace the origin of the bones, which turned out to be a Xiǎotún Village (小屯村 Xiǎotún Cūn) near today's Ānyáng (安阳/安陽) city of Hénán (河南) Province.

Decades later, continued excavations in Xiǎotún Village and the vicinity uncovered hundreds of thousands of oracle-bone pieces. Remarkably, scholars were able to decipher part of the oracle-bone script and construct a Shāng king genealogy that matched what was recorded in the *Records of the Great Historian* (史记/史記 Shǐjì) written by the Hàn dynasty historian Sīmǎ Qiān (司马迁/司馬遷 ca. 145 or 135–86 BCE).

Even more remarkable was that the excavations led to the discovery of the remains of the Shāng (1200–1050 BCE) capital, including palaces, temples, tombs, and bronze workshops. The name of the Shang capital was Yīn (殷), and the Shāng dynasty is also known as the Yīn dynasty. This site of the Shāng capital ruins, therefore, is referred to as Yīn Xū (殷墟), "Yīn Ruins." Today, you can visit the Yīn Ruins. It is one of China's oldest and largest archeological sites and a UNESCO World Heritage Site.

Bronze script

The Shāng (商) and the Zhōu (周) dynasties (16th–3rd centuries BCE) saw the use of the bronze script (金文 jīnwén, 金 'metal'). This style is also known as zhōngdǐngwén (钟鼎文/鐘鼎文: 钟/鐘 zhōng 'bell,' 鼎 dǐng '(a type of ceremonial vessel)') because it is most often seen on ritual bronze vessels cast during the Shāng and Zhōu dynasties. As shown in Figure 21.3, characters may be inscribed on the inside of a bronze vessel, arranged in a way that complements the design of its exterior, achieving an overall aesthetic harmony.

The vessel in Figure 21.3, called Duke Máo's Cauldron (毛公鼎 Máogōng Dǐng), in fact bears a prime example of the bronze script. The inscribed essay records how the King Xuān of the Zhōu (周宣王), in a time of unrest, charged his uncle Duke Máo with governing state affairs and bestowed on the Duke a wealth of gifts. The Duke had the cauldron cast to record the honor given by the king and intended for the vessel to be used with respect by his descendants for generations to come. The nearly 500-character inscription inside the cauldron is not only the longest text on a bronze vessel but also one of the most elegant. Figure 21.4 is a rubbing of half of the inscription inside the vessel. As we can see, compared with the oracle-bone script, the broze script appears more elaborate. The characters tend to have a greater number of strokes, and their structure is more complex. They also make more use of curved lines and less of angular lines, giving the characters a softer look. The sizes of the characters have become more uniform by this stage, even though they may not all fit in equal-sized square cells. Like the oracle-bone script, the characters are usually arranged in columns and do not yet form clear rows.

FIGURE 21.3 Duke Máo's Cauldron with bronze script inscription on the inside
Source: Collection of National Palace Museum, *Táiwān*

FIGURE 21.4 Rubbing of inscription inside Duke Máo's Cauldron (half)
Source: Collection of National Palace Museum, *Táiwān*

Great seal script

The great seal script (大篆 *dàzhuàn*) is the name given to the style of writing used before the *Qín* (秦 221–206 BCE) dynasty, that is, before China was unified, especially during the Western and early Eastern *Zhōu* dynasties. The script was named retroactively by those in the *Hàn* dynasty (汉/漢 206 BCE–220 CE), when a later script, the clerical script, became dominant. Before the creation of the clerical script, the First Emperor of the *Qín* had the small seal script (小篆 *xiǎozhuàn*) designed to replace the great seal and be used across the unified China. The later clerical script was much faster to write, and thus in the *Hàn* dynasty neither the great seal nor the small seal script was widely used in ordinary writing, and they were relegated almost entirely to seal carving – the inscription of personal names or short phrases on stone stamps. This was the origin of the name "seal script." The great seal script was in use during the time of Confucius and his disciples. Some of the Confucian Classics might have been written in this script.

An example of the great seal script is the inscription on a set of ten drum-shaped stones (石鼓文 *shígǔwén* 'stone-drum script') that belonged to the state of *Qín*.[8] Dated to around the 5th century BCE, the stone-drum inscription is the earliest existent stone inscription in China. Each stone drum had on its surface a poem about the hunting or military expeditions of the *Qín* monarchs. Each of the ten poems had 70 characters, amounting to a total of 700 characters, 272 of which are still legible today.[9] You can see the rubbing of the inscription on one of the stone drums in Figure 21.5.

FIGURE 21.5 Inscription on stone drum
Source: Collection of the Metropolitan Museum of Art

The great seal script synthesized the stylistic features of previous scripts and further matured from the bronze script. Stone-drum characters appear even more sophisticated than the characters on Duke Máo's Cauldron. As we can see from Figure 21.5, the characters in general have a greater number of strokes and contain more curved strokes. Each character is well balanced in structure and is roughly the same overall shape and size. The characters are not only aligned in columns but are also neatly arranged in rows. Since their discovery in the 7th century, the stone drums, extolled for the distinctive beauty of their inscription, have been a source of inspiration for many calligraphers.

Small seal script

The small seal script (小篆 *xiǎozhuàn*) is a product of systematic standardization after the First Emperor, Qínshǐhuáng (秦始皇), conquered all the other Warring States and established the *Qín* dynasty in 221 BCE. The emperor took measures to unify the writing system as well as currency, weights, measurements, and so forth to be used across the newly united China.

FIGURE 21.6   *Qín* brick with 12 characters
Source: Collection of China National Museum

A simplified version of the great seal script, the small seal script does not represent a drastic stylistic departure from the great seal. The individual characters are more refined and balanced, but the strokes are still curved and are still of even thickness. Figure 21.6 shows a *Qín* dynasty brick with 12 characters cast on its surface. Like the great seal script, the small seal cannot be written quickly. It was soon replaced in official use by the clerical script designed for more expedient writing.

Clerical script

The development of the clerical script (隶书/隸書 *lìshū*) is a critical step in the calligraphic evolution of the Chinese writing system. It marks the transition of the Chinese script from the archaic style to the modern style. Chinese characters written in the clerical script and onward are more easily recognizable to today's readers educated in contemporary characters, because they bear significantly more visual resemblance to the contemporary script than do any of the previous styles. Figure 21.7 shows a rubbing of the Cáo Quán (曹全) stele[10] of the Eastern *Hàn* dynasty, a representative work in clerical script. The curved lines of the seal scripts are replaced by straight or slanted strokes or sharp bends. Circles have entirely disappeared. The width of the strokes now varies, adding another dimension of artistic expression. For example, a phrase often used to highlight the stylistic feature of the horizontal stroke in the clerical script is "silkworm head and goose tail (蚕头雁尾/蠶頭雁尾 *cán tóu yàn wěi*)," vividly capturing the dynamic change in contour as the stroke proceeds from the beginning to the end.

FIGURE 21.7   Partial rubbing of the Cáo Quán (曹全) stele (185 CE)

FIGURE 21.8   "Silkworm head and goose tail" – horizontal stroke of the clerical script

Companion Website

Exercise 21.1 Writing speed

Following the clerical script, the stylistic repertoire of Chinese calligraphy dramatically expanded. Three major variants of the clerical script developed almost concurrently from the 2nd to the 4th century CE. These were cursive script (草书/草書 *cǎoshū*), running script (行书/行書 *xíngshū*), and standard script (楷书/楷書 *kǎishū*). The standard script is the style used commonly today in printing and careful handwriting and is also the style Chinese children are first taught in school. More experienced writers may use the running script in handwriting. As previously mentioned, students of Chinese calligraphy usually start their practice with the standard script and then move on to running and cursive scripts. We will follow this order in the following sections as we take a closer look at each of these styles.

Standard script

The so-called standard (aka regular) script (楷书/楷書 *kǎishū*) has been the standard style of writing in China for thousands of years, and it remains so today. You may recall that, in imperial China, candidates taking the civil service exams (604–1904) were required to write their exam papers in the standard script. Being able to write a good hand in the style was believed to enhance one's chance of passing the exams. In modern China, schoolchildren learn to read and write in the standard script. It is also the style people use in handwriting for formal purposes, such as in filling out official paperwork. Print media, including books, newspapers, and magazines, generally use typefaces of the standard script as well.

The standard script is visually close to the clerical script. Perhaps the most distinctive difference between them is in the proportion of the characters. In the standard script, the characters are almost perfectly square, while those of the clerical script tend to be longer in the horizontal dimension than the vertical, looking almost like a squished-down version of the standard script. Another difference is in how certain strokes begin and end. Horizontal strokes in the standard script do not usually have "silkworm heads" or "goose tails" but are written in a more subdued manner compared with the clerical script.

That said, calligraphers of the standard script have considerable freedom in developing their individual styles. Works of the "four grandmasters of the standard script" (楷书四大家/楷書四大家 *kǎishū sìdàjiā*) – Yán Zhēnqīng (颜真卿/顏真卿 709–785 CE), Liǔ Gōngquán (柳公权/柳公權 778–865), Ōuyáng Xún (欧阳询/歐陽詢 557–641), and Zhào Mèngfǔ (赵孟頫/趙孟頫 1254–1322) – are the most well-known. Although the majority of these works are thousands of years old, calligraphy students today, more likely than not, still begin their practice modeling on one of the four masters. Printed models of these works are also readily available in Chinese bookstores.

Running script

It is easy to recognize the running script (行书/行書 *xíngshū*) in comparison with the standard script. Characters written in the standard script have distinctly separate strokes, each carefully executed and deliberately positioned within an imaginary square. By contrast, as its name suggests, the running script uses brush strokes written in swift motion in a manner that creates continuous energy from one stroke to the next. As a result, strokes are semi-connected within the characters, although the overall integrity of individual strokes is largely preserved and the strokes are clearly discernable. The size of the characters may vary, and they may not always conform to a square shape.

The famed calligraphy sage (书圣/書聖 *shū shèng*) Wáng Xīzhī (王羲之 321–379 CE) is credited for having created the running script. He also wrote in this script, in the year 353, what is perhaps the most well-known piece of work throughout the Chinese calligraphic history, *Preface to the Poems Composed at the Orchid Pavilion* (兰亭集序/蘭亭集序 *Lántíngjí*

Xù). The script allows the artist considerable freedom in modifying the strokes or the overall structure of the characters, encouraging an inventive use of brush and ink. For example, in *Preface*, Wáng wrote the character 之 (*zhī* '(grammatical marker)') 21 times, each in a different form. Such spontaneous variation is highly prized. However, it is also believed to be inimitable. It is said that Wáng wrote the *Preface* after having had a few drinks with his friends. He liked it so much and tried to replicate it later on but could not do so to his own satisfaction. Nonetheless, the *Preface* is widely regarded as a masterpiece – legendarily so, in fact – and it has served as a model for numerous calligraphers and amateurs to this day.

Cursive script

The cursive script (aka grass script,[11] 草书/草書 *cǎoshū*) was originally invented during the *Hàn* dynasty as a quicker version of the clerical script. Characters are routinely simplified by replacing components with single, continuous strokes. Often, several characters are written in one unbroken stroke as the brush moves continuously downwards. As you can imagine, the cursive script is the most expressive of spontaneous, free-flowing energy. Perhaps for this reason, it is the preferred script for poetic inscription in paintings during the *Táng* dynasty (唐 618–907 CE).

The *Táng* monk Huái Sù (怀素/懷素 737–799) was a grandmaster of the cursive script. Only a few pieces of his works survived, among which his *Autobiography* (自叙帖 *Zìxù Tiē*) represents the epitome of cursive-style calligraphy for its unparalleled artistic accomplishment and influence (Figure 21.9). The surviving copy is now housed at the Palace Museum in Taipei and is on view once every 16 years.

FIGURE 21.9   *Autobiography* (partial) by Huái Sù
Source: Collection of the National Palace Museum, Taipei

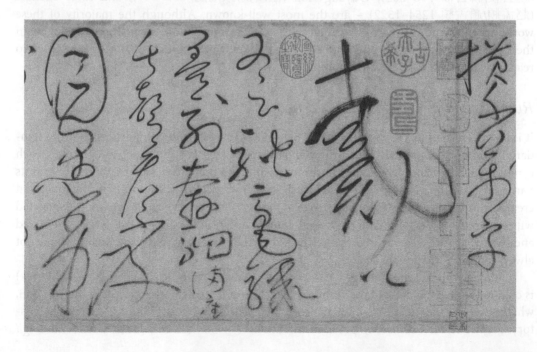

We have taken a brief survey of the major script styles in the history of Chinese calligraphy. To conclude, it is important to keep in mind the following two points. First, these styles did not develop in a strict linear order. For example, there was significant overlap between the great seal, small seal, and clerical scripts, as well as between the clerical, running, cursive, and standard scripts in terms of their predominant time periods. The running, cursive, and standard scripts have coexisted from their inception to this day. Second, although we have learned about the script styles as distinct categories, they are not strict, mutually exclusive categories. In practice, calligraphers may choose to blend two or more styles and write in a manner that falls somewhere between, for example, the typical running and the typical cursive scripts. Therefore, not all calligraphy work ever created could be clearly labelled with one of the script names we have reviewed above. There are also sub-styles within the major categories. In daily writing, standard and running scripts are the most commonly used styles, but all the major script styles find their place today in works created by practitioners of traditional and modern calligraphy.

Notes

1 The *Shāng* dynasty divination inscription is dated to 1250–1050 BCE (Wilkinson, 2015, p. 681).
2 See Sullivan (1999).
3 Practitioners of water calligraphy (aka ground calligraphy) often use extra-large brushes dipped in water to write on cement surface of public areas, such as on sidewalks or in public parks, as a form of physical exercise.
4 Chiang (1973, p. 110).
5 Chapter 7.
6 Wilkinson (2015, p. 684).
7 Ibid., p. 682.
8 The state of *Qín* defeated the other states and united China to establish the *Qín* dynasty.
9 Wilkinson (2015, p. 693).
10 A stele is a stone slab, usually taller than it is wide, that is erected as a memorial. It generally carries inscription on at least one side (the side considered to be the front) of its surface.
11 The name "grass script" for cursive script may have come from the idea that the brush strokes look like leaves of grass blowing in the wind.

22 A calligraphy workshop

I F YOU HAVE NEVER had the experience of writing with brush and ink, in this chapter, you will get a taste of what it is like. As you can imagine, developing highly refined skills in East Asian calligraphy takes an enormous amount of training. Many accomplished calligraphers start their practice in childhood and persist over a lifetime. Without substantial experience handling calligraphy tools and materials, it is nearly impossible to produce highly skilled works. This practice, however, will be useful for you to gain direct and personal understanding of East Asian calligraphy through hands-on experience. The end-product may or may not be exactly the way you want it, but it will be a remarkable piece of work nonetheless as an earnest attempt at a challenging art form.

▢ Getting ready

Tools and materials

The main instruments and materials you will need for calligraphy practice are commonly referred to in Chinese as *wénfáng sì bǎo* (文房四宝/文房四寶), "four treasures of a scholar's studio." These are brush (笔/筆 *bǐ*), ink (墨 *mò*), paper (纸/紙 *zhǐ*), and inkwell (砚/硯 *yàn*). In pre-modern times, they were indispensable items for students and scholars in the East Asian cultural sphere. The manufacturing of these items became highly developed both technically and aesthetically, so that the finest examples, especially of brushes and inkwells, became valuable collector items and find their places in museums and auction houses. With the adoption of Western writing tools from the mid-19th to the early 20th centuries, brushes and inkwells have long been replaced by fountain pens or ballpoint pens for daily writing purposes. However, the sustained popularity of traditional art ensures that these items are readily available today from stationery sellers or in art supply stores. In the West, they can usually be purchased at Asian bookstores, large art supplies shops, or online sellers based in East Asia.

For this workshop, we will use student-grade tools and materials. They are reasonably good in quality, quite affordable, and possibly the most readily available. The following guidelines aim to help you select the right types of "treasures" to use for this practice.

The brush you choose should be medium to large, with a bristle length of 1.5–2 inches. Brushes of this size are ideal for writing characters that fit comfortably in square cells of 3–4 inches in width and height. Although this is much larger than the characters used in actual writing for everyday purposes, big characters are considered a wise choice for beginners, because writing big makes it easier to grasp the characteristics of individual strokes and to appreciate the composition of whole characters. In fact, practicing calligraphy is colloquially referred to as *xiě dàzì* (写大字/寫大字) "writing big characters" in Chinese.

Calligraphy ink comes in two main forms: solid ink sticks and bottled liquid ink. Ink sticks are the traditional form. They need to be ground and mixed with water right before writing takes place. Compared with ready-mixed liquid ink, solid sticks allow the calligrapher more control over the ink's consistency. The action of ink grinding can also be a calming and meditative process that prepares the artist for the writing. For our purpose, however, bottled ink is a better choice. It is more convenient and affordable, and it also saves the worry about achieving the right consistency.

Calligraphy paper, in Chinese, is commonly referred to as "*Xuān* paper (宣纸/宣紙 *xuān zhǐ*)." Although in English it has the common name "rice paper," rice is not its main ingredient. *Xuān*, in fact, comes from the ancient place name *Xuānzhōu* (宣州 '*Xuān* prefecture,' today's 宣城 *Xuānchéng* '*Xuān* city'), where a highly prized kind of calligraphy paper has been produced since the *Táng* dynasty (618–907 CE). Authentic *Xuān* paper uses the bark of elm trees indigenous to the area as its main ingredient. Many calligraphy students start with writing on gridded practice paper that is of a lesser quality than *Xuān* paper. The printed grids are an excellent aid for beginners, so we will also use this kind. Such practice paper is gridded either with a rectangle inside each cell like the character 回 (*huí*) or with crossing lines like the character 米 (*mǐ*), as shown in Figure 22.1 Our calligraphy model uses the *mǐ*-grid, so it is better to use the *mǐ*-gridded paper. Each sheet usually contains 12 or 15 cells. For today's practice, you will need 8–12 sheets.

FIGURE 22.1 *Huí* gridlines and *mǐ* gridlines on typical calligraphy practice paper

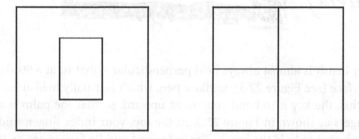

Since we will not be grinding ink, a dedicated inkwell or ink stone may not be necessary and can be substituted by a small, shallow container for liquid, such as a ceramic saucer.

In addition, there are a few items you may consider using to make the writing process smoother. You may use a piece of felt underneath the calligraphy paper to keep the ink from seeping through onto the desk surface or use a couple of sheets of newspaper for the same purpose. You may also want to use a paperweight to keep the paper in place while writing. A few sheets of paper towel may come in handy when you need to wipe ink off the desk.

Before you start writing, take your time to arrange the tools and materials on your desk. If you are right-handed, place the calligraphy model to the left of the practice paper, and the brush, ink, and inkwell to the right, as is shown in the diagram (Figure 22.2). If you are left-handed, then you may want to switch the items on the two sides.

Gesture and posture

It is important for beginners to carefully learn how to hold the calligraphy brush, as the configuration of your fingers, palm, and wrist is quite different from holding a pen. First of all,

FIGURE 22.2　Setting up the writing space
Source: © Cheryl Crowley; used with permission

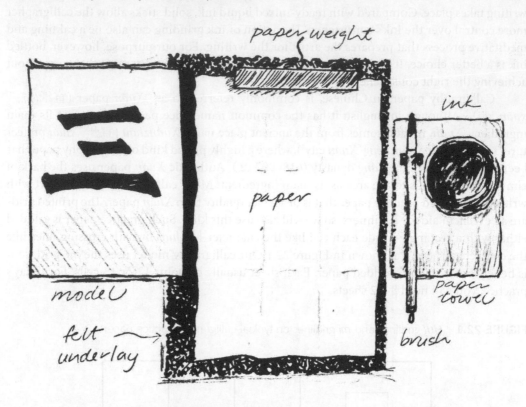

the calligraphy brush is almost always held perpendicular – that is, at a 90-degree angle – to the writing surface (see Figure 22.3), unlike a pen, which is usually held at a 30- to 45-degree angle. To do this, the key is to bend your wrist upward, so that the palm is almost upright. Place your fingers as shown in Figure 22.3. At the top, your index finger, middle finger, and thumb work together to hold the brush. The index and middle fingers are on the same side of the brush, while the thumb counterbalances them from the opposite side. The index and middle fingers may spread apart from each other to give a steadier hold. Below them, the brush rests against the top knuckle of the ring finger. Then, the little finger rests against the inside of the ring finger to provide additional support. The five fingers assume different angles in relationship to the writing surface: the index finger is more or less horizontal, while the others are almost vertical. The middle, ring, and little fingers point downwards, while the thumb points upwards. Note that your fingers naturally curve around the brush without touching the palm. They do not clench together to form a fist; rather, they should be quite relaxed, leaving an empty space between them and the palm, and the size of this space is – in conventional pedagogical lingo – large enough to fit in an egg.

Holding the brush in this manner, you should be able to move its tip forward and backward relatively freely. When you do so, the thumb and the index finger are stationary, making a pivot where they touch the brush. The other three fingers then move in coordination to bring the brush away from you and then toward you. This is the basic gesture used when writing a vertical stroke. In writing a horizontal stroke, most of the movement is accomplished by moving the entire hand left to right, with the wrist or the elbow as the pivot. To help keep a steady

FIGURE 22.3 Holding the brush (left handed, right handed)

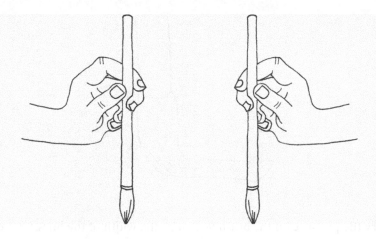

hand, beginners may wish to rest the wrist on the desk while writing. This will limit the size of the characters, however, and is why sometimes more strict training may require a "hanging wrist" with the wrist hanging a few inches above the writing surface instead of resting on it.

It is also important to sit in a correct posture when practicing calligraphy. Sit with a straight back. Do not lean forward against the edge of the desk. There should be a two- to three-inch distance between your body and the desk. Your forearms should naturally rest on the desk. If you are right-handed, you can use your left hand to hold down the calligraphy paper as you write, and vice versa. Do not cross your legs. Place both of your feet flat on the ground without extending your legs forward or bending them backward. Your overall body posture should be straight yet relaxed to avoid fatigue or overstraining your muscles. Do not hold your breath. Keep breathing naturally while you write.

Warm-up

Writing using a soft brush may feel very different from using a pen. Before we start writing Chinese characters, let's do a few exercises to warm up.

We will use the center-tip technique (中锋/中鋒 zhōng fēng) in these exercises. Pay attention to how the mark you make changes as you alter the pressure and direction of the brush tip. One constant factor is that the tip of the brush should always remain in the center of the mark you make. For example, when writing a vertical stroke, the brush tip always makes a symmetrical contact on the paper along the direction of its movement without leaning either to its left or to its right. This is what is called the center-tip technique. It is the most commonly used brush technique.

First, make some straight and even lines. Start by making a few horizontal lines across the width of your paper. Maintain steady pressure so that the width of the lines remains even. Then make a few vertical lines that cross the horizontal lines at even intervals. Keep the width of the vertical lines constant and consistent with the horizontal marks. Do this repeatedly until you feel comfortable using the brush to create straight and even lines.

FIGURE 22.4   The center-tip technique

Then, vary the pressure on the brush to change the width of the lines. Use less pressure for thinner lines and more pressure to make the lines thicker.

In the next exercise, use the brush to make half circles, still keeping the width of the lines even. Do this in a variety of directions.

In the last exercise, make diagonal lines and vary the pressure of your brush as you write. Start out relatively thin and then make the line thicker while you put more pressure on the brush tip. Then, reduce the pressure again until eventually lifting the brush off of the paper.

Basic strokes

Chinese characters are composed of a variety of strokes. Although the number of characters is enormous, the types of strokes are quite limited. The most basic ones include horizontal (横/橫 *héng*), vertical (竖/豎 *shù*), down-left sweep (撇 *piě*), down-right sweep (捺 *nà*), bent (折 *zhé*), hook (钩/鉤 *gōu*), and dot (点/點 *diǎn*). Let's practice writing each one of them.

First, the horizontal stroke. Before we start, look at the model (Figure 22.5) carefully. What characteristics do you see in the form of this stroke? Is it even in width? Is it perfectly horizontal? Is it positioned right in the center of the square cell? You will notice that the two ends of the stroke are slightly thicker and the middle portion is relatively thin. The stroke slants subtly upward as it goes from left to right. The overall stroke is in the center of the cell. Therefore, it begins somewhat below the middle line and ends a little bit above it. Written in this manner, the horizontal stroke is shaped almost like a piece of bone, demonstrative of its inner strength.

Now let's write the horizontal stroke. Start off by pressing down the tip of the brush at a 45-degree angle. Then drag the brush toward the right while slightly and gradually lifting it as it goes toward the middle. As it passes the middle point, slightly press it down as it moves forward. To end the stroke, lift the brush so that only the tip lightly touches the upper right edge of the stroke, press down on the brush at a 45-degree angle, and then bring it back up to round off the corner, resulting in a somewhat rounded end of the stroke.

There are two types of vertical strokes: one with a rounded ending called "hanging dew-drop" (垂露/垂露 *chuí lù*; see Figure 22.6), and the other with a sharp tapered ending referred to as "suspended needle" (悬针/懸針 *xuán zhēn*; Figure 22.7). The beginning of both of the

FIGURE 22.5   Horizontal (*héng*)

vertical strokes is the same and similar to that of the horizontal stroke. The ending of the "hanging dewdrop" is similar to the ending of the horizontal stroke. The "suspended needle" ends somewhat differently: instead of lifting and pressing the brush to round off the end, it simply lifts to form a sharp needlepoint at the end. This kind of vertical stroke is usually used when it is the last stroke of a character.

FIGURE 22.6   Vertical (*shù*): "hanging dewdrop" (*chuí lù*)

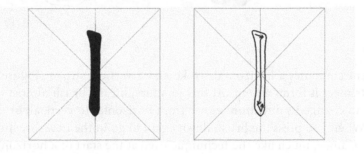

FIGURE 22.7   Vertical (*shù*): "suspended needle" (*xuán zhēn*)

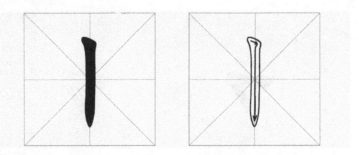

The down-left (Figure 22.8) and down-right (Figure 22.9) sweeps are similar to the suspended-needle vertical stroke in terms of brush technique. The one exception is the ending of the down-right sweep. As you see in Figure 22.9, the stroke has a smooth curve on its upper edge and an angular shape on its lower edge. This effect is achieved by changing the direction of the brush while maintaining a smooth top edge.

FIGURE 22.8 Down-left sweep (*piě*)

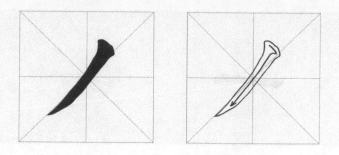

FIGURE 22.9 Down-right sweep (*nà*)

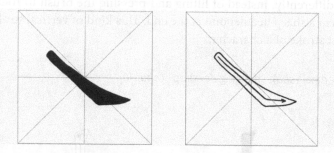

The bent combines a horizontal stroke and a vertical stroke (Figure 22.10). Where the two parts meet it forms a bent. At this juncture, lift the brush almost but not entirely off the page to change its direction, either from horizontal to vertical, or from vertical to horizontal. When you press the brush down again to go in the new direction, it should be at a 45-degree angle, much like the technique used at the start of a horizontal or a vertical stroke.

FIGURE 22.10 Bent (*zhé*)

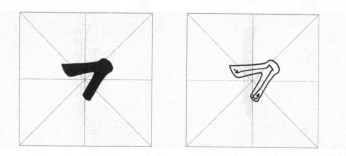

The hook might be one of the most difficult strokes to write for beginners. It is similar to the bent in that the brush needs to change directions. However, it is also different because it usually tapers off into a pointed ending at an angle greater than 90 degrees. The hook can be attached to a horizontal or a vertical, as shown in Figures 22.11 and 22.12.

FIGURE 22.11   Horizontal and hook (*héng gōu*)

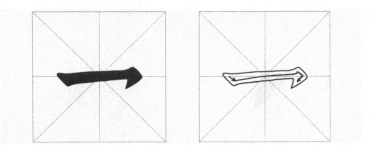

FIGURE 22.12   Vertical and hook (*shù gōu*)

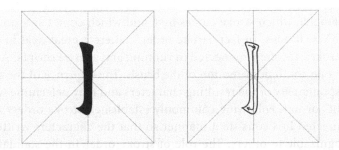

The "dot" is really a cover term for a variety of short strokes. Unlike what the term may imply in English, a "dot" in Chinese calligraphy is almost never round. Rather, it is sometimes shaped like a raindrop, sometimes appears to have a hook coming out of it, and at other times looks more like a shorter vertical stroke, all depending on which part of the character it composes. What these various shapes have in common is their brevity. They are so much shorter than a regular horizontal, vertical, or sweep that conceptually it is natural to think of them all as dots. Figure 22.13 is what can be called a "left dot" and Figure 22.14 is a "right dot."

FIGURE 22.13   Left dot (*zuǒ diǎn*)

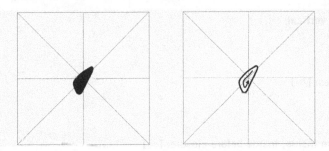

A single stroke can also be a combination of several of the basic stroke types. For example, the character 力 (*lì* 'strength, power') consists of two strokes, a simple *piě* (down-left sweep) and a more complex *héng-zhé-gōu*, that is, a combination of horizontal, bent, and hook.

FIGURE 22.14 Right dot (*yòu diǎn*)

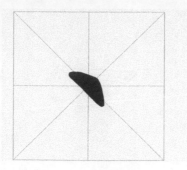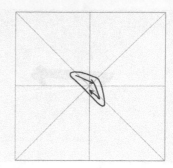

Stroke order

In writing a character, which stroke comes first, and which comes second? Does stroke sequence matter? Yes, it does. In fact, stroke order matters a great deal in calligraphy. One reason is that strokes are often connected in running and cursive scripts. A group of strokes may be done in one continuous motion of the brush. The sequence of the strokes thus contributes to the spontaneity of the resulting characters and may determine whether the characters "feel right" or not. Following commonly established stroke orders also ensures that strokes are connected in a consistent manner so that the characters written by one calligrapher are recognizable to others. The role of stroke order in the standard script may be less apparent but is just as important, since mastering the standard script, for perhaps the majority of calligraphy students, serves as the foundation for progressing to the running and cursive scripts.

There are a few major patterns or principles when it comes to stroke order:

Top before bottom: [三]

一　二　三

Left before right: [人]

丿　人

Horizontal before vertical: [十]

一　十

Center before sides: [小]

亅　小　小

Outer frame before inside, inside before closure: [回]

丨　冂　冋　冋　回　回

Inside before outside: [道]

丶 丷 丷 丷 产 产 首 首 首 ̇首 辶首 道 道

It may not always be completely straightforward to determine the exact stroke order of a character. Even native writers sometimes vary among themselves in how they write certain characters. That said, are you up for a few challenges? See the companion website for stroke-order exercises.

Companion Website

Exercise 22.1 Stroke orders

Composition

Writing well does not only require beautiful execution of individual strokes. It also demands close attention to the spatial relationship between the strokes. In general, calligraphers may consider it better to have imperfect strokes but a balanced arrangement of the strokes than the other way around, which shows how important it is to master the composition of characters.

At this stage of your practice, learning to use the printed guidelines on your calligraphy paper will be particularly beneficial. Before you start to write, observe closely, and when you write, imitate as much as possible. Take the following character 山 (*shān*, 'mountain, hill') as an example (Figure 22.15). What do you notice? First of all, there is a great amount of empty space around it within the area defined by the gridlines. None of the strokes are touching or even approaching the outer frame of the square cell. Then, notice how the three vertical strokes are arranged, and how they are spaced in relation to each other. The middle stroke is right in the center, with almost equal length above and below the middle horizontal gridline. The two shorter verticals are about equal distance from the middle one, and along the horizontal dimension each is positioned at about the middle point of its half of the grid. On the vertical dimension, the two shorter verticals sit at about the same level, yet they are not the same height. The one on the left is somewhat shorter, not quite coming up to the middle gridline, while the one on the right crosses slightly over the gridline. Finally, notice how the horizontal stroke is positioned. Is it perfectly horizontal? It is easy to see that it is not, if you compare the distance between this stroke and the middle gridline on the left end versus the right end of the horizontal stroke. The horizontal stroke in fact slants upward as it goes from left to right. This subtle curvature gives it a tension – and thus an unyielding inner strength – like that in a piece of bone or in a bamboo stem that would only slightly curve while under pressure. As you have seen, the gridlines are very useful if you take the time to "read" the character. Reading the character in this manner will no doubt train your eyes to see. Being able to see the defining characteristics of a character is the prerequisite to producing the desired result, so do take the time to look closely before you start writing.

FIGURE 22.15   Character composition

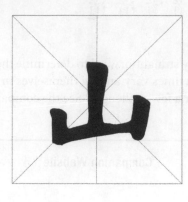

■ Writing exercise

Now you are ready to do some hands-on practice. Use Figures 22.16 to 22.19 as a model to write the four characters we have already looked at in the stroke-order exercise: 日 (rì), 心 (xīn), 永 (yǒng), and 道 (dào).

FIGURE 22.16   Model: 日 (rì)

FIGURE 22.17   Model: 心 (xīn)

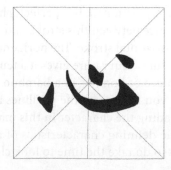

FIGURE 22.18   Model 永 (*yǒng*)

FIGURE 22.19   Model 道 (*dào*)

If you are interested in practicing more, you can ask your instructor for additional models to make a complete piece.

Enjoy!

23 Modern calligraphy in China

B Y THE MID-1980S, the grand tradition of Chinese calligraphy had been increasingly seen as a rigid, limited, and outdated form of expression by some calligraphers in China who we now refer to as the Modernists. Through theoretical debates, technical exploration, and artistic innovation, these calligraphers launched a movement to modernize the tenets and practice of calligraphy, challenging and redefining its boundaries. They also created and exhibited new works that were drastically different from the classical style. In this chapter, we will learn about the sociocultural background of the Modernists' endeavors and look at a few of their works.

The '85 New Wave

The attempts to modernize calligraphy were part of a much larger and highly influential artistic movement toward Modernism that had been burgeoning in China since the adoption of the new economic reforms and "open door" policy (改革开放政策/改革開放政策 *gǎigé kāifàng zhèngcè*, ca. 1978). Chinese artists were gaining increasing access to Western works, trends, and ideas. Many in the artistic and intellectual circles took every opportunity to immerse themselves in learning about the West, especially its modern cultural theory and literary criticism theory. Being able to do so shortly after the decade-long restriction of the Cultural Revolution (文化大革命 *Wénhuà Dà Gémìng* 1966–1976) had an enormous impact on how artists viewed and valued traditional art forms and their associated social hierarchy and ideological control. The younger artists who were coming of age during that time, in particular, longed for new means of expression as individuals and freer and more democratic ecosystems as communities. They devoted themselves to the pursuit of these ideals with extraordinary enthusiasm.

The year 1985 is considered a landmark in the history of contemporary Chinese art. It was the beginning of an unprecedented artistic movement that passionately and courageously opened a new path towards internationalization and contemporaneity.[1] From 1985 to 1989, a group of more than a thousand young artists engaged in creating and exhibiting artworks and organizing academic forums. Hundreds of new artist groups sprouted in major cities around China, giving the young artists collective voices in advocating for new art forms different from the dominant, conservative ideology and, in practical terms, making it possible for them to show their works outside the government-sponsored museum and gallery system that rarely approved of the New Wave.

A microcosm of the New Wave movement, Modern Calligraphy (现代书法/現代書法 *Xiàndài Shūfǎ*) – so-called by its practitioners to distinguish it from the time-honored tradition of classical calligraphy – also gained momentum in the 1980s. In October 1985, the

First Modern Calligraphy Exhibition (现代书法首展/現代書法首展 *Xiàndài ShūfǎShǒu Zhǎn*) was held in Beijing, marking the beginning of the Modern Calligraphy movement. Inspired by Western artistic and intellectual trends to innovate in their work, the Modernists took a critical view of the strict conventions Chinese calligraphy had formed and perpetuated in its artistic form over the millennia. To them, completely following the tradition was staying on a dead-end path; to make the archaic art form relevant again to modern life, calligraphers must break free from the constraining rules. However, to modernize calligraphy was not to negate or eradicate tradition – Modern Calligraphy shared with traditional calligraphy the same cultural foundation; instead, it was to continue the legacy of classical calligraphy in a form that was more compatible with the modern spirit.

The Modernists advocated seeking new means of calligraphic expression by looking outward – in particular, by drawing inspiration from other forms of art, both Eastern and Western. In the early 1980s, thanks to increased communication with Japanese calligraphers, Chinese calligraphers were exposed to Japanese Avant-garde calligraphy that advocated freeing calligraphy from the restraints of textual legibility and experimented with new media and materials in their works. The Japanese genre had a direct and profound impact on the development of Modern Calligraphy in China. Experimentations and explorations continued from there to develop a rich new calligraphic vocabulary. Indeed, as one scholar has pointed out at the beginning of the 21st century, "over the past fifty years, there have been greater changes in the art of calligraphy than in the previous thousand years."[2] We will look at a few examples of these changes below.

THE STORY BEYOND

Trends in today's Chinese calligraphy

The "Modern" in "Modern Calligraphy," in our discussion, refers to an artistic genre rather than a time period. It by no means implies that all – or even most of – the calligraphy works produced in recent decades are of a monolithic, Modernist style. In fact, the traditional style has been and still is the predominant form of calligraphy in China, and there is not a simple dichotomy between "Modern" and "Classical."

So, what kinds of works do calligraphers create in this day and age in China? According to Barrass (2002), there have been four distinct trends: the Classicists, the Neo-classicists, the Modernists and the Avant-garde. The Classicists uphold the grand tradition of Chinese calligraphy and seek to preserve as many of the old values as possible. They are the majority of calligraphy practitioners and are also the most influential. Schoolchildren, when first introduced to calligraphy, follow the classical tradition. The Neo-classicists by and large maintain the same aesthetic values and principles as the Classicists. However, they are usually much younger and are interested in reviving and refreshing the classical tradition by giving it a new context (pp. 25–39).

The Modernists and the Avant-garde calligraphers both explore radically new approaches to calligraphy. One difference between them is that the Modernists largely resort to "ink on paper" as their primary media, while the Avant-garde often integrate calligraphic techniques and imagery with conceptual or performance art, incorporating non-conventional techniques and materials.[3] Today, their works continue to push the limits of what constitutes calligraphy.

Although the four approaches are distinct, they are not mutually exclusive. Many artists creating modern or Avant-garde works have been classically trained and enjoy crossing boundaries in the various genres.

■ The Modernists and their works

How exactly did the Modernists innovate? Let's explore this question by looking at the works of a few artists, Gǔ Gān (古干 1942–), Sà Běnjiè (萨本介/薩本介 1948–), Qiū Zhènzhōng (邱振中 1947–), and Wáng Dōnglíng (王冬龄 1945–).

Gǔ Gān was one of a few who spearheaded the Modern Calligraphy movement and produced a large number of high-quality works. His books, *The Construction of Modern Calligraphy* (1987) and *The Three Steps of Modern Calligraphy* (1990), were important works on Modern techniques. He believed that calligraphy in modern times should focus on the concepts or ideas behind the works rather than the textual meaning of what was written. As a result, many of his works contained only one or two characters. These characters were not written in the traditional manner. Rather, they were given a more painting-like form, sometimes by restoring the characters to their pictographic origin. The pictorial form, in turn, reinforced the meaning of the characters and built additional layers of complexity into the calligraphy.

Let us look at two examples. You can see images of these works on the companion website. In *Coil*, the character 绕/繞 *rào*, which means "to coil, to detour, to circle," is written in cursive strokes that resemble a coiling, thorny vine or a barbed wire. The image directly reinforces the meaning of the character. The character 開 *kāi* "to open" in *Opening Up* is written in thick strokes striding across the width of the piece. The viewer is invited to peek through the opening door – the 門 *mén* component of the character – and see an ancient Chinese-style building behind it. Closer to the viewer and perched atop the pointy, fence-shaped stroke of 开 *kāi*, the inside component of the character, is a bird. Aside from the integration of painterly elements in the calligraphy piece, both the bird and the building are in red, a departure from the "black ink on white paper" tonal scheme of traditional calligraphy. The artist also made use of painting techniques to create a rugged ink effect for the background against which the character is set. It is not difficult to see that these examples demonstrate an approach to calligraphy that integrates the visual styles and technical elements of painting into brush writing.

Companion Website

Exercise 23.1 Interpreting a calligraphy work

Another approach of the Modernists was to play with the characters – taking them apart, recombining them, and generating new or additional meaning in the process. The piece by Sà Běnjiè consists of two characters, 覺 (*jué* 'to be aware') and 悟 (*wù* 'to understand'), with their components reconfigured into one coherent image. The parts in red compose the character 悟, which has 心 (*xīn* 'heart,' written as 忄 as a radical) on the left and 吾 (*wú* 'I, my') on the right. The bottom-left component in black, 見 (*jiàn*, 见 in simplified script), meaning "to see," is the bottom element of 覺. The top-right black component is the top part of 覺 and does not constitute a stand-alone character. By recombining the components of the two characters into one image, this piece may convey synthesized meaning derived from the characters. As the artist explains, it shows that the meaning of the word 覺悟, "consciousness," consists of "to see" (見), "my" (吾), and "heart" (心). Therefore, being conscious can be understood as being able to see one's heart.

Companion Website

Exercise 23.2 Reconstructing characters

Qiū Zhènzhōng's Modernist calligraphy works sought to break the rules of traditional calligraphy, but only one or two at a time. While retaining the general look of classical pieces – his works appear to contain a number of characters, words, or phrases written in black ink on white paper – they were undeniably modern. One example is his *New Poetry Series – Promise* (新诗系列-保证/新詩系列-保證 *Xīnshī Xìliè – Bǎozhèng*; Figure 23.1). Unlike classical calligraphy, in which a poem is written in columns arranged from right to left, in this piece the characters appear from left to right in rows arranged from top to bottom, consistent with the page layout of modern texts. Qiū also allowed the brush to be almost completely drained of ink before recharging, creating a highly dynamic ink effect. Another example is his *Characters to be Deciphered Series – No. 9* (待考文字系列 – No. 9 *Dài Kǎo Wénzì Xìliè*; Figure 23.2). The characters in this piece are unrecognizable to viewers because they are ancient characters that have not been deciphered. The content of the piece would be an unlikely choice for traditional calligraphy, which was used to record and present important textual information. In addition, the way the characters are scattered on the writing surface instead of being arranged in columns or rows also breaks the convention.

FIGURE 23.1   *New Poetry Series – Promise*, Qiū Zhènzhōng, 1989
Source: Courtesy of the artist

FIGURE 23.2 *Characters to be Deciphered Series – No. 9*, Qiū Zhènzhōng, 1988
Source: Courtesy of the artist

Wáng Dōnglíng, in some of his modern calligraphy works, took yet another approach to innovation. These works contain very few – or perhaps no – characters. They seem to shift the visual scale of calligraphy by having the viewer zoom in so close as to see only part of a calligraphic stroke. One example, *Being Open and Empty* (守白 *Shǒu Bái*), is shown in Figure 23.3. In this type of work, there are no discernable characters, only abstract shapes and lines that suggest some resemblance of characters. The visual quality of calligraphy clearly exists – there are traces of the brush made with black ink on white paper – yet at the same time it is no longer calligraphy in the traditional sense. To the artist, breaking away from the traditional form allows for the freedom to fully express his feelings and his understanding of the calligraphy art.[4]

FIGURE 23.3 守白 *Being Open and Empty*, Wáng Dōnglíng, 2005
Source: Courtesy of the artist

Wáng is also a master of cursive calligraphy written on a grand scale. Figure 23.4 shows him writing the four-character phrase 道法自然 (*dào fǎzìrán* '*Dao Operates Naturally*') in 2014 at the The Metropolitan Museum of Art. Such works are often done with a large crowd of spectators on site. The act of writing thus becomes a performance characterized by an ebullient outpouring of energy, making the creative process as integral a part of the artwork as the final product.

FIGURE 23.4 Wáng Dōnglíng creating 道法自然 *Dao Operates Naturally* at The Metropolitan Museum of Art, January 11, 2014
Source: Courtesy of the artist

Accompanying the changes in calligraphy was an intense debate between the Modernists and the traditionalists about its essence: what was calligraphy, and what was it for? One of the central questions was whether or not calligraphy must purely be the writing of Chinese characters. On this issue, the Modernists held a much more liberal view than the traditionalists. As you have seen, some of them created works that integrated non-textual elements or rendered characters into illegible forms. These works bore much resemblance to Western abstract painting and were thus more approachable to Western viewers than traditional Chinese calligraphy. In this sense, it might be appropriate to say that such works were the result of cross-fertilization between traditional Chinese art and Western modern art. As for the question of whether the calligraphy Chinese artists create without using legible characters can still be considered "calligraphy," it may remain a matter of debate for the foreseeable future.

Notes

1 Fei (2007, p. 7).
2 Barrass (2002, p. 15).

3 Some art historians, for example Liu (2010), do not distinguish between the Modernists and the Avant-gardists and consider them both modern.
4 Wáng Dōnglíng talks about the tension between his classical training and his efforts to continuously innovate in calligraphy in a video interview by the Creative Thinking Project (2017). In this interview, he also discusses his "chaotic script" (luànshū 乱书/亂書), an outcome of calligraphic innovation for the past three decades.

24 Chinese characters in Avant-garde art

In THE PREVIOUS CHAPTER, we learned about the Modern Calligraphy movement that came to fore in the 1980s. Given the sociocultural conditions of that time, it was no co-incidence that calligraphy practitioners were pushing for change and innovating for new forms of expression. Of course, such artistic experimentation was not limited to calligraphers. In fact, thousands of painters, sculptors, print makers, mixed-media artists, performers, and other artists launched an unprecedented Avant-garde art movement that eventually turned Chinese contemporary art into a global phenomenon. Some of the most interesting works created during and since the '85 New Wave make use of Chinese characters or calligraphy. In this chapter, we will look at a few examples with a focus on the period during and not long after the New Wave, that is, from 1985 to 2000. We will examine the fascinating new perspectives these works produced and reflect on some of the questions they raised.

Background

Several factors contributed to the flourishing of new concepts, perspectives, and approaches to making art during and after the New Wave. Besides the ending of the Cultural Revolution and the implementation of an economic reform and open policy, more direct impact on artists came from the increasing accessibility of Western intellectual works translated into Chinese and made available through bookstores. Books on Western philosophy, literary criticism, and cultural theory became increasingly popular in Chinese intellectual communities and provided fertile stimuli for artists eager to speak the language of modernity and internationalization.

THE STORY BEYOND

Reading fever

The following is an excerpt from an interview with artist Huáng Yǒngpíng (黄永砅 1954–), who was at the forefront of the '85 New Wave.[1] Huáng's personal account illustrates the impact of Western texts on contemporary artists working in the 1980s.

At the end of the 1970s and through the beginning of the 1980s, there was an up-surge in reading. What had happened during the Cultural Revolution, as many of you know, was that books were limited and mostly banned, and people were encouraged to read only one, the little red book, consisting primarily of quotations by Chairman

Mao. At the end of the 1970s, policies changed and bookstores re-opened, offering an increasing number of translations of Western texts, as well as some traditional Chinese texts. This period has been called "Reading Fever." At this time, the intellectual community was gripped with a desire to read a wide range of texts.

I love reading and read quite a lot during that period. Bookstores would constantly be changing the titles on their shelves, so one had to read really quickly before the next set of books replaced the old books on the shelves. I could read really fast, but the information wouldn't always stick! [Laughter.] I loved reading about philosophy, but philosophical texts took quite a bit of time to absorb so I would spend a lot of my free time focusing on these texts. I especially enjoyed reading Wittgenstein. Most of us [artists] would eagerly await new translations of books and when they were made available, we would immediately devour them.

At the same time, Chinese philosophical and literary works also became available again. Books on Daoism and Buddhism – in particular *Chánzōng* (禅宗/禪宗, 'Zen sect') Buddhism – as well as Confucianism were especially sought after. Artists continued to draw ideas from classical Chinese intellectual works but began integrating them with Western concepts and approaches in their artworks.

Artworks

Companion Website

Exercise 24.1 Analysis of artworks

Book from the Sky (1987–1991)

One of the most influential artworks of the period was Xú Bīng's (徐冰 1955–) *Book from the Sky* (天书/天書 *Tiānshū*), an installation composed of a large number of hand-printed books and scrolls. Figure 24.1 is an image of this work. Since its initial exhibition in Beijing in 1988, it has been shown in a number of locations around the world, including several museums in the United States. As you can see, in this initial show the exhibition hall was filled with printed text presented in a variety of formats – bound books on the floor and scrolls mounted on the wall and draping from the ceiling. Walking into this space enveloped in text, viewers could not help wanting to read and understand what was in front of them. They looked and stared, only to discover that none of the characters was comprehensible. Only then did they realize that, indeed, those were not regular characters but characters that the artist had invented.

FIGURE 24.1 *Book from the Sky*, mixed media installation
Source: Courtesy of Xú Bīng Studio

The title of this work, *Tiānshū* (天书/天書: 天 'sky, heaven,' 书/書 'book'), literally means "sky book," or "book from the sky." In Chinese, this term is used to refer to writing that is incomprehensible to ordinary people due to either its divine nature, or, in a joking manner, its poor execution. In the case of this artwork, of course, the writing is unreadable for yet another reason – none of the seemingly Chinese characters is real. Invented by the artist by reassembling the original strokes in new ways compatible with the compositional principles of Chinese characters, they look authentic even to native eyes. But they are not associated with any sounds or meanings in the Chinese language and are not actually used for functional communication between any writers or readers of Chinese.

FIGURE 24.2 *Book from the Sky* (details), hand-printed book page from wooden blocks inscribed with false Chinese characters
Source: Courtesy of Xú Bīng Studio

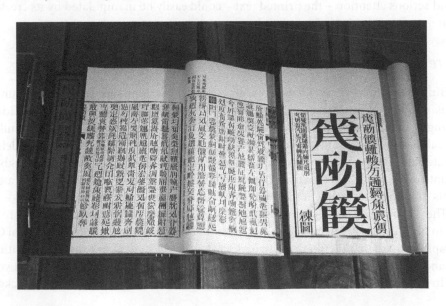

In fact, Xú Bīng invented some 4,000 characters. Not only that: he hand-carved each character on a wooden block, printed the text using the movable blocks, created books strictly following the bookbinding conventions of the *Sòng* dynasty (960–1279), and made exquisite wooden boxes to hold the books. The entire project took him more than four years to complete.

You may have all kinds of questions to ask by this point: Why did Xú Bīng create so many unreadable characters? Why did he put in so much effort to create a text that is utterly incomprehensible? What did he intend to say with this artwork? It is natural to want to know the artist's intention when the artwork is so provocative and puzzling at the same time. However, the artist did not provide us with responses to any of these questions. His job was done as soon as the artwork was completed, and he has done his job well when you, the viewer, start asking questions. As for answers, you will need to come up with your own.

Imagine yourself walking into the exhibition hall that houses this installation. How will you react to *Book from the Sky*? If you are like one of the viewers at the first show in Beijing, you may feel a variety of emotions, depending on whether you consider yourself Chinese or non-Chinese, whether you read and write the Chinese script, or whether you have learned Chinese as a native speaker or a second-language learner. Perry Link (2006) analyzed these reactions in his essay "Whose assumptions does Xu Bing upset, and why?"[2] He found that viewers who could read Chinese naturally tried to comprehend the text but then were disappointed, frustrated, and even angered upon realizing that the characters were not real. To them, looking for meaning where no meaning could be found was a rather irritating experience.[3] To those who did not read much or any Chinese, however, it could be a relief. This was because not knowing the characters no longer constituted a deficiency, and they knew as much or as little as any other viewer.[4] To yet another group of viewers with a rebellious spirit, the work could be exhilarating in its subversive nature: characters were created by an individual instead of sanctioned by the nation-state, the use of characters represented a lack of meaning rather than the creation of meaning, and books filled with characters were printed but not to be read.[5] The work called into question the fundamental idea of communication through writing, demonstrating how something that looked official and seemed to demand serious attention – the printed text – could easily be manipulated by its creators and ultimately end up manipulating its readers.

Square Calligraphy Classroom (1994)

If Xú Bīng's *Book from the Sky* challenges our assumptions about writing and communication, his *Square Calligraphy Classroom* continues to do so in an almost parallel yet paradoxically opposing manner. *Square Calligraphy Classroom* is a mixed-media installation, a fully functional calligraphy classroom equipped with tables, seats, calligraphy manuals, models, tools, and materials. The walls are furnished with instructional charts, and even the blackboard in the front of the room is covered with written characters that appear to demonstrate to the students how writing is done in the "square-word" script.

The classroom is there not merely to be seen, but to be experienced, and, more importantly, to be figured out. The installation appears to be a perfect model of a traditional Chinese calligraphy classroom. Viewers are invited to step in, sit down, and do some writing with brush and ink. Imagine yourself doing so. Sitting at the table, you observe what is at your disposal. In front of you is a book of model calligraphy – white characters on black background, typical of models made from rubbings of ancient stone steles. On the table is a practice book with the same characters as in the model printed in red outlines, guidelines for you to trace as you write, also a typical practice for beginners. For your reference is a calligraphy manual, black characters on white paper, with drawings illustrating the shapes of certain brush strokes. That is also typical of traditional calligraphy manuals. You pick up the brush and are ready to write.

So, what is there to figure out? You look at the model, and this is when you realize – wait a minute, what is it I am writing? What is this script? It looks Chinese, but a native reader or someone with knowledge of Chinese characters can tell that it is *not* Chinese. The characters are not readable in Chinese. Are they invented characters again like those in *Book from the Sky*? You look again, and again, and perhaps you take a glance at the calligraphy manual. You notice the English letters in the manual, and it dawns on you that the script is no other than that of English. Each letter is made to look like a component in a Chinese character, and each English word is written as though it is a Chinese character. At this moment, you discover that you can in fact read what is in the model: "Little Bo Peep/Little Bo Peep/Has lost her sheep and can . . ." *Voilà*, you figured it out. What appears mysterious now becomes completely comprehensible, and what seems strange turns out extremely familiar.

Companion Website

Exercise 24.2 Nature of the Square Calligraphy script

Square Calligraphy Classroom, like *Book from the Sky*, challenges our assumptions about language, writing, and identity. To Western viewers uninitiated to the content, norm, and styles of Chinese calligraphy, the classroom, at least at first glance, may represent an unfathomable world of a different culture. To Chinese viewers who have grown up practicing calligraphy, the brush, ink, red-lined tracing book, white-on-black characters of the printed model, and nature-inspired metaphors in the manual are all cues of a familiar cultural experience. Indeed, both groups of participants come with their own culturally acquired assumptions; however, both are likely surprised in the end. The English-speaking participants would realize that they can actually read what is written, while the Chinese viewers would find themselves puzzle over the incomprehensible script. Despite the differences in reaction, the message may be one and the same: we are only constrained by our own culture. As we realize that we have fallen into another one of *Xú Bīng*'s "traps," we may start to contemplate – what other cultural traps are we in that we have yet to recognize, and how do we free ourselves from them?

Printing on Water (1996)

Printing on Water is a photo-documented performance. The artist Sòng Dōng (宋冬 1966–) sat in the water of the Lhasa River in Tibet, in his hands an ancient wooden seal bearing the Chinese character 水 (*shuǐ* 'water'). For about an hour, he stamped the wooden seal repeatedly onto the surface of the river as if trying to leave a mark of the 水 (*shuǐ*) character on the water surface. The artwork consists of a series of 36 photos documenting this performance.

In Chinese culture, seal stamping is a traditional practice by which the owner of the seal claims authorship or ownership or an artwork. When looking at examples of calligraphy works, you may have noticed the red marks of the artists' personal seals. The ones bearing the artists' names indicate authorship. Besides the artists, collectors may also stamp their own seals on a work of calligraphy or painting they own. The painting in Figure 24.3, for example, is a highly prized masterpiece, as shown by the great number of collectors' seals.

FIGURE 24.3 *Night-Shining White* by Hán Gàn (active ca. 742–756), ca. 750. *Source*: Collection of the Metropolitan Museum of Art

Sòng Dōng's action to repeatedly stamp the surface of the river with a seal may be understood as an attempt to impose a certain kind of human authority over nature. However, the character 水 (*shuǐ* 'water') is semantically identical to the receiving surface of the stamping, making it a pointless action. Nature exists regardless of human recognition of its existence. Furthermore, as one can imagine, the action in itself is only futile. Any imprints on the water's surface are only temporary and instantly disappear as the river flows on. Perhaps the very inability of the character to maintain any lasting existence on the river surface suggests to us nature's resistance against linguistic categorization – or any kind of artificial classification. This may be one of many interpretations of this work.[6]

Copying the "Orchid Pavilion Preface" a Thousand Times (1990–1995)

As the title suggests, Qiū Zhìjié's (邱志杰/邱志傑, 1969–) *Copying the "Orchid Pavilion Preface" a Thousand Times* involved repeated ink writing on a single surface. Over the course of several years, the artist copied Wáng Xīzhī's (王羲之 321–379 CE) famous calligraphy work on the same sheet of paper more than a thousand times. He recorded the first 50 or so iterations on video and took photographs throughout the process. As shown in Figure 24.4, as the artist copied the same text for a second, third time, and so on, writing over the existing characters, the text became increasingly illegible and the calligraphic lines took on the quality of an abstract ink painting. By the time he reached about the fiftieth iteration, the paper had turned solid black. The end product was a sheet of paper bearing a thick layer of black pigment.

FIGURE 24.4 *Copying the "Orchid Pavilion Preface" a Thousand Times* by Qiū Zhìjié
Source: Courtesy of the artist

What is the significance of this work? The meaning is, of course, open to interpretation. In Qiū's own words, once the characters became indistinguishable from each other and merged into one block of blackness – that is, for about 95% of the copying process – the act of writing became a meditative practice of Zen.[7] If you know something about the practice of copying in traditional calligraphy training, the act of copying itself might not seem strange to you. After all, almost all calligraphy students start by copying the works of the masters and usually do so for years before writing without a model. There was also nothing unusual about the choice of the model. As one of the most celebrated masterpieces, the *Preface* had been used by numerous students as a model. What was unusual, however, was that each iteration of the copying was done on top of the previous ones. With sufficient repetitions, the written words began to disappear into the blackness; that is, with sufficient repetitions, even the best masterpiece turned into nothingness. Could this be a critical analogy for blindly following cultural conventions? Could this be a warning against mindlkess reproduction without innovation? What else do you think could be the message?

Notes

1   Asia Art Archive (2010).
2   Link (2006).
3   Ibid., pp. 47–48.
4   Ibid., p. 48.
5   Ibid., pp. 49–51.
6   Vinograd (2011, p. 107).
7   Qiu (1995).

25 Chinese characters and Western Modernist poetry

YOU MAY WONDER: WHAT have Chinese characters got to do with Western Modernist poetry? They appear to be very different subjects rooted in vastly distant traditions. It is also true that, we have so far almost always examined the Chinese writing system within the Asian context. Only occasionally have we made comparisons between the Sinitic script and the Roman alphabet – and in that case, the relevance is obvious. What can possibly be the connection here? In fact, the connection is an important and fascinating one, and we will delve into the details in this chapter. To understand the role Chinese characters have played in the development of Modernist poetry in the English language, however, we first need to know something about Imagism, the movement that marked the beginning of Modernist poetic aesthetics in the West.

Imagism and Modernist poetry in the English language

In the early 20th century, a group of British and American poets working in London launched the Imagist movement in reaction against what had become of Romanticist poetry by that time: in their eyes, it had been overtaken by muddy abstraction, verbose language, and rigid prosody. Writing in free verse, these poets devoted themselves to "clarity of expression through the use of precise visual images."[1] An **image**, as defined by Ezra Pound (1885–1972), who spearheaded the movement, was "that which presents an intellectual and emotional complex in an instant of time."[2] The concept was an amalgamation of such key tenets as treating the subject directly, rendering the exact particularities rather than dealing with vague generalities, using the language of common speech, always choosing the exact word with no excess verbiage, and composing in free verse rather than in conventional rhyme and meter. Even though the Imagism movement lasted for only about five years (1912–1917), its poetic principles had a profound impact on English-language writing for the remainder of the 20th century.

THE STORY BEYOND

A poem

In a Station of the Metro
The apparition of these faces in the crowd;
Petals on a wet, black bough.
                    —Ezra Pound, 1913

In this poem, Pound presents a vivid image – a glimpse of faces appearing amid the crowd at a dimly lit subway station in Paris – through a metaphoric equation. Instead of describing what he sees, he has the image speak for itself. He compares the faces to bright and delicate petals on a dark, wet tree branch. The concrete and exact details of the observation evoke a crisp image in the reader's mind's eye. The language that he uses is akin to common speech, free of ornate diction or verbose phrasing. This poem exemplifies the precise observed details, concrete metaphors, and concise language that the Imagists aimed to pursue.

Chinese characters came to serve as illustrative support for Imagist poetics because of Ernest Fenollosa and Ezra Pound's collaborative work on Chinese poetry. The collaboration was a rather unusual one. Pound, who was at the front and center of the Imagist movement, had been actively promoting the work of Imagist poets by anthologizing and publishing their poetry since 1912.[3] By that time, Ernest Fenollosa (1853–1908) had already passed away. In 1913, Fenollosa's widow contacted Pound and handed him her husband's unpublished notes on Chinese poetry. Fenollosa was an American art historian with a focus on Japanese art. While in Japan, he wrote about poetic aesthetics based on his study of Classical Chinese poetry. His widow found that Imagist ideas – their emphasis on clarity, precision, and economy of language – resonated with those of Fenollosa's, and she wished for Pound to complete the manuscripts her husband had left behind. In 1915, despite the fact that he had never studied the Chinese language, Pound published *Cathay*, a collection of Classical Chinese poems translated into English based on Fenollosa's word-for-word rendering in his notes. This work received critical acclaim for its "supreme beauty."[4] T. S. Eliot even called Pound "the inventor of Chinese poetry for our time."[5] In 1918, Pound edited and published in London Fenollosa's essay titled "The Chinese Written Character as a Medium for Poetry." This essay, as you probably have understood by now, was where the Chinese script and Western Modernist poetry came together. Although Pound's poetry translation and the essay were criticized by Sinologists for their inaccuracy or misunderstanding of the Chinese language and script, they were tremendously influential on the development of Modernist aesthetics for English-language poetry. In the remainder of this chapter, we will take a closer look at Fenollosa's essay.

Chinese characters and Imagist poetry

Fenollosa's essay is a philosophical discussion of poetic aesthetics inspired by – to a great extent – misunderstandings about the nature of the Chinese writing system as well as some linguistic universals. Assessing the essay from a linguistic perspective will allow us to get down to the "nitty gritty" of his arguments and unveil some of the misunderstandings and mistakes. These mistakes offer us valuable insights into how misconceptions about the Chinese writing system arise so that we can be cautious not to help create or spread such misunderstandings in the future. As you have seen more than a few times in this book, myths about the Chinese script, especially the ideas that Chinese characters are pictures or ideograms, still abound in scholarly and non-scholarly publications. This book – and perhaps this chapter in particular – hopes to help you detect and debunk such claims when you see them.

Characters as visual shorthand of motion

In Fenollosa's view, Chinese characters are different from English in that they "have no basis in sound."[6] Rather, they are "shorthand pictures"[7] that capture movement or the succession of time in nature. This perceived visual quality of Chinese characters led him to question the compatibility of Chinese with the art of poetry.

> In what sense can verse, written in terms of visible hieroglyphics, be reckoned true poetry? It might seem that poetry, which like music is a time art, weaving its unities out of successive impressions of sound, could with difficulty assimilate a verbal medium consisting largely of semi-pictorial appeals to the eye.[8]

In other words, Fenollosa suggests that Chinese poetry is primarily made of written characters – what he terms "semi-pictorial appeals to the eye" – rather than speech sounds.[9] Poetry, on the other hand, is an art of sounds, consisting of "successive impressions of sounds" strung together. Thus, he doubts that Chinese poetry written in characters can be considered true poetry.

Fenollosa has in this instance confused Chinese writing with the Chinese language (speech) and has taken the written symbols of the Chinese language as its essential form of existence. He seems to have failed to see that Chinese characters represent speech sounds as much as any other full writing systems do and failed to understand that the Chinese language or speech is not essentially different from the English language or speech, regardless of whether it is written in characters or in an alphabetical script. The choice of words in a line of Chinese poetry, for example, is not in a significant way determined by their picturesque qualities, but rather, as in English poetry, by their sound and semantic values. Despite being represented by a writing system that appears more "pictorial" than the Roman alphabet, the Chinese language is as much speech in essence as the English language, and Chinese poetry is as much a "verbal medium" as Western poetry.

Drawing from the observation that the earliest Chinese characters are predominantly pictographic, Fenollosa claims that many of the simple pictograms and radicals contain "a verbal idea of action"[10] and are "shorthand pictures of actions or processes."[11] He gives one example to illustrate this idea: the character 言 (*yán* 'to speak'), as he describes, consists of a mouth (口) on the bottom with two words and a flame coming out of it.[12] He suggests that, with concepts pictorially coded in this manner, expressing one's thoughts in Chinese would be as easily accomplished by drawing pictures as by speaking, and reading Chinese would be like "watching things work out their own fate."[13] As fascinating as these ideas may seem, they are hardly corroborated by the actual experience of native Chinse writers and readers. Decomposing characters and taking into account the meaning of individual components are hardly part of their natural writing or reading process. Rather, characters are perceived as symbols representing speech sounds in much the same way that Roman letters are processed in the minds of English writers and readers.

The verbal quality encoded in Chinese written symbols, Fenollosa argues, is even more pronounced in compound characters. He believes that when two or more components are put together, a relationship between them emerges that is both fundamental and poetic. "Things in motion, motion in things, and so the Chinese conception tends to represent them."[14] He supplies five examples to illustrate this point:

伙 'messmate' is a 'man' (人) and a 'fire' (火).

春 'spring' is the 'sun' (日) underlying the bursting forth of plants.

東[15] 'east' is the sun sign (日) tangled in the branches of the tree (木).

男 'male' is 'rice field' (田) plus 'struggle' (力).

洲 'ripple' is 'water' (氵) plus 'boat' (舟).[16]

Fenollosa seems to suggest that the meaning of the compound characters is the sum of their components. This view, however, does not entirely hold up. As we know, the great majority of Chinese characters are semantic-phonetic compounds. At least two of the examples Fenollosa gives, 伙 'messmate' (huǒ) and 洲 'ripple' (zhōu), belong to this category. From our earlier discussion in Part II Chapter 3, we also know that the so-called semantic-semantic compounds are most likely a retrospective category made up for pedagogical purposes and may not represent the true etymology of the characters. The most plausible semantic-semantic compounds may be characters with reduplicated components such as "森" (sēn 'forest') and "林" (lín 'woods'), and the others are more likely semantic-phonetic compounds for which the phonological clues have become opaque due to historical sound changes. If this is true, then春 (chūn 'spring') and男 (nán 'male') are more likely semantic-phonetic compounds as well. The remaining example, 東 (dōng 'east'), is generally considered a simple character, not a compound. All in all, it is more likely than not that none of the examples above can serve as valid evidence for Fenollosa's argument.

For Fenollosa, the visual poetic quality of characters extends to larger segments, such as phrases, and adds additional layers of meaning through a mechanism he calls the "pictorial method."[17] For example, in 日昇東 (rì shēng dōng 'sun rises [in the] east'), the 日 component occurs in all three characters, creating a visual connection that may be difficult to achieve in Roman alphabetical writing. In Fenollosa's imagination, the composition in Chinese characters is varied enough for the poet to choose "words in which a single dominant overtone colors every plane of meaning," and he even goes so far as to call this "the most conspicuous quality of Chinese poetry."[18] Of course, given what we have discussed up to this point, it is not difficult to see that the pictorial method arises from Fenollosa's imagination and is not something known to have been used as a creative device in composing classical Chinese poetry.

Overall, Fenollosa's misguided claims may remind us of the ideographic myth (see Chapter 8) that is at the root of much of the misunderstanding about the Chinese writing system. He has greatly exaggerated the pictographic origin of the writing system and mistakenly considered Chinese characters as pictures representing ideas, actions, or processes directly without referencing speech sounds. As we have previously learned, it is crucial to understand that the Chinese writing system, like any full writing systems, is essentially visual representation of speech sounds. Without the language (speech) behind the writing, it would be impossible to read the script, and writing would also be devoid of reliable meaning or communicative function.

Sentences as transitive processes

Fenollosa argues that good writing should make use of strong, transitive verbs because a natural sentence form dictates transitive verbs. He considers the sentence pattern "agent act-object" universal to all non-inflected languages, as exemplified by the "subject-verb-object" word order typical in both Chinese and English (while saying that languages that make use of inflections, such as Japanese and Spanish, do not have to follow this order), for example, "farmer – pounds – rice." He reasons that such universality of the "agent-act-object" form must imply its naturalness: it "was forced upon primitive men by nature itself. It was not we who made it; it was a reflection of the temporal order in causation."[19] If the sentence denotes a fact, then the verb is "the very substance of the fact denoted" and "erects all speech into a kind of dramatic poetry." According to Fenollosa, the dominance of the verb in a Chinese sentence gives us the model of a terse, fine style.

Companion Website

Exercise 25.1 Shakespeare's English and Chinese poetry

Fenollosa does not agree with professional grammarians' definition of what constitutes a sentence. First of all, he thinks it is problematic to define a sentence as something that "expresses a complete thought," because in nature there is no completeness. "Acts," as Fenollosa sees it, "are successive, even continuous; one causes or passes into another."[20] Therefore, he argues, there can be no complete sentences, and recognizing this gives the poet the creative license to employ phrases, rather than grammatically complete sentences, for their succinctness and sharpness.

Fenollosa thinks it is also problematic to define a sentence as something that "unites a subject and a predicate" as grammarians do. He thinks of this definition as an artificial construct out of "pure subjectivity," because the subject and the predicate are both decided by the speaker. In that sense, "the sentence . . . is not an attribute of nature but an accident of man as a conversational animal." If so, "then there could be no possible test of the truth of a sentence."[21]

The distrust Fenollosa has of grammarians applies similarly to logicians. In fact, he considers the study of logic developed in the Middle Ages the source from which prescriptive grammarians have derived their linguistic theories. Both logic and grammar deal with abstraction, while Fenollosa believes that thought deals with concrete things and that the language of poetry must therefore also strive for concreteness.

Freedom from grammar

Fenollosa sees prescriptive grammar as abstract and deadening, something that drains "the sap of nature"[22] out of poetry. Chinese, to him, offers an example of a language less constrained by grammar. According to his understanding, there is a general lack of distinction between parts of speech in the Chinese language. Of course, there are verbs, in particular transitive verbs. He believes, however, that the other forms of verbs – intransitive, passive, the verb "to be," and negative – all derive from the transitive. "The beauty of Chinese verbs is that they are all transitive or intransitive at pleasure."[23]

Fenollosa argues that Chinese has no grammar and that words are one and the same when it comes to parts of speech – that nouns, adjectives, prepositions, and conjunctions are in fact all verbs. "Almost every written Chinese word is . . . not exclusive of parts of speech, but comprehensive; not something which is neither a noun, verb, or adjective, but something which is all of them at once and at all times."[24] Nouns, adjectives, prepositions, and conjunctions all derive from verbs, and even prepositions contain "secrets of verbal metaphor."[25]

As an example, Fenollosa explains that the Chinese character 明 (*míng* 'bright') serves as a verb, a noun, and an adjective. The compound consists of two parts, 日 (*rì* 'sun') and 月 (*yuè* 'moon'). Thus, when writing "the cup's brightness," one is literally writing "the sun and moon of the cup." In this case, 明 serves as a noun. It can also function as a verb to mean "the cup shines."[26] It is unclear what expressions Fenollosa is referring to in this case. "The cup's brightness" could be 杯之明 (*bēi zhī míng*; 之 *zhī* indicates possession), but "the cup shines" cannot be *杯明, as this is not a legitimate word. Fundamentally, however, this again reveals Fenollosa's confusion between language and writing. He seems to have failed to recognize that the part of speech of a morpheme is determined by how it functions in the language and has little to do with how the morpheme is visually represented in writing.

Fenollosa thinks that parts of speech are not natural and are invented by grammarians. He also believes that grammar for Chinese is imposed by foreigners. The idea that certain words are nouns and certain others are verbs or adjectives is indeed a recent Western import for describing the Chinese language.[27] Fenollosa's observation about the flexibility in the parts of speech of Chinese also has some merit. However, the concept of a morpheme functioning in multiple parts of speech may be more applicable to Classical Chinese, when words are more often monomorphemic. In modern Chinese, however, significantly more words are polymorphemic, so different parts of speech of related words do tend to be in different forms.

Fenollosa's essay makes for an excellent lesson for us – students of the Chinese writing system. Given that the purpose of Fenollosa's essay is philosophical, it might seem beside the point to scrutinize the linguistic details it uses as evidence, since the inaccuracy of the evidence does not necessarily invalidate the principal arguments. Yet, there is a difference between knowing and not knowing just what makes the linguistic evidence questionable in this essay. Only when we know what the linguistic problems are can we fully appreciate the merit of the essay in a context beyond linguistics. Critiquing Fenollosa's understanding of Chinese writing requires us to be able to tease apart "truth" from "fiction" before drawing conclusions that may be founded on more solid evidence. Finally, it is worthwhile to note that despite the many linguistic errors in Fenollosa's analyses, his vision of what counted as good poetry was remarkable and invaluable in the development of Modernist poetic aesthetics. It is in this spirit that we have examined closely a few of the key arguments raised in his essay.

Notes

1 Academy of American Poets (2004).
2 Ibid.
3 In 1914, *Des Imagistes: An Anthology* (Aldington, Flint, Pound, Lowell, & Williams, 1914) was published. Assembled and edited by Pound, it was the first anthology of the Imagism movement. Poets collected in this volume include Ezra Pound, William Carlos Williams, Richard Aldington, James Joyce, H.D., F.S. Flint, and Amy Lowell.
4 From a comment made by Ford Madox Ford in a June, 1915 review of *Cathay* in *Outlook*.
5 Eliot (1928).
6 Fenollosa, Pound, Saussy, Stalling, and Klien (2011, p. 44).
7 Ibid., p. 46.
8 Ibid., p. 42.

9 Fenollosa does seem to also recognize the representation of speech sounds by Chinese characters: "Chinese poetry has the unique advantage of combining both elements [sound and image]. It speaks at once with the vividness of painting, and with the mobility of sounds. It is . . . more dramatic. In reading Chinese we do not seem to be juggling mental counters, but to be watching *things* work out their own fate" (Fenollosa et al., 2011, p. 45). But his focus is so overwhelmingly on the written characters that consideration on the sound component is nearly non-existent.

10 Ibid., p. 45.

11 Ibid., p. 46.

12 Ibid., p. 46.

13 Ibid., p. 45.

14 Ibid., p. 46.

15 Fenollosa's essay obviously refers only to traditional characters. Because it references a large number of characters and often focuses on their appearance, to avoid confusion, simplified forms of the Chinese characters are not provided for this chapter as they are in the other chapters of the book.

16 Modified from examples on p. 46 of Fenollosa et al. (2011).

17 Ibid., p. 59.

18 Ibid., p. 60.

19 Ibid., p. 47.

20 Ibid., p. 47.

21 Ibid., p. 47.

22 Ibid., p. 51.

23 Ibid., p. 48.

24 Ibid., p. 51.

25 Ibid., p. 52.

26 Ibid., p. 51.

27 The first scholarly work written by a Chinese that systematically described the grammar of Chinese was Mǎ Jiànzhōng's (马建忠/馬建忠) book Mǎshì Wéntōng (马氏文通/馬氏文通, '*Basic Principles for Writing Clearly and Coherently by Mister Ma*') published in 1898. Prior to that there were several works on Chinese grammar written by Westerners.

References

Academy of American Poets. (2004). A brief guide to imagism. Retrieved December 28, 2018, from www.poets.org/poetsorg/text/brief-guide-imagism

Aldington, R., H.D., Flint, F.S., Pound, E., Lowell, A., & Williams, W.C. (1914). *Des imagistes: An anthology.* New York, NY: Albert and Charles Boni.

Alves, M.J. (2001). *What's so Chinese about Vietnamese?* Papers from the Ninth Annual Meeting of the Southeast Asian Linguistics Society. Arizona State University, Program for Southeast Asian Studies, pp. 221–242.

Alves, M.J. (2009). Loanwords in Vietnamese. In M. Haspelmath & U. Tadmor (Eds.), *Loanwords in the world's languages: A comparative handbook.* Berlin: Mouton de Gruyter.

Asia Art Archive. (2010). Conversation with Huang Yongping. Retrieved December 28, 2018, from www.aaa-a.org/programs/conversation-with-huang-yongping/

Attané, I. (2012). Being a woman in China today: A demography of gender. *China Perspectives, 2012,* 5–15.

Barrass, G.S. (2002). *The art of calligraphy in modern China.* Berkeley, CA: University of California Press.

Bergman, J. (2010). China's TV dating shows: For love or money? *Time,* June 30, 2010.

Berwick, R., & Chomsky, N. (2016). *Why only us: Language and evolution.* Cambridge, MA: Massachusetts Institute of Technology Press.

Bodde, D. (1991). *Chinese thought, society, and science: The intellectual and social background of science and technology in pre-modern China.* Honolulu: University of Hawaii Press.

Boltz, W.G. (1993). "Shuo wen chieh tzu 說文解字". In M. Loewe (Ed.), *Early Chinese texts: A bibliographical guide,* Early China Special Monograph Series, 2 (pp. 429–442). Berkeley, CA: Society for the Study of Early China, and the Institute of East Asian Studies, University of California.

Boltz, W.G. (1996). Early Chinese writing. In P.T. Daniels & W. Bright (Eds.), *The world's writing systems* (pp. 191–199). New York, NY: Oxford University Press.

Bouchot, J. (1925). *Pétrus Truong-Vinh-Ky, érudit cochinchinois, 1837–1898.* Saigon: Bouchot.

Brannigan, M.C. (2015). *Japan's March 2011 disaster and moral grit: Our inescapable in-between.* Lanham, MD: Lexington Books.

Brown, L., & Yeon, J. (2015). *The handbook of Korean linguistics.* Chichester: John Wiley & Sons.

Campbell, L., & Mixco, M.J. (2007). *A glossary of historical linguistics.* Salt Lake City, UT: University of Utah Press.

Camus, Y. (2007). *Jesuits' journeys in Chinese studies.* Paper presented at the World Conference on Sinology 2007, Renmin University of China, Beijing, March 2007.

Chen, P. (1999). *Modern Chinese: History and sociolinguistics.* Cambridge: Cambridge University Press.

Chiang, W. (1995). *We two know the script; we have become good friends: Linguistic and social aspects of the women's script literacy in southern Hunan, China.* New York, NY: University Press of America.

Chiang, Y. (1973). *Chinese calligraphy: An introduction to its aesthetic and technique* (3rd revised and enlarged edition). Cambridge, MA: Harvard University Press.

Chinese Academy of Social Sciences. (2007). *Contemporary Chinese dictionary* [*Xiàndài Hànyǔ cídiǎn*] (5th edition). Beijing: The Commercial Press.

Chung, Y. (2008). Use hangeul, not hangul. *The Korea Times,* January 2, 2008.

DeFrancis, J. (1950). *Nationalism and language reform in China.* Princeton, NJ: Princeton University Press.

DeFrancis, J. (1977). *Colonialism and language policy in Viet Nam.* The Hague: Mouton.

DeFrancis, J. (1984). *The Chinese language: Fact and fantasy.* Honolulu: University of Hawaii Press.

DeFrancis, J. (1989). *Visible speech: The diverse oneness of writing systems.* Honolulu: University of Hawaii Press.

Eliot, T.S. (1928). Introduction. In *Selected poems by Ezra Pound.* London: Faber & Gwyer.

Endo, E. (1999). *Endangered system of women's writing from Hunan, China.* Presentation given at the Association of Asian Studies Annual Conference, March 1999.

Fan, C.C. (1996). Language, gender, and Chinese culture. *International Journal of Politics, Culture, and Society, 10*(1), 95–114. doi:10.1007/BF02765570.

Fei, D. (2007). *85 New Wave: The birth of Chinese contemporary art*. Shanghai: Shanghai People's Publishing House.

Fenollosa, E., Pound, E., Saussy, H., Stalling, J., & Klein, L. (2011). *The Chinese written character as a medium for poetry: A critical edition*. Ashland, OH; London: Fordham University Press.

Fincher, L. H. (2013). China's entrenched gender gap. *New York Times*, May 20, 2013.

Fisher, S. R. (2001). *A history of writing*. London: Reaktion Books.

Foust, M. A. (Ed.). (2016). *Feminist encounters with Confucius*. Leiden; Boston, MA: E. J. Brill.

Frank, H. (2001). Identity and script variation: Japanese lesbian and housewife letters to the editor. In K. Campbell-Kibler, R. J. Podesva, S. J. Roberts, & A. Wong (Eds.), *Language and sexuality: Contesting meaning in theory and practice*. Stanford, CA: CSLI Publications.

Goldin, P. R. (2000). The view of women in early Confucianism. In C. Li (Ed.), *The sage and the second sex: Confucianism, ethics, and gender* (pp. 133–161). Chicago, IL: Open Court.

Gottlieb, N. (1995). *Kanji politics: Language policy and Japanese script*. London; New York, NY: Kegal Paul International.

Gu, G. (1987). *The construction of modern calligraphy*. [*Xiàndài shūfǎ gòuchéng*]. Beijing: Běijīng Tǐyù Xuéyuàn Chūbǎnshè.

Gu, G. (1990). *The three steps of modern calligraphy*. [*Xiàndài shūfǎ sān bù*]. Beijing: Zhōngguó Shūjí Chūbǎnshè.

Gulik, V. (1974). *Sexual life in ancient China*. Leiden: E. J. Brill.

Hannas, W. C. (1997). *Asia's orthographic dilemma*. Honolulu: University of Hawaii Press.

Hannas, W. C. (2003). *The writing on the wall: How Asian orthography curbs creativity*. Philadelphia, PA: University of Pennsylvania Press.

He, Z., & Jiao, H. (2014). Shàng shìjì wǔshí niándài Táiwān *Zìyóu Zhōngguó* zázhì duì hànzì jiǎnhuà de hūyù. [Taiwan's *Free China* periodical advocates for character simplification in the 1950s]. *Fujian Forum (Humanity and Social Sciences Edition)*, *2*, 115–119.

Hoosain, R. (1991). *Psycholinguistic implications for linguistic relativity: A case study of Chinese*. Hillsdale, NJ: Lawrence Erlbaum.

Huang, H. (1996). Portuguese settlement in Macao and cultural exchange between China and the outside world. *Review of Culture, Macau, S.*, *2*(29), 67–84.

Hue, C., & Hu, Z. (2003). Number of characters a college student knows. *Journal of Chinese Linguistics*, *31*(2), 300–339.

Idema, W. L. (2009). *Heroines of Jiangyong: Chinese narrative ballads in women's script*. Seattle, WA: University of Washington Press.

Idema, W. L., & Grant, B. (2004). Reality. In *The red brush: Writing women of imperial China* (pp. 542–566). Cambridge, MA: Harvard University Asia Center.

Iwahara, A., Hatta, T., & Maehara, A. (2003). The effects of a sense of compatibility between type of script and word in written Japanese. *Reading and Writing: An Interdisciplinary Journal*, *16*, 377–397.

Jeon, J. (2015). Some pushing for more elementary school instruction of Chinese characters. *Hankyoreh*. Retrieved September 16, 2018, from http://english.hani.co.kr/arti/english_edition/e_national/704331.html

Joshi, R. M., & Aaron, P. G. (2006). *Handbook of orthography and literacy*. London: Taylor & Francis.

Kaiho, H., & Nomura, Y. (1983). *Kanjijōho no shori no shinrigaku*. [*Psychology of kanji information processing*]. Tokyo: Kyōiku.

Kim, B. (2017). Hanja in elementary textbooks is still controversial. *Korea National University of Education Bulletin*, Vol. 77, May 31, 2017.

Kim, S.-J. (2015). Debate grows over teaching Chinese characters. *Korea Times*, September 14, 2015.

Kindaichi, H. (2017). *The Japanese language*. North Clarendon, VT: Tuttle Publishing.

King, R. (1996). Korean writing. In P. T. Daniels & W. Bright (Eds.), *The world's writing systems* (pp. 218–227). New York, NY: Oxford University Press.

Koichi. (2011). The ultimate Kanji test: Kanji Kentei. *Tofugu*. Retrieved December 10, 2018, from www.tofugu.com/japanese/kanji-kentei/

Kornicki, P. F. (2018). *Languages, scripts, and Chinese texts in East Asia*. Oxford: Oxford University Press.

Kraus, R. C. (1991). *Brushes with power: Modern politics and the Chinese art of calligraphy*. Berkeley, CA: University of California Press.

Kubler, C. C. (2011). *Basic written Chinese: An introduction to reading and writing for beginners*. North Clarendon, VT: Tuttle Publishing.

Le, M., & O'Harrow, S. (2007). Vietnam. In A. Simpson (Ed.), *Language and national identity in Asia*. Oxford; New York, NY: Oxford University Press.

Lee, I., & Ramsey, S. R. (2000). *The Korean language*. New York, NY: State University of New York Press.

Lee, K., & Shim, J. (2015). Use of Chinese characters in primary school textbooks. *Korea Focus*. Retrieved September 16, 2018, from www.koreafocus.or.kr/design2/layout/content_print.asp?group_id=105802

Lee, L. (2002). Creating a female language: Symbolic transformation embedded in nushu. In X. Lu, W. Jia, & D. R. Heisey (Eds.), *Chinese communication studies: Contexts and comparisons* (pp. 101–118). Westport, CT: Greenwood Publishing Group.

Lee, T.H.C. (2000). *Education in traditional China: A history*. Leiden: E. J. Brill.

Li, C. (Ed.). (2000). *The sage and the second sex: Confucianism, ethics, and gender*. Chicago, IL: Open Court.

Lin, J. Y. (1995). The Needham Puzzle: Why the industrial revolution did not originate in China. *Economic Development and Cultural Change, 43*(2), 269–292.

Lin, Y. (1977). *My country and my people*. Heinenmann: Asia.

Link, P. (2006). Whose assumptions does Xu Bing upset, and why? In J. Silbergeld & D.C.Y. Ching (Eds.), *Persistence-transformation: Text as image in the art of Xu Bing*. Princeton, NJ: Princeton University Press.

Liu, C. (2010). *Zhōngguó xiàndài shūfǎ shǐ*. [*The history of modern Chinese calligraphy*]. Nanjing: Nanjing University Press.

Liu, M. (1957). *Zhōngguó yīnbiāo zì shū*. [*Chinese phonetic script*]. Beijing: Script Reform Publishing [Wénzì Gǎigé Chūbǎnshè].

Liu, Y. (1991). Difficulties in Chinese information processing and ways to their solution. In V. H. Mair & Y. Liu (Eds.), *Characters and computers* (pp. 1–8). Amsterdam; Washington, DC: IOS Press.

Logan, R. K. (1986). *The alphabet effect: The impact of the phonetic alphabet on the development of western civilization*. New York, NY: Morrow.

Mair, V.H. (1991). Preface: Building the future of information processing in East Asia demands facing linguistic and technological reality. In V. H. Mair & Y. Liu (Eds.), *Characters and computers* (pp. 1–8). Amsterdam; Washington, DC: IOS Press.

Mair, V. H. (1996). Modern Chinese writing. In P. T. Daniels & W. Bright (Eds.), *The world's writing systems* (pp. 200–208). New York, NY: Oxford University Press.

Mair, V. H. (2000). Advocates of script reform. In W. T. De Bary, I. Bloom, W. Chan, J. Adler, & R. J. Lufrano (Eds.), *Sources of Chinese tradition* (Vol. 2, pp. 302–308). New York, NY: Columbia University Press.

Mair, V. H. (2002). Sound and meaning in the history of characters: Views of China's earliest script reformers. In M.S. Erbaugh (Ed.), *Difficult characters: Interdisciplinary studies of Chinese and Japanese writing* (pp. 105–123). Columbus, OH: National East Asian Languages Resource Center, Ohio State University.

Man, B. (1990). *Backhill/Peking/Beijing*. Sino-Platonic Papers, p. 19.

Needham, J. (1956). *Science and civilization in China* (Vol. 2). Cambridge: Cambridge University Press.

Needham, J. (2013). *Grand titration: Science and society in East and West*. London: Routledge.

Nguyen, N. B. (1984). *The state of Chữ Nôm studies: The demotic script of Vietnam*. Fairfax, VA: Indochina Institute, George Mason University.

Ni, H. (1948). *Zhōngguó pīnyīn wénzì yùndòng shǐ*. [*History of Chinese phonetic script movement*]. Shanghai: Shídài Shūbào Chūbǎnshè [Times Publishing].

Ni, H. (1987). *Lādīnghuà Xīn Wénzì yùndòng shǐmò hé biānnián jìshì*. [*Chronical of Latin Xua Sinwenz movement*]. Shanghai: Zhīshí Chūbǎnshè [Knowledge Press].

Noguchi, M. S. (2009). The crafty names of Japan's cleverest companies. *The Japan Times Online*, June 17, 2009.

O'Mochain, R. (2012). Listserv communication by LGBT and heterosexual Japanese youth: A survey of three features. *US-China Foreign Language, 10*(11), 1734–1744.

Otis, E. (2015). Inequality in China and the impact on women's rights. *The Conversation*, March 19, 2015.

Peng, H. (2010). Xu Teli and the new characters movement of Latinization. *Journal of Changsha Normal College, 2010*(2), 14–18.

Penney, M. (2012). The Fukushima anniversary: Japanese press reactions. *The Asia-Pacific Journal*. Retrieved from http://apjjf.org/-Matthew-Penney/4710/article.html

Qian, X. (1999). *Qian Xuantong anthology* (Vol. 3). Beijing: Renmin University Press.

Qiu, Z. (1995). A one-thousand-time copy of Lantingxu. Retrieved July 26, 2017, from www.qiuzhijie.com/worksleibie/calligraphy/e-lanting.htm

Renmin chuban she. (1956). *Zhōngguó wénzì gǎigé de dìyī bù*. [*First step in China's script reform*]. Hong Kong: Zhōngguó Yǔwén Xuéshè.

Rogers, H. (2005). *Writing systems: A linguistic approach*. Malden, MO: Blackwell.

Sampson, G. (1985). *Writing systems*. Stanford, CA: Stanford University Press.

Seaton, P. (2016). Japanese war memories and commemoration after the Great East Japan Earthquake. In A. L. Tota & T. Hagen (Eds.), *Routledge international handbook of memory studies* (pp. 345–356). London; New York, NY: Routledge.

See, L. (2014). *Snow flower and the secret fan*. London: Bloomsbury Publishing.

Seeley, C. (1991). *A history of writing in Japan*. Leiden; New York, NY: E. J. Brill.

Seybolt, P.J., & Chiang, G.K.-K. (1979). *Language reform in China: Documents and commentary*. White Plains, NY: M.E. Sharpe.

Shibatani, M. (1990). *The languages of Japan*. Cambridge [England]; New York, NY: Cambridge University Press.

Smith, J.S. (1996). Japanese writing. In P.T. Daniels & W. Bright (Eds.), *The world's writing systems* (pp. 209–217). New York, NY: Oxford University Press.

Smith, J.S., & Schmidt, D.L. (1996). Variability in writing Japanese: Towards a sociolinguistics of script choice. *Visible Language, 30*(1), 47–71.

Snow, D. (2004). *Cantonese as written language: The growth of a written Chinese vernacular*. Hong Kong: Hong Kong University Press.

Sohn, H. (2001). *The Korean language*. Cambridge [England]; New York, NY: Cambridge University Press.

Sohn, H. (2011). *Korean language in culture and society*. Honolulu: University of Hawaii Press.

Song, J.J. (2005). *The Korean language structure, use and context*. London: Routledge.

State Council, The (2013). Guówùyuàn guānyú gōngbù "Tōngyòng guīfàn hànzì biǎo" de tōngzhī. [The State Council's notice about the publication of the "List of standardized characters for general use"]. Retrieved from http://www.gov.cn/zwgk/2013-08/19/content_2469793.htm

Su, J. (1999). Sexism in Chinese characters. [Hànzì zhōng de xìngbié qíshì]. *Journal of Chinese, 1999*(4), 38–41.

Sugimoto, T., & Levin, J.A. (2000). *Global literacies and the World-Wide Web*. London: Routledge.

Sullivan, M. (1999). *The three perfections: Chinese painting, poetry, and calligraphy*. New York, NY: G. Braziller.

Tahara, S. (2012). 'Fukushima' o 'Fukushima' to yobu no wa, mō yameyou! [Let's stop calling "Fukushima (福島)" "Fukushima (フクシマ)!] Retrieved from www.taharasoichiro.com/cms/?p=789

Tang, D. (2013). 5,000-year-old primitive writing generates debate in China. *NBC News*, July 11, 2013.

Taylor, I., & Taylor, M.M. (1995, 2014). *Writing and literacy in Chinese, Korean and Japanese*. Amsterdam; Philadelphia, PA: John Benjamins.

Taylor, K.W. (1983). *The birth of Vietnam*. Berkeley, CA: University of California Press.

Taylor, K.W. (2013). *A history of the Vietnamese*. Cambridge: Cambridge University Press.

Tranter, N. (2008). Nonconventional script choice in Japan. *International Journal of the Sociology of Language, 2008* (192), 133–151. Retrieved from https://doi.org/10.1515/IJSL.2008.040

Tsu, J., & Ellman, B.A. (Eds.). (2014). *Science and technology in modern China: 1880s-1940s*. Leiden: E.J. Brill.

Tuminez, A.S. (2012). *Rising to the top? A report on women's leadership in Asia*. Lee Kuan Yew School of Public Policy (Singapore) and Asia Society (New York City).

Unger, J.M. (2001). Functional digraphia in Japan as revealed in consumer product preferences. *International Journal of the Sociology of Language, 150*, 141–152.

Unger, J.M. (2004). *Ideogram: Chinese characters and the myth of disembodied meaning*. Honolulu: University of Hawai'i Press.

Vinograd, R. (2011). Making natural languages in contemporary Chinese art. In H. Tsao & R.T. Ames (Eds.), *Xu Bing and contemporary Chinese art: Cultural and philosophical reflections* (pp. 95–115). Albany, NY: State University of New York Press.

Vovin, A. (2014). Out of Southern China? Philological and linguistic musings on the possible Urheimat of Proto-Japonic. *Journées de CRLAO*, June 2014.

Walle, W.V. (2013). The encounter between Europe and Asia in pre-colonial times. In J. Cauquelin, P. Lim, & B. Mayer-König (Eds.), *Asian values: Encounter with diversity* (pp. 164–200). New York: Routledge.

Wang, H.-C., Hsu, L.-C., Tien, Y.-M., & Pomplun, M. (2014). Predicting raters' transparency judgments of English and Chinese morphological constituents using latent semantic analysis. *Behavior Research Methods, 46*(1), 284–306.

Wang, J. (2009). *Dāngdài Zhōngguó de wénzì gǎigé*. [*Writing reform in contemporary China*]. Beijing: Dāngdài Zhōngguó Chūbǎnshè [Contemporary China Publishing House].

Wang, L. (2002). Hànyǔpīnyīn yùndòng de huígù jiānjí tōngyòng pīnyīn wèntí. [On Chinese pinyin's history and Romanization issues]. *Zhongguo Yuwen, 2*, 165–173.

Wang, X., & Liu, Y. (2016). *Hànzì wénhuà yǔ shūfǎ yìshù*. [*Chinese character culture and the art of calligraphy*]. Beijing: Zhōngguó Wénlián Chūbǎnshè [China Federation of Literary and Art Circles Publishing].

Wilkinson, E.P. (2015). *Chinese history: A new manual* (4th edition). Cambridge, MA: Harvard University Asia Center.

Xiang, Y., Wu, J., & Yang, J. (Eds.). (2016). *Shūfǎ sānshí liù kè*. [*Thirty-six lessons on calligraphy*]. Guilin: Líjiāng Chūbǎnshè [Lijiang Publishing House].

Xing, J.Z. (2006). *Teaching and learning Chinese as a foreign language: A pedagogical grammar*. Hong Kong: Hong Kong University Press.

Xiong, V.C. (2006). *Emperor Yang of the Sui dynasty: His life, times, and legacy*. Albany, NY: State University of New York Press.

Yamada, H. (1991). Is logography a better writing system? In V. H. Mair & Y. Liu (Eds.), *Characters and computers* (pp. 141–145). Amsterdam; Washington, DC: IOS Press.

Yang, F. M. (2001). Luó Míngjiān hé Lì Mǎdòu de *Pú-Hàn cídiǎn* (lìshǐ yǔyánxué dǎolùn). [Michele Ruggieri and Matteo Ricci's *Portuguese-Chinese Dictionary* (A historical-linguistic introduction)]. In J. W. Witek (Ed.), *Dicionário Português-Chinês* [*Portuguese-Chinese Dictionary*]. Biblioteca Nacional Portugal. San Francisco, CA: Ricci Institute for Chinese-Western Cultural History (University of San Francisco).

Yang, J. (2015). Jiǎng Jièshí wèihé fàngqì "jiǎntǐ zì"? [Why did Chiang Kai-shek give up "simplified characters"?]. *Téngxùn Wǎng Duǎn Jì* [*Tencent Brief History*], March 9, 2015. Retrieved September 25, 2017, from http://view.news.qq.com/original/legacyintouch/d313.html

Yen, Y. (2005). *Calligraphy and power in contemporary Chinese society*. London ; New York, NY: Routledge-Curzon.

Yin, B. (1990). *Chinese romanization: Pronunciation & orthography = Hanyu pinyin he zhengcifa*. (M. Felley, Ed. & Trans.). Beijing: Sinolingua.

Yin, B. (1991). Pinyin-to-Chinese character computer conversion systems and the realization of digraphia in China. In V. H. Mair & Y. Liu (Eds.), *Characters and computers* (pp. 26–36). Amsterdam; Washington, DC: IOS Press.

Yuan, L. (2005). *Reconceiving women's equality in China: A critical examination of models of sex equality*. Lanham, MD: Lexington Books.

Zhang, S. (2016). Chinese characters are futuristic and the alphabet is old news. *The Atlantic*, November 1, 2016.

Zhang, S., Wang, T., Li, Q., & An, N. (Eds.). (1997). *Jiǎnhuà zì shù yuan*. [*The origins of simplified characters*]. Beijing: Yǔwén Chūbǎnshè.

Zhang, T. (2005). *Literacy education in China*. Paper commissioned for the EFA Global Monitoring Report 2006, Literacy for Life, UNESCO.

Zhao, S., & Baldauf, R. B. (2008). *Planning Chinese characters: Reaction, evolution or revolution?* Dordrecht: Springer.

Zhong, X. P. (2009). Four interpretations for the slogan "Women hold up half the sky." *Nankai Journal, 2009*(4). doi:10.3969/j.issn.1001–4667.2009.04.007

Zhou, Y. (1961). *Hànzì gǎigé gàilùn*. [*Script reform overview*]. Beijing: Wénzì Gǎigé Chūbǎnshè [Script Reform Publisher].

Zhou, Y. (1991). Intrinsic features of Chinese language as applied in word processing on computers. In V. H. Mair & Y. Liu (Eds.), *Characters and computers* (pp. 20–25). Amsterdam; Washington, DC: IOS Press.

Zhou, Y. (2003). *Zhōngguó yǔwén de shídài yǎnjìn*. [*The historical evolution of Chinese languages and scripts*]. Columbus, OH: National East Asian Languages Resource Center, Ohio State University.

Zhu, W. (1956). Wǒ hé "Jiāngsū xīn zìmǔ" ["Jiāngsū xīn zìmǔ" and I]. *Yǔwén Jiànshè, 4*, 3–5.

Zhuang, G. (2016). Shūfǎ jiànshǎng fāngfǎ lùn [On approaches to calligraphy appreciation]. *China Fine Arts Education, Visual Art, 8* [造型艺术卷(8)], 446–449.

Index

Note: Page numbers in *italics* refer to figures; page numbers in **bold** refer to tables.